THE

LAST ANGRY

PRINCIPAL

Howard L. Hurwitz

Halcyon House

FIRST PRINTING

Published by
HALCYON HOUSE
333 SW PARK
PORTLAND, OREGON 97205

Library of Congress Catalog No. 88-80826
ISBN 0-89420-255-3
Printed in United States of America

For
NETTIE *and* **DONALD**
my home front in the school wars

CONTENTS

ACKNOWLEDGEMENTS

IT WAS AT the urging of my wife, Nettie, that I wrote this book. I ill-rewarded her by having her read every line of it, not once but several times, since she is an expert in sentence structure and fearlessly sends me back to the drawing board when she thinks I can do better.

I am also indebted to Betty Wein, a topnotch writer and editor, who read the entire book, chapter by chapter as it progressed, and caused me to rewrite many parts of it.

Louis A. Schuker, retired principal of Jamaica High School, New York, a brilliant educator, read the final two chapters on the reform movement. He insisted, rightly, that I strengthen my positions at some points.

Carl W. Salser, my good friend and publisher, encouraged me to get on with it every step of the way.

As you might suspect, I am not easily swayed. This should make it obvious that all the mistakes are mine.

H.L.H.

FOREWORD

IT WAS MY GOOD OR BAD FORTUNE to be the principal player in one of the most dramatic confrontations in the history of education in America. Never before in the history of the school had a principal been barricaded in his office by a community in a successful effort to prevent him from being fired for an action he took to maintain discipline in his school.

I became a national symbol for upholding school discipline. I was hailed as "THE LAST ANGRY PRINCIPAL" in the *San Francisco Examiner* and in *New York* magazine; "Champion of School Discipline" in *The New York Times*; featured by CBS on "60 Minutes."

While this book starts with my being barricaded in my office during the Bicentennial Year 1976 and recounts other dramatic experiences such as my arrest by a federal judge for refusing to submit to him data on the race and ethnic origins of teachers and students at Long Island City High School, it is more, much more. It is an insider's view of the school saga, 1938–1988, a half-century in which the public schools rose to the highest point in public perception of its strengths and fell to its nadir.

I spin off in this book from personal involvements to an assessment of where we are going after two decades of decline. I react to the avalanche of reports, including *A Nation at Risk*, that cover failure of the schools. My reactions to proposed reforms do not square with the prevailing views.

Our schools are marred by both violence and student apathy that disfigure much of the good work that goes on in some schools. Discipline remains the Number 1 problem as it has been for more than a decade. In the 1940's the discipline problems were talking, chewing gum, making noise, running in the hallways, getting out of place in line, wearing improper clothing and not putting paper in the wastebaskets. In the 1980's our sneakered, jean generation, attending school or dropping out, is decimated by drug abuse, alcohol, pregnancy, suicide, pornography, rape, robbery, assault, vandalism and arson.

The breakdown of order is not confined to the 300 metropolitan school districts but spreads across the 15,500 school districts in cities, towns, suburbs and rural areas.

Schools are suffering loss of support that follows from the precipitate rise in single-parent homes, mothers employed full-time outside the home, a changed school population in which the minorities are the majorities in many schools. The social problems are pervasive and schools are leaned on to solve the problems of society.

Ours is a time when teacher retirements and resignations require replacement by the mid-nineties of one-half the 2.2 million teachers in the public schools. The stepped-up recruitment is already scraping the bottom of the college barrel.

There is the endless cry for more money for schools, although the cost of education has doubled during each ten-year period since 1950, after adjusting for inflation. Currently, we are spending $310 billion a year for all levels of education, an investment far greater than our expenditures for national defense. There is widespread concern that we are not only failing to get the bang for the buck but that we remain "a nation at risk."

In the past 10 years I have kept up a steady commentary in my national education column (two times weekly, 104 columns a year). In the past year, I have written about Joe Clark, principal of Eastside High School, Paterson, New Jersey, whose symbols of discipline are bat and bullhorn. I wish I might say, "We've come a long way, baby." It appears that we have not.

In addition to my columns, I have been a national lecturer, radio-tv commentator on the schools, member of a national education council and president of University Professors for Academic Order.

THE LAST ANGRY PRINCIPAL

I mention my post-barricade career because this book is not only an autobiography, it is a critical analysis of a major concern of the American people—education of our children.

It is not enough to tell my story. I have distilled from dramatic episodes in my front-line experience lessons we must learn if we are ever again to recapture the high regard in which our schools were once held.

Now, to the barricades!

HOWARD L. HURWITZ
Jamaica, New York
June 1988

I

BEHIND THE BARRICADES

THE SCHOOL SECURITY supervisor who entered my office at 3 p.m., on Monday, March 22, 1976, was a huge man. Tears were in his eyes, and his voice choked as he said, "I'm sorry to give you this, Dr. Hurwitz."

He handed me a letter signed by the New York City schools chancellor. It ended my career in the schools after almost 40 years of service, which the chancellor himself agreed was superior. He ordered me to report at once to the superintendent of Queens high schools to await trial on charges of insubordination.

I read the letter as John Meehan sat by my desk. We had come to know each other during the years that he supervised security guards assigned to Queens schools. We had talked many times about guards whom I dismissed because of poor service and poor attendance. He always cooperated and assured me that if all schools had the security problems of Long Island City High School, he would have no worries. I once reflected that he would have no job, and he laughed.

John Meehan was not laughing that afternoon. I told him that because he was delivering the letter did not suggest to me that he agreed with it; that I would handle the matter. John shook my hand and was on his way. I was to catch glimpses of him during the battle that was reported throughout the nation.

I was being brought up on charges of insubordination because I had refused to readmit to my school a student with a long record of disruptive behavior. I knew instantly that if I left my

1

office as ordered, I would never again be the principal of Long Island City High School, or any school. I could not live with that thought.

I reached for my phone and called Peter Vallone. Over a ten-year period I had established close links with the community that reflected the composition of our neighborhood high school—Italians, 40 percent; Greeks, 15 percent; Hispanics, 15 percent; blacks, 10 percent; others, 20 percent, including about 2 percent Asians.

Vallone, a city councilman, was the prime mover in the Astoria Civic Association, a large and strong community group. Pete, then about 40, had deep roots in the community where his father had been a judge.

"Hello, Pete. I'm calling to let you know that I've been fired."

Pete dismissed such nonsense with a quip.

"Let me read you a letter from Irving Anker that was just hand-delivered to me."

I read the whole letter. ". . . This will inform you that pursuant to Section 105 of the By-laws of the Board of Education . . . I have this day charged you with . . . conduct prejudicial to the good order, efficiency and discipline of the service . . . substantial cause that renders you unfit . . . in that you were insubordinate in your refusal to comply with a direct instruction . . . and I hereby suspend you from your duties as Principal of Long Island City High School effective as of the close of business, Monday, March 22, 1976. . . ."

"What do you want me to do, Pete?"

"Stay there."

Within a half-hour, six men entered my office. I recognized a few of them as parents of students in the school. Gerald Nozilo, who was to be the field commander of the operation, told me that I was being barricaded in my office. "No children are coming to this school, Doc, unless you're the principal." They placed a long bench outside of my secretary's office and piled chairs on top of it. We had begun three days and nights of a 'round the clock defense of discipline in the schools that electrified the nation.

BEHIND THE BARRICADES

The episode which made me a national symbol of discipline in the schools was triggered by the outburst of a 16-year-old girl. She screamed at a secretary in the general office who had objected when she took a magazine from the librarian's letter box without permission. Her loud, vituperative shouts had startled the clerks, students, teachers and parents who were in the office at the time.

The Dean of Girls brought the student to my outer office and gave me the girl's file. There was a long record of disruptive behavior going back to the third grade. She had been reported as "hostile" and requiring treatment in an "outside clinic." Up to the time she entered her senior year at LIC, she had interfered with the education of others. She was the kind of student who is being tolerated in all too many schools with the result that education is suffering throughout the country.

In junior high school when she was questioned by a teacher about being in the hall without a pass (permission to leave a classroom), her response was "I don't need a pass for a piss." Not so funny when you are on the receiving line as a teacher. Contempt of teachers is a greater cause of teacher grief than physical assaults. The latter is not the order of the day. The former has become a way of life in many schools.

At LIC the girl abused teachers, cut classes, was late excessively and a truant. Her mother told a LIC counselor that she had lost control of the girl.

Our Dean of Girls told me that she could no longer control the student. She had talked with the girl many times and the record showed that she had met with counselors frequently. Her mother had been to school following the more serious outbreaks. Although there were times when she was relatively quiet, her increasingly frequent temper tantrums had brought her to a point of no return.

I told the dean to send the girl into my office. I asked Jane Doe (the name used in subsequent hearings) to tell me what had happened that required the dean to bring her to me. We talked about her long record of misbehavior. I told her that on the basis of the record and her outburst a few minutes earlier, I was going to talk to the superintendent and ask that he suspend her. I would notify her mother, who would receive a letter from the superintendent within a few days.

I phoned Mrs. Doe and told her that I was sending Jane home, directly.

I then phoned the superintendent who agreed to the suspension. He had been in charge of Queens high schools for seven of the 10 years during which I was the principal. There had not been a single occasion in which he had refused to suspend a student at my request. He knew that I suspended fewer students than any other high school principal in the city. When I did ask for a suspension the documentation I sent forward in support of my request was complete and irrefutable.

In the 10 years previous to the Jane Doe suspension I had asked for 25 suspensions. Other principals had asked for hundreds during the same time span. Usually, a student who is suspended at the superintendent's level is transferred to another school.

Virtually no student is expelled from any school system as an outcome of suspension. This nationwide fear of expelling 16-year-olds with long records of disruptive behavior is another cancer eating into the school system.

About an hour after I sent Jane home I phoned to find out whether she had arrived. Jane answered and asked for a transfer to Bryant, a neighboring high school. I told her that the suspension was in the superintendent's hands but I would do what I could to obtain the transfer.

I phoned the superintendent to tell him that Jane would accept a transfer, and he said he would make the arrangements. This procedure is resorted to often in order to avoid the long, adversarial hearings mandated by the state legislature. Jane's mother agreed to the transfer.

I had no reason to expect that Jane would be returned to my school. This had never taken place in the past, and my determination to keep the school safe from disrupters was well known at 110 Livingston Street, headquarters of the Board of Education.

I placed the case on a backburner and occupied myself with the many details that contribute to decision-making at the principal's level.

Two days later, after the superintendent had agreed to the suspension and said he would arrange for the transfer, he phoned and left word that I must contact him on "a most urgent matter." It was his decision to return the suspended student to LIC.

I reminded him that he had never before changed his mind about a suspension after giving me his word. I had sent him, as requested, Jane's anecdotal record in accordance with the regulations governing student suspensions. In the case of Jane, it was a four-page, single-spaced description, giving the dates and the details of incidents and counseling intended to bring about improvement in Jane's conduct. I stressed that his decision would have the effect of weakening my authority in the school.

"Howard," he countered, "how can you talk that way? You're the strongest principal in the city. What's one student? Do me a favor. Take her back."

I told him that he had not been a principal for 10 tough years. Therefore, he could not understand how a single student could undermine even a strong principal. This is a point that is not understood today. A single student in a school who can tell a teacher off in four-letter words and finish the day is evidence that the authority of the principal has been destroyed.

The word had gone out that Jane would not be returning. She had been given innumerable chances to behave reasonably. If she were to return, I told the superintendent, I would have my hands filled with the marginal discipline cases who were quiet so long as they knew my authority was firm.

Nevertheless, the superintendent insisted that I accept the girl. I told him flat out that I would not permit her to enter the school. He asked me to reconsider and to phone him the next morning. I agreed and asked in return that he reconsider his order.

The next morning I talked separately with the Assistant Principal (Guidance), two counselors, the Attendance Coordinator, the Cutting (truancy from class) Coordinator, and the Dean of Girls. All opposed the return of Jane Doe and urged me not to agree to her return. The Dean of Girls developed a hysterical ball in her throat when I stated that Jane might be returning the next day. In the 10 years that she had been dean, she had never reacted in such a way to a discipline case.

I phoned the superintendent and described my conversations with the people to whom I had talked about Jane Doe. I then read to him a paragraph from a confidential report in which Mrs. Doe told a counselor that she could not control her daughter's "big mouth" and temper; that Jane had been under the care of a psychiatrist, but did not continue because she was unresponsive. I referred to other documents that I did not read over the phone, but that I sent forward to the superintendent. I concluded by reaffirming my determination not to accept Jane's return.

The superintendent replied: "All right. We'll take care of it here."

The next morning I found Jane Doe, her mother, and a man and woman from the local federally funded poverty agency seated on a bench outside my office door. They had been placed there by the Dean of Boys who had refused to permit Jane to go to classes.

I had learned to take careful notes and to write out the precise language used in sensitive situations. Perhaps it is my training as a historian and my preference for primary sources. In any event I returned to the bench of unexpected visitors with a hand-held tape recorder. I identified myself as principal and asked the male poverty worker for his name.

I explained that I had refused to readmit Jane to the school. I asked him to leave with the group. He refused to do so. I advised him to take his business to the chancellor. I called for the assistance of the police officer assigned to the vicinity of the school. When he arrived, I said: "Officer, I am asking you to persuade these people to leave this school. Failing that, I must regretfully ask you to arrest them and my complaint will be criminal trespass." I made clear the circumstances to the officer. "They are preventing me from doing my job and they are creating a situation in the hall."

I left the group with the officer and returned to my office. A few minutes later I saw that only the male poverty worker remained on the bench. I ignored him and went about my business. The officer, too, at my request left the corridor. After about two hours the bench was empty. I knew then that a major confrontation lay ahead, but could not imagine the deep, sharp turn it would take.

Before noon the superintendent's assistant phoned and read a letter from the superintendent to me. In the afternoon, it was hand-delivered and I signed for it. The final paragraph stated: "It is now my judgment that [Jane] be returned to Long Island City High School, effective Friday morning, March 12, 1976. You are, with this communication, instructed to permit [Jane Doe] to attend her classes at Long Island City High School."

The thought of wavering never entered my mind. I phoned the police precinct captain and asked him to be sure to have an officer at the school by 7:30 a.m., the next day.

I arrived at school at 6:30 a.m. and was joined at the main entrance an hour later by two officers. As a further precaution I stationed one of the deans at a side door which was the regular student entrance. He was to direct Jane Doe and anyone who accompanied her to the front of the building.

This time Jane arrived without her mother, but with the same male poverty worker and another woman. It was a cold March day with no promise of spring, but I remained outdoors with the group. We talked with the poverty workers. The woman added to the exchange: "We want to get rid of you as principal." It took me two hours to get rid of *them*.

The weekend intervened. On Monday, at 7:30 a.m., I was ready again with the police officers. No one showed.

Early in the afternoon the superintendent's assistant phoned to say that Jane would be arriving and that the superintendent had ordered me to admit her. I reiterated my refusal to do so.

I phoned the superintendent and repeated the message about his "order." He said that he had been misunderstood; that he was merely inquiring as to whether Jane Doe would be admitted by me.

The superintendent then said: "Well, I transferred her to Bryant."

This is exactly what I had suggested and the superintendent had said he would do in the first place. I remarked, "You never told me that."

"I thought I had." This was a lie, and I wondered what new

form the game was taking. I was to find out soon enough.

I arranged for the police to be on hand the next morning. This time the two officers were joined by a detective and sergeant. My firm ties with the police were a comfort. School principals these days who do not have a solid relationship with the local police are in poor shape. Police officers should not be assigned *in* a school, but in the vicinity or on quick call.

When Jane did not appear, I asked a guidance counselor to phone Bryant to find out whether she was on their register. She was. The incident was closed—or so it seemed.

The very day that I verified the transfer of Jane to Bryant, I received another hand-delivered letter from the superintendent, dated March 16, 1976. The letter called for me to be present at a hearing on the Jane Doe case. It was a mild missive compared with the missile the chancellor launched against me a week later.

The superintendent directed me to report to his office on March 19, at 11 a.m., to respond to his charge that I had refused to obey his "direct instruction." I was advised of my right to be accompanied by a school employee who was not a lawyer.

The letter was unexpected and I answered it with a letter of my own. "How can you," I asked, "after praising me in our conversation on March 15, as a principal who has 'the support of 99.99 percent of the Long Island City community' send me such a letter? . . . . I believe that your actions against me may be found in your determination to placate [the poverty group] and the New York Civil Liberties Union, who have for a decade sought with no success to oust me as principal of Long Island City High School. You have sided with them before and you are aiding and abetting them now.

"Your charges are not in accord with the facts and ignore totally the decency of my motives, the proved effectiveness of my school administration to which you have attested, and the overwhelming support of children, parents and community leaders whose confidence inspires me.

"The people who support me know that I must refuse to accept your judgment in the [Jane Doe] case, if Long Island City High School is to remain the kind of school to which neighborhood children can come without fear and with a chance to learn in a peaceful atmosphere."

Poverty workers and the New York Civil Liberties Union were united in protecting the right of the vilest miscreant to attend school. They invoked every conceivable procedure to harass me and other principals in the city. The easy out was to give in to them. And I must say sadly that it is the easy out that has driven schools up and over the wall. I resisted them every inch of the way and was supported by the community.

My letter to the superintendent had no effect. The superintendent phoned to say that he "momentarily expected to be served with papers" by the poverty lawyer; that I had to readmit Jane in order to avoid an order to do so by the court.

I retorted that there was not a court in Queens county that would issue such an order. Jane had not begun to exhaust her administrative remedies—appeal to the chancellor, to the Board of Education, the State Commissioner of Education. A judge would have to ignore precedent to listen to any poverty or civil liberties union lawyer on this kind of case.

The superintendent's fear of legal action stemmed from a combination of ignorance and cowardice. He failed to comprehend the effect readmitting Jane would have on the school. Unwittingly, he was escalating what was to become a national cause célèbre.

In a separate note I had asked the superintendent to postpone for a few days the hearing on the charge of insubordination. He refused. The representative "who is not a lawyer," whom I planned to bring with me was Peter O'Brien, then president of the Council of Supervisors and Administrators of which I was a vice president and one of the founders.

O'Brien insisted on a delay. He wanted time to consult our union's lawyer. More so than I, he felt that things were getting very serious. Over the years he had warned me that they were going to try to get you on something that they think will stick. I could not believe that this was the one. I naively assumed that it would be absurd to suspend me in order to readmit a 16-year-old with a horrendous record.

9

THE LAST ANGRY PRINCIPAL

When I did not appear for the hearing, the superintendent sent me another letter, again hand-delivered, informing me that on Monday morning, March 22, Jane Doe would be accompanied by an assistant whom he named in the letter. I knew that she was a black woman and I phoned to excoriate him for this tactic. The girl was black and I believed that the superintendent had decided to build the incident into a racial issue.

While I was behind the barricades, Jane was interviewed in the office of a poverty group by Ken Auletta who was doing the story for a national magazine. He asked Jane: "Was this incident racially motivated?" She paused and then said, "No, I think he'd do it to anybody. He doesn't care what color you are" (*New York*, May 3, 1976, page 48).

On Monday morning, March 22, Jane Doe was accompanied to school by a black woman. I inadvertently addressed the administrator as Mrs. Doe. She was affronted and I apologized. I told her that she could enter the building but I would not admit Jane Doe. I observed a group of poverty workers across the street. As in the past, police officers were at the main entrance with me, along with an assistant principal and dean. There were always plenty of witnesses to my action, and I sometimes made a written report of the event that an assistant principal and teacher would sign to attest to its accuracy.

Jane Doe's companion for the morning asked for permission to phone the superintendent. Immediately after the call, she left the building taking Jane with her. They joined the poverty workers across the street and left together with them.

All of these events took place while the school was going on peacefully. Students who saw me with police at the main entrance did not crowd around during change of classes. Television crews who had visited the school before and after the barricading never failed to express astonishment that students did not crowd around them and interfere with their work. True, there is the natural curiosity of kids, but they understood that a quick look was all they had time for if they were to get to their classes.

In battles it is wisdom to anticipate the enemy's next act. I did not anticipate that the chancellor would suspend me. No high school principal had ever been suspended. Of course none had ever behaved the way I did. I determined during those terrible years in which students were taking over schools and colleges to run a school with dignity or not at all. Daily reports of school violence in the city and nation only sharpened my vigilance.

I did not expect suspension because I attributed some intelligence to the chancellor. How could he fire a principal with almost 40 years of superior service? Only the previous year—1975—I had been commended by the New York State Assembly and Senate in separate unprecedented resolutions for "leadership in the performance of his duties as principal of Long Island City High School" during "a turbulent decade." How could he remove me as principal because I refused to readmit to the school a student with an execrable record of behavior? Apart from such compelling considerations, he would be taking action against me at a time when schools in the city, state and nation were suffering the after-effects of the Vietnam War protest.

Surely the chancellor would not justify my dismissal on the ground that everyone must obey the law—no exceptions. I had not broken any law. I had differed with the judgment of a superintendent and refused to obey his irrational order.

As for lawbreaking, Irving Anker, before he became chancellor, had hailed lawbreakers in the South who had refused to ride in the back of the bus. At worst, I reasoned, he must equate my refusal to obey with acts of civil disobedience that have lent lustre to this nation's past.

I had known Anker for 20 years. We had both been history teachers. He was about 10 years older than I and had started up the ladder earlier. I thought of him as a mediocrity with the charisma of a rabbit. He was as out of place at the head of a troubled school system as a rabbit leading lions.

Boards of education in New York and elsewhere are often uneasy with strong superintendents. Often there is a prima donna on the board who seeks the limelight. To the extent that boards interfere in the day to day operations of the schools, they damage operations. They have not been notably successful in selecting superintendents as evidenced by the fact that the average life in office of a superintendent is three years. The decline in public schools is owing in part to poor policy-making by boards of education and weak leadership of superintendents. (The title "Chancellor" in a public school system is an affectation. The duties are those of a superintendent. Superintendents of New York City high schools are really assistant superintendents.)

The chancellor suspended me on the afternoon of March 22, 1976. As the barricades went up, I realized that I was in a life and death struggle in which my career could be ended in a matter of hours. I thought of the terrible hurt to my wife and son.

I have written elsewhere of my retarded son and the tremendous effort and courage my wife had shown in helping him to approximate normalcy. He had reached the age of 32, two days before my suspension. My book, *Donald, The Man Who Remains A Boy*, had touched a sensitive chord, even among parents with normal children. We have received letters about Donald from teenagers and parents all over the nation.

My worst fears about the effect of my struggle on my wife and son were realized almost instantly. Donald had heard about his father on radio. He was home because he had lost his job. The W.T. Grant Company, which I had described in the book as the "corporation with a heart" had failed. Grant had employed Donald for 10 years prior to suffering a billion dollar bankruptcy, the greatest up to that time in the history of the nation's retail business.

Nettie phoned to tell me what Donald had asked her.

"Has Daddy lost his job?"

"Will we lose the house, Mom?"

"Will I lose my room? Will I have to give back my bed?"

We had just bought Donald a new bed for his birthday.

I can take on an army of Ankers. I become vulnerable when I feel that I am causing my wife and son to suffer for causes which I undertake because of my ego and determination to do what I think is right no matter what the risk.

Nettie told me that she could not leave Donald to come to me in school. He had been out of work for a month despite my efforts to get him a job. He was unhappy. Nettie sent pajamas, shirts and a toothbrush with a teacher who lived nearby. I kept a blanket and pillow in school, since I sometimes took a nap before an evening meeting.

Through the early part of the three days and nights that I was the "prisoner of the community," I was hurt more by the pain I was inflicting on my wife and son than by the action of the chancellor.

There was a point when Peter O'Brien, who was at my side for hours, became concerned. Pete, who tipped the scale at 250, stands over six feet and sports a heavy red beard and dark glasses, has a heart tailored to size.

"Howard, you look depressed. Is there anything I can do?"

"Pete, how would you like to save three lives?"

Pete had sensed that my depression had nothing to do with the battle we were in. As the father of a deaf son, who knew my family, he was sensitive to my thoughts.

I had decided to ask Pete for help, because I was near the breaking point. I could not take both the destruction of my career and the devastation of my wife and son. Since I was too choked up to talk, I gave Pete a note I had written.

In the note I asked Pete to give my son a job. I promised to write for CSA for the rest of my life without any compensation, if he would do that for me.

Pete had started for a corner of the office while reading the note. He wheeled around and came back to my desk.

"How can you think of giving me such a promise? Tell Donald to report for work tomorrow morning."

The next morning Donald phoned his mother from work.

"Don't worry, Mom. I have a job now. Daddy doesn't have to work anymore."

Nettie phoned to tell me what he said. We both cried, as we have so many times when we have faced a crisis with Donald.

Pete called me twice during the day to tell me how well Donald was doing and how happy the office staff was to have him with them.

As I write, Donald has completed 12 years at CSA where he regards the mail room as his private preserve. He also runs errands. On his fortieth birthday, officers and staff gave Donald a surprise party. He is easily the happiest worker in America.

THE LAST ANGRY PRINCIPAL

His enthusiasm for his job is known to everyone. When asked by the office manager, "Donald, what is it that you don't like about working for CSA?" Donald answered: "Saturday and Sunday."

Peter O'Brien's kindness in giving Donald a job relieved me of much of the tension generated by our resistance to the chancellor's order. My office was invariably filled with televison crews, radio and press reporters. Len Buder of *The New York Times* was with me most of the time. Ken Auletta of *New York* magazine spent at least 25 hours with me and had dinner at my home, after the ordeal. His article, "The Last Angry Principal," brought letters from the West Coast where I was hailed as a "folk hero."

Buder described me as a "Champion of School Discipline"; Owen Moritz of the *New York Daily News* as "a principled principal"; Tom Buckley in *The New York Times* as a "national figure"; the editor of the *Richmond* (Virginia) *News Leader* as the "Man of the Year"; Mort Young, in the *San Francisco Examiner*, wrote he "just doesn't scare." Pictures of me with an accompanying story appeared in small town newspapers nationwide. More than a thousand letters reached me, some with newspaper clippings. I was interviewed on television and radio by reporters in Toronto, Boston, Pittsburgh and other cities. The story was carried in the European press. Later, my articles on the event and views on education appeared in newspapers in Los Angeles, San Francisco, Chicago, Philadelphia and Boston.

The unfolding drama was seized upon by metropolitan and network television because of the thousands who marched in the streets outside the school and the evening mass meetings in the community. Hand-lettered signs and sheets carried such slogans as "No Doc. No School." There were signs in Greek, Italian and Spanish. Blacks and whites marched together. Students paused in their march around the building to sing lyrics that they had written about me. I was so exhilarated by the outpouring of good will that I had no time to be exhausted.

Two years after the event, some of the street scenes were included as background when I was interviewed by Mike Wallace on "60 Minutes" (Feb. 26, 1978, with a repeat in June).

14

BEHIND THE BARRICADES

On the very first night that I was to sleep in, there were hundreds of parents and friends in the corridor outside my office. As the hour grew late the festive atmosphere heightened. But, they were working men and women and I did not want them to lose any sleep on my account. I suggested to Gerald Nozilo, field commander of the operation, that everyone go home since nothing would happen during the night.

It was not the first time that my miscalculations, if they had been permitted to prevail, would have ended in disaster for me. Nozilo told me, "O.K., Doc, but 20 of us are sleeping outside your door."

II

BARRICADES REMOVED

THE COMMUNITY LEADERS were right and I was wrong. Had I been permitted to hold to my judgment that I needed no protection during the night, my day as a high school principal would have been ended.

After midnight, on March 23, 1976, two Board of Education security guards appeared with a court order that directed them to remove me from the building. They had gained entrance through a side door that had been opened for them by a board security guard who had remained in the building.

The board guards were stopped by Gerald Nozilo and his men. They did not reach me and were persuaded to post the court order on the door that they had used to enter the building.

The court order was taken from the door by Robert Robson, a young giant who acted as my aide-de-camp. Bob had been graduated from Long Island City High School two years earlier and was attending the John Jay College of Criminal Justice. He noted that the court order was not signed and gave it to my lawyer who found other errors in the order. We thus gained two days during which we made plans for leaving the school and setting up headquarters in the Young Men's Christian Association building across the street. It had been offered to us by Frank Tempone, the YMCA director who has been my friend for over two decades.

Bob, at 6 feet 6 inches and 225 pounds, was highly visible at the height of the action in my office, but went about his work quietly. He timed the interviews with reporters and the camera crews so that the office was not too crowded and scheduling conflicts were avoided. He assisted my superb secretary, Eva Stern, on the telephone. He brought me water and coffee and tried to get me to eat. I lost 10 pounds in three days. My wife, Nettie, lost 25 pounds and was down to a mere 95 pounds. She had started worrying weeks before I knew what hit me.

There was always food in the office—mounds of sandwiches and coffee. Susan Biolchini, a cafeteria supervisor, had kept me well fed for 10 years. She was now prepared to feed every media man in the city. Women in the community were not to be outdone. There was an ethnic smorgasbord. The Greeks brought in spinach pie, Feta cheese, Pita bread and baclava; the Italians, lasagna, ravioli, meatball heroes and Bola wines.

Although I ate without appetite and slept little, an Associated Press wirephoto showed me munching a sandwich and drinking coffee contentedly. At that I was barely able to prevent the photographer from cajoling me into lying down on the couch in the office so that he could show me sleeping.

I came much closer to priests, ministers and rabbis during those three days than ever before in my life. During much of the day and many evening hours, there was at least one clergyman with me. My relationship with St. Patrick's, the parochial school across the street from our schoolyard, had been close. Reverend Francis J. Fahey was with me for many hours. The ladies in his parish organized letter writing and telephone calls to the board in my support. It was not the first time they stood by my side in a crisis.

I saw in the first hours that the neighborhood people were determined to keep me as their principal. Hundreds were in the halls and thousands in the streets. There was not a single act of violence from the beginning to the end of the confrontation. The police told me later that there was not even a near arrest. I had said to Nozilo: "Jerry, if a single kid or parent is hurt out there, I'm going over these benches and head for Worth Street to put in my retirement papers."

Everyone around me was confident that we would win. I had my doubts. A chancellor who could not see that my stand on discipline would be sure to gain national support might be stubborn enough to try to wear the community down. I saw, however, that our people were prepared to stay in the trenches indefinitely. Their stake was even greater than mine. I could retire under generous pension provisions and suffer no loss of income. They stood to lose a safe school for their children. Parents had told me that they were saving money by sending their children to a public school; that if I were not the principal, they would not send their children to a public high school. Their confidence in me was flattering, but it was sad to know that the schools of which I had once been proud were on a toboggan.

During the days that students were boycotting classes and parading, the teachers were in school. They let the press know that they were supporting me. The teachers' union sent in George Altomare, a vice president, to see what he could do to help restore me to authority in the school. The union had been inveighing for almost a decade against assaults on teachers, and I stood high with the union on the basis of our safety record.

The chancellor sent in the Queens high school superintendent and the Executive Director of High Schools. I was informed of their every move by Nozilo and others who were on the scene constantly. They sought unsuccessfully to use the public address system. It had been made inoperative by Bob Robson, who had anticipated just such use. The custodian-engineer, Joseph Johnson, was not available to assist the superintendent. Mr. Johnson had worked with me closely to make our building so dignified that it took on the appearance of an aged but handsome museum. He guarded the hundreds of framed paintings on the walls as though he were in charge of the National Gallery of Art.

By scurrying about the halls the chancellor's emissaries were able to convene a faculty meeting in the student cafeteria on the morning of the second day of the boycott. I was given a written report of the meeting by my secretary who had obtained the information from a parent.

Parents along with the teachers attended the meeting and shouted the superintendent down when he started to say that classes would resume. He could not finish the sentence which started, "We have every intention to conduct. . . ." When he began again, "I am here at Long Island City, a high school which is an example of law and order . . . . ," he was reminded that it did not exist elsewhere. Parents rose to demand that Dr. Hurwitz be returned as principal immediately.

Both the superintendent and director were flustered by the hostile reception. They received no encouragement from the teachers. The meeting was ended by the superintendent.

After their failure with teachers and parents, the superintendent and director sent in word that they wished to meet with me. I agreed to meet with them in my office. The community people would not remove the benches piled up at the entrance to my secretary's office which led into mine. I had indicated that the benches should be moved aside, but was ignored. I watched the two clamber clumsily over the barricade.

Already in my office were Peter O'Brien, president of the Council of Supervisors and Administrators, and City Councilman Thomas Manton, representing the community.

We sat around the light oak, rectangular table. No pleasantries were exchanged. The superintendent spoke first:

"Dr. Hurwitz, you are disobeying official orders, and you must leave this building at once."

Before I could respond, Councilman Manton, roared: "Dr. Hurwitz is not going to leave this building. You are! The chancellor has shown us that he doesn't care about safety in our school when he ordered the return of a student who caused a lot of trouble. Dr. Hurwitz has the complete confidence of our community. You had better get his suspension lifted because this school boycott will continue until you do."

When I was able to get a word in, I said, "Anyone reading Jane Doe's record would have to agree that I acted in the interest of the children in the school. You, Abe, agreed immediately to her transfer."

To our amazement the director let us know, "I haven't yet seen the record." The superintendent had seen some of the record, but not the confidential part about which I had talked with him on the phone at the time he arranged the transfer of Jane to nearby Bryant High School. It was her return to LIC that I had refused to accept when the superintendent succumbed to the pressures of the poverty group and the New York Civil Liberties Union.

Manton tried to reason with the board officials. The director responded: "An order is an order, and we have to obey it regardless of what we think of it."

Manton again laced into the two for their failure to understand that the community was determined to keep me as the principal. "We'll never yield," he declared. "We want the kids back in school, but they're not coming back on your terms." They had said they wanted me to report to board headquarters to stand trial for insubordination. An assistant principal would be the acting principal in my absence.

The superintendent and director left the table. Again, they climbed awkwardly over the barricade. I had moved to push aside a bench, since I didn't want them to break their necks. A community man said, "No way, Dr. Hurwitz."

When Manton and O'Brien left, the barricades were pushed aside for the moment.

In the evening I talked with Altomare, who represented the teachers' union, O'Brien, City Councilman Vallone, State Senator Anthony Gazzara, and others who explored with me a way out of the impasse. Vallone and Gazzara had been busy during the day rallying legislative support for my stand. The Queens legislators in the City Council, State Senate and State Assembly were unanimous in communicating to Chancellor Anker their determination that I be restored as principal so that school could resume. They were coordinated by Serphin Maltese, Executive Director of the New York State Conservative Party. It was clear that partisan politics was no factor in supporting me. All political parties affirmed that the schools must be kept safe for the children, and I had worked to this end with legislators regardless of their party affiliation.

Vallone and Gazzara, the key negotiators for the community, were able to arrange a meeting at board headquarters. Chancellor Anker told them he could not be at the meeting because he had to be in Albany, but he would be represented by the superintendent and executive director. When I heard this, I told

Vallone and Gazzara that I could see no hope for a binding settlement with the chancellor's lackies.

Plans for the meeting at the board went ahead. Altomare and O'Brien had suggested to Vallone and Gazzara an ingenious compromise in which the chancellor would save part of his face and I would be restored to duty.

The Board of Education resolution confirming my suspension contained a clause as unprecedented as the suspension itself. It must have been drafted by someone who sensed that the chancellor's suspension of me might have to be revoked quickly. The clause gave the chancellor the right to restore Dr. Hurwitz to duty without returning to the board for approval. Since the board meets only twice a month, a great timesaving had been made possible.

Vallone and Gazzara, after the first negotiating session, came to me late in the afternoon emotionally exhausted. They looked haggard. "Pete, Tony," I said, "Before you say anything, let's have some coffee and cake. I have some idea of what you must have gone through with those characters."

Vallone started by saying: "Dr. Hurwitz, we want to offer you a compromise. But, if you don't want it, just say so. We're with you one hundred percent. We'll back you, no matter what you decide."

Gazzara added his personal assurances. Both spoke for the community, they said, and the community would settle for nothing less than my return as principal; but, the chancellor had to save face.

Vallone explained the proposed compromise: "The suspension will be lifted and you must obey the chancellor's orders in the future. You must stand trial at the Board of Education after your return to duty. The trial will be held in such a way that your duties at the school will not be interfered with excessively. Finally, and most important, the girl is to be readmitted, but she is to be accompanied by a special security guard, paid for by the board, who is to be with her at all times while she is in school."

I did not for a moment envisage a security guard walking around with a student, but I did see that the principle of discipline would be served by the compromise. The chancellor had recognized that the girl posed a special problem and that I was justified in identifying her as such. No such arrangement for a discipline problem had ever been made—and no other such arrangement has been made since that time.

If I refused the compromise, it seemed that the kids would be out of school for weeks or months. I could not bring myself to say "no" to the compromise. I loved the people in the community. I could not be so selfish as to demand complete capitulation by the chancellor.

The promise to obey the chancellor in the future gave me no pause. I had been obeying orders for years. It was only when the order meant a sacrifice of principle that I balked. As for the trial on an insubordination charge, I thought that it might give me the chance to establish for the record why I had insisted that Jane Doe be transferred to another school. No principal, including me, ever asked for expulsion of a severe discipline case. So reasonable an action is unthinkable in an era when individual rights are sacrosanct and those who suffer from abuse by a culprit must take it—no matter what.

I told Vallone and Gazzara that I accepted the compromise. They said they would get back to me with plans for my meeting with the chancellor's representatives at the board. I learned later in the evening that Nozilo and two other men, Mike Partridge and Joe Florio, would call for me at 7 a.m., the next morning, before any sizable number of students and parents might assemble for the day's parade around the building.

Our cloak and dagger routine went off as planned. We drove from Queens to Brooklyn in comparatively light traffic. I had the chance to talk in a more relaxed way to the men who were making it possible for me to remain in the school system. They were men in their thirties. Nozilo and Florio had children in my school. Partridge, a Greek Cypriote, had children who were attending elementary schools. All could afford homes in the suburbs, but their parents lived in the community and their roots were in the community. They looked forward to their children remaining in the community. In fighting my fight, they were fighting for their children and their community.

We arrived early at board headquarters for the meeting that we expected would produce a written agreement whereby my suspension would be lifted. We had some coffee in the small cafeteria just inside the main entrance and were joined by the elevator starter, Bob Schmaltz, whose long service and lively talk had made him an institution at Livingston Street.

Schmaltz had not recognized me. He talked about the terrible situation at Long Island City High School. "Everybody," he told us, "supports Dr. Hurwitz, a brave man who stands for safe schools." He asked whether we knew him. Nozilo, Partridge and Florio assured Schmaltz that they were admirers of Dr. Hurwitz. I remarked, thinking as I talked that I would make it up to Schmaltz at the first opportunity, "I don't know Dr. Hurwitz as well as I should, but I'm getting to know him better." We could not tell Schmaltz who we were because the press room was only a few feet from where we were talking and we were not about to pledge Schmaltz to secrecy.

In my subsequent visits to Livingston Street, where my trial was held, Schmaltz, who did not reach five feet and weighed under a hundred pounds, did everything but carry me up on his shoulders. It was embarrassing, but Schmaltz was all heart, and his enthusiasm was shared by the riders.

For the secret meeting, we decided that Partridge, a real estate operator with negotiating experience, would sit on my side of the table. Nozilo would remain in the outside corridor, and Florio would be at the main entrance. We had not forgotten that I was under a court order to vacate my office. That very day, I was being represented in court by my CSA attorney, accompanied by Vallone and Gazzara who were also attorneys.

Partridge and I sat down in the superintendent's office expecting to consider at least a draft of the compromise that Vallone and Gazzara had said they had reached. We learned at once that Anker's spokesmen denied having promised that a security guard would accompany Jane Doe in school. They told us that so far as they were concerned the school had officially opened at the very time we were seated in the room. They said the chancellor had sent five teachers to the school and this signified official opening of the school. The magic number "five" had no precedent in my experience, and I seethed inwardly as I contemplated the deceit of Abe and Sam, men whom I knew on a first-name basis for over a decade.

"We are asking you," the director said, "to phone the school and give the word that students are to report for classes. You will remain here for a few weeks to write a syllabus on constitutional law. You are restored to the payroll from which we removed you two days ago when you failed to report to me as ordered."

The syllabus-writing was intended to please me since they had read much that I had written, including *The Principal, School Discipline, and the Law*, in which I analyzed the constitutional law affecting student behavior in the nation's schools.

Partridge was composed but incredulous. He would not accept their denial that the details of an agreement had been fleshed out with Vallone and Gazzara.

I spoke up: "I did not ask the students to leave school, and I shall not ask them to return. As for writing a syllabus, you know what you can do with that idea. As for the pay, I'm a long way from being down to my last dime. And, as for your outright lying, I believe Vallone and Gazzara—not you."

I got up from the table and walked to my coat. The superintendent and director pleaded with me to remain. I could not bring myself to so much as look at them. I said nothing further and left the room. Partridge remained.

I joined Nozilo in the hall. He was perturbed. He told me, "I've seen two of the process servers who tried to get into the building." As we spoke, the two passed us hurriedly.

"Let's get the hell out of here," Nozilo said.

"How will Partridge know we've gone?"

"Don't worry. He'll know."

We took the elevator down, picked up Florio at the door, and walked to the parking lot for our car.

Five minutes later, Partridge joined us. We drove back to Queens and I was shielded by the three men as I entered the school by the side exit. I was seen only by the community people who were on guard outside my office. They removed the barricade for us.

I phoned Vallone and told him what had happened.,

"Impossible," he responded. "I'll get back to you."

My wife had come to school on the second night. Nettie quickly made friends with people in the hall and office. A marvellous raconteur, she delighted them with stories about her mother, patriarchal father, and 12 brothers and sisters. I have often thought of taping her as she talks and weaving the stories into a saga of an immigrant family whose children became doctors, lawyers, teachers and furriers in a worldwide business. The basic story is not new to the American Dream, but the details are something else again.

Nettie had told me stories about my own school on her visits during Christmas parties and was to tell me what she learned while I was behind the barricades. She sees as a weakness of mine—and I agree—my deaf ear to the liaisons among faculty members.

On a sad note, she told me of one girl who when she learned Nettie was my wife told her, "I love your husband." She added, "Dr. Hurwitz spoke to the kids in my classes. I have to go to the bathroom very often, but no one makes fun of me anymore. I have a colostomy."

By 4 p.m., the third and final day of the boycott, Vallone was back in my office with the written agreement. The chancellor may have learned of the community plan to close 30 more schools in the district if I were not restored as principal by the end of the week.

I did not like the tone of the agreement which, in effect, said that I was being returned to duty on condition that I be a good boy in the future. However, the facts were clear. I had been suspended by the chancellor who three days later revoked my suspension. The student who had stirred the confrontation was being returned to school, but a security guard was being assigned as a guarantee of her good behavior for the remainder of her stay in school.

On Friday morning, March 26, 1976, the students streamed back into school. I stood in the main corridor, visible to all who entered. The boys shook my hand or smiled and waved as they walked to class. Some called to me, "We won."

THE LAST ANGRY PRINCIPAL

Many girls stopped to kiss me on the cheek.

When I returned to my office, I expressed astonishment to my secretary, Eva Stern.

"I'm not the kind of principal whom girls kiss."

"You don't understand, Dr. Hurwitz. They love and respect you because they're safe here. No boy would dare to touch a girl in this school."

At noon on the first day of school the superintendent and director arrived for lunch. They were visibly relieved that it was all over. Susan added to the festive atmosphere by preparing my favorite shrimp. The table in my office was set tastefully as always when I entertained guests.

The director told me about his three highly successful children. The superintendent told me about his five grandchildren. I told them about my only child, Donald. "He has a job with CSA that he loves. Peter O'Brien gave him the job a couple of days ago when he saw how blue I looked. No, it wasn't what you were doing to me. Nettie is so happy now that Donald is working again." I told them that Nettie is an inveterate worrier who sees me as a warrior in the school wars. She fears the risks I take, but has never once counseled surrender. "I could not have resisted with such determination if my support on the home front had been anything but strong."

As I spoke, I thought that I was overdoing things a bit, sitting at the same table with them. Even Susan had asked, "Should I put down the tablecloth, Dr. Hurwitz? I know you don't like those people."

I find it hard to compartmentalize my life. I know that lawyers can oppose each other bitterly in court. I have seen them chat amiably during recess. Legislators, too, can be at the antipodes on issues and seem quite friendly outside the chamber.

There are some people in the school system whom I have not spoken to for years, and I shall not speak to again. They include Anker, who faded into oblivion when his contract was not renewed, the superintendent who retired, and the director, fired by the chancellor who succeeded Anker. I despise them on two counts and cannot bring myself to mention them by name, lest they derive some benefit from the recognition.

First, they placed me on the wrack along with my wife and son when they would be the first to admit that I have always been a superior teacher and principal. To pillory me and protect a miscreant, typical of thousands nationwide who are destroying our schools, was unconscionable.

"It's nothing personal, Howard. I must do my duty." Cattle-car talk so far as I'm concerned.

Second, these people headed an imperilled school system of which I was proud up to the time I became a principal in 1966. They were people of modest abilities who rose to the top because they could be counted on to do as they were told. They were cultured cowards. They knuckled under to the poverty panderers and New York Civil Liberties Union. They were bleeding hearts, but it was not their own blood they shed. They drained principals who could not maintain discipline during troubled times without vigorous support from the top. As a consequence the learning climate in our schools has evaporated.

I am a great believer in leadership and these people are nonleaders; even worse, they are misleaders. To the extent that the Ankers have facsimiles in the school world, we can explain the decline of American public education.

On the first day of my return to school, I visited Livingston Street in the late morning, as part of the agreement. I busied myself in the superintendent's office for an hour making phone calls to radio and television stations that had asked me to return calls and arrange for appearances. Barry Farber and Bob Grant, who continue to host popular talk shows, had me on several times during and after the crisis. I was also interviewed by Robert MacNeil on his network Public Broadcasting System news report. It was to lead to a new career as a national lecturer, radio-tv commentator and education columnist.

The school settled down from the first morning that my suspension was lifted and the boycott ended. Jane Doe did not appear the first day. When she did come to school two days later, accompanied by a security guard, I assigned the security guard to the girls' toilet on the first floor. As noted, the idea of any student in my school walking around with a security guard was unthinkable—to me.

THE LAST ANGRY PRINCIPAL

I sent Jane to the Assistant Principal's office for a pass to class and told her to return to my office before going to class. I seated her alongside my desk and before I could say anything, she said, "My lawyer told me not to speak to you."

This is the advice published by the New York Civil Liberties Union in its *Student Rights Handbook*. Students are informed that they need not speak to school officials when charged with offenses. No student had told me "See my lawyer," and Jane Doe was not going to make it to class with that approach. It was outrageous of the lawyer for the poverty group to give Jane such advice.

I told Jane, "You can tell your lawyer that if you do not speak to the principal, you cannot stay in school. Either you tell me now that you will speak to me, or I am taking you to the door and sending you home."

Jane changed her tone. I explained that I did not hold her responsible for the closing of the school for three days. "If you control your temper, you will have no problem here. I do not want to embarrass you by having a security officer escort you from class to class. I have assigned the security guard elsewhere."

Jane seemed chastened by her experience. She was to leave school about three months later at the end of June to enroll in an evening high school where she completed her high school education.

Jane's case was kept active by the poverty lawyer who sought to have her failing marks changed and notation of the suspension removed from her permanent record card. The failing marks had been entered before the incident that precipitated her transfer to another school. She had been failed in all subjects during a term in which she had been absent excessively without a legitimate excuse. She had not been treated any differently from other students who had absented themselves without excuse (truancy).

The correspondence initiated by the poverty lawyer was voluminous and my replies detailed. The chancellor sustained my refusal to change the record. After my retirement, all records were changed.

Part of the agreement under which I had been restored as principal included my trial on charges of insubordination. I have never doubted that if I had yielded to the original order to leave my school and report to Livingston Street, I would not have resumed the principalship of LIC or of any school no matter what the outcome of the trial. I knew also that months would have elapsed before the start of any trial. The appeals that I would surely have undertaken would have meant years in the courts.

Notice of the start of my trial came with unusual swiftness. I had started the school anew on March 26, 1976, and within a week was notified that the trial would start on April 12.

The trial, too, was to be unique.

III

KANGAROO COURT

I WAS THE ONLY HIGH SCHOOL PRINCIPAL in the history of the City of New York to be suspended. As an added twist, I was the only school employee placed on trial while *not* suspended. My suspension had been lifted after three days that shook the system as part of the agreement with the chancellor whereby the school was reopened with me as principal.

During the trial which started with unprecedented promptness after my restoration to duty, my attorney, Max Frankle, and I listened to witnesses called by the chancellor's attorney. The hearing was presided over by a retired civil court judge, Charles Gold, retained by the board as the trial examiner.

It was apparent from the first that Judge Gold knew on which side his bread was buttered. His conduct of the trial moved Frankle to style the proceeding as "bloodletting by a kangaroo court."

On the sixth day of the trial Frankle stunned Judge Gold by withdrawing from the case. I left with him. The trial examiner had refused to permit any testimony about my nearly 40 years of superior service and refused to admit as relevant the confidential Jane Doe record. Frankle could not sustain any cross-examination of witnesses for the chancellor, so frequent was the trial examiner's interruptions. The trial record was subsequently shown by Frankle to be replete with errors so fundamental and pervasive that no lawyer could be expected to defend his client.

The judge, evidently disturbed that our withdrawal from the case might reflect on his ability to conduct a hearing and thereby prevent further employment by the board, entreated Frankle and me to return. He wrote and phoned us. We would not return.

The judge continued the hearings without us for several weeks and compiled a record in support of his recommendation that I be fined $3,500 for failing to obey an order of the superintendent. He also wrote: "No consideration may be given to the demonstrations and the school boycott by pupils which went on for a number of days, as this was not one of the charges, and, of course, there was no proof that the Respondent had organized it or generated it directly.

"Had there been such a charge and actual convincing proof thereof the Trial Examiner would unhesitatingly have recommended dismissal of the Respondent."

In his 58-page Reply to the trial examiner's recommendation, addressed to the board, Frankle characterized Judge Gold's contemplated dismissal of me as "a final transcendently outrageous comment." He took exception to numerous errors made by the trial examiner and concluded, "The aura of hostility and vituperation spread over the findings and recommendations by this hypothetical commentary results in a biased and unalterably prejudicial presentation. . . ."

The community was outraged by the recommendation that I be fined. Father John Poulos, pastor of St. Demitrios Greek Orthdox Church in Astoria, the largest Greek community in North America, came to me and offered to pay the fine. I had won the high regard of the Greek people when I introduced modern Greek into the curriculum during my first year as principal. No one had asked me to do so.

Years later, when I had become well known in the community, a local newspaper, *The Greek American*, hailed me as "A Man of the Hour." Although I have never been accused of modesty, I cannot bring myself to quote at any length from the long biographical piece. I was especially pleased with the reporter's observation of the school. "The halls," she wrote, "are neat and the lunch room is a marvel in itself—you can almost hear a napkin drop—and you'll see it picked up also." Of me, she wrote: "He seldom says 'no' if it's a worthy or important cause.

THE LAST ANGRY PRINCIPAL

He can be stern but his warmth and understanding overshadow that sternness. . . ." She noted that of the 2,600 students in the school, 15 percent were Greek-American and of the 167 teachers, 13 percent were Greek-American.

At about the same time as Father Poulos' visit, Mike Partridge, a Greek layman, came to me after the fine was reported in the press. He told me how much the community appreciated my leadership of the school for ten years and how glad they were that I had decided to stay even after the horrible suspension experience. They knew of my wife's strong desire that I retire and be free of the harassment to which I was being subjected by the chancellor right up to the moment he was talking to me. He held in his hand a check for $3,500 and offered it to me.

I thanked Partridge for the community's generous assessment of my work. I said that the board had not yet accepted the trial examiner's recommendation and that if it did, as I was sure it would, I could take the case to the State Supreme Court. In no event, however, would anyone—not even my union—pay the $3,500 fine. I would pay the fine myself.

Actually, I doubted the desirability of carrying the case beyond the board to the courts. My union had already undertaken considerable expense in defense of my actions. I phoned Peter O'Brien and suggested that I pay the fine so that we could concentrate on other issues. I was convinced by the press and community that payment of the fine would not suggest that I had been in the wrong. I had virtually 100 percent support for my stand on discipline and the effect of the chancellor's acts had been to make me a national hero. In that connection a board public relations employee, whom I met in the elevator carrying me to the hearing room, had asked facetiously, "How much are you paying Anker to do your public relations?"

In response to my offer to drop the appeal and pay the fine, O'Brien, a giant, thundered, "No!" He held to the principle. The union was behind me and we were not going to permit the board to get away with any technical victory.

From September 3, 1976, when Frankle filed his Reply to the Trial Examiner's findings and recommendations, to December 15, there was no board action. For a time I thought the board had decided sensibly to push the recommendation for a fine under the heavily carpeted board office. Not so.

I learned shortly before the Christmas holiday that the board had placed the trial examiner's recommendation on its calendar. They had ignored Frankle's detailed reply. My letter to individual board members had set forth reasons why my counsel withdrew from the trial and why we were prevented from presenting a defense.

It is the record of Jane Doe, I wrote, that "is the basis for my refusal to accept the order of the Queens superintendent of high schools to readmit the suspended student. His order was arbitrary and capricious. If I had readmitted the suspended student at his command, my authority as principal would have been undermined. . . .

"The arbitrary nature of the superintendent's order is clear from the undeniable fact that in no previous instance during my 10 years as principal has this superintendent or his predecessors refused to suspend a student at my request; nor has any student so suspended ever been returned to Long Island City High School.

"In the instant, 'Jane Doe' case, the superintendent did transfer the suspended student to another high school where she was on register and in attendance. He ordered 'Jane Doe' back to Long Island City High School when a local poverty lawyer threatened him with a suit. The superintendent phoned me to urge that I accept the return of the student, saying: 'I am expecting momentarily to be served with papers.' I told him he was capitulating to a poverty agency bent on its usual mischief. . . .''

The poverty agency had sought to make a racial issue of Jane Doe's suspension, but the girl herself, as previously noted, said that race was not a factor in my decision. I believed then and now that poverty groups do black youths a disservice when they impute racial motives to school authorities.

I treated black students as I would any others. The biggest mistake a school administrator can make with black youths is to patronize them. The black parents at LIC worked closely with me. They wanted their children to be held to the same standards as white children. This was clearly the feeling of the presidents of the parents' association, almost always black women, during my tenure as principal.

My letter to board members continued:

"Although I have been heartened by the support of people everywhere who applaud our stand at Long Island City High School for a safe school in which students can learn to the best of their abilities, this commitment has taken a personal toll. It is not an experience that will be made more indelible by additional undeserved punishment.

"I have been denied due process by a biased, incompetent Trial Examiner. Therefore, my counsel in our Reply has asked for a new trial. But, I know from the instant case that it will deprive the school of a principal during the year which is already the most difficult in the history of the New York City public schools. . . . [Thousands of teachers had been dismissed during the City's financial crisis.]

"We are three months into the new school year, and it is my hope that you will let the matter rest. I ask that you leave me to carry on my duties free from the litigation and controversy which will follow surely from any implementation of the Trial Examiner's outrageous findings and recommendations. You were resourceful in anticipating the need for moderation in these events. We should like to count on your good sense again."

Anyone who would count on the good sense of that board would also believe in the tooth fairy. I did not receive so much as an acknowledgement from any of the seven board members. They no more cared for my feelings, the feelings of the Long Island City people—and indeed the nation's—than a boa constrictor for the feelings of sheep.

The community was again aroused. Signs were lettered and affixed to long sticks to increase their visibility—"Support A Principled Principal Dr. Hurwitz," "Reward Don't Punish Dr. Hurwitz," "Dr. Hurwitz and L.I.C., Stand for Safe Schools." The picketers at board headquarters, on the evening of the meeting, were photographed by the press and topped the reports. In addition, there was radio and television coverage.

On December 15, 1976, a bitter cold night, bus loads of Long Island city residents and people from all over the city—

Italians, Greeks, Hispanics, blacks (including the president of Long Island City High School Parents' Association, a black woman)—assembled at 110 Livingston Street. They jampacked the auditorium in which the board met and overflowed into the streets.

I did not enter the building. I stood on the steps at the entrance, shielded partly by a corner, where I was interviewed by reporters, including Bob Grant on whose talk show I was to appear from time to time during the decade following my retirement.

The board president refused to permit Councilman Peter Vallone, State Senator Anthony Gazzara, or Peter O'Brien to talk on my behalf. The decision was greeted with outraged cries by my supporters. For once the Hall of the Board of Education was not filled with militants who influenced the board's decisions.

The board meeting hall had become off-limits for decent citizens, who despaired of persuading the poverty-controlled and New York Civil Liberties Union-dominated Board of Education. It had been conceded generally that the public schools were a lost cause, except for an individual school here and there. The exodus of the middle class, black and white, from the public schools had been widely reported. By the late 1980s, 80 percent of the system's almost one million children were black and Hispanic.

Max Frankle was the only supporter permitted to address the board. He was allotted five minutes. He said, ". . . permit me to tell you that for the first time in 50 years of practice, I found it necessary to walk out of a hearing after several weeks of long and tedious participation. This I did with great hesitation, knowing full well that the reputation of an educator of 38 years standing was at stake, and that I carried the responsibility as counsel to advise him that he was not receiving due process, that I was being deprived of the right to cross-examine witnesses, and the fact that a trial examiner is merely one who sits to gather information and to make a report does not exclude the obligation on his part or the part of this board in reviewing the record that he be impartial—which he was not, that he conduct a fair hearing—which he did not, and more and above all, not to be a hatchet man, which his report disclosed because he acted contrary to law, contrary to the record and in contradiction to every ruling he himself made during the course of the hearing."

We knew that the board had made its decision before the public hearing. This is invariably the case, but we were determined to make as strong a public appeal as possible.

The audience was quiet during most of the proceedings, except for sustained applause when Frankle completed his address. He was followed by the only board member who voted against accepting the trial examiner's recommendation. Joseph Barkan, the Queens member of the board, remarked that Long Island City High School was "a fully integrated school . . . and the third highest in utilization in the city."

Mr. Barkan spoke of "an administrator that has a rapport with his parents that is the envy of many of his colleagues. He has come through the ranks and by dint of hard work, further study, has achieved one of the highest posts in education. . . . This is a man who, according to his supervisors, is 'a principal who is far above average,' and against whom 'no previous charge appears from the evidence ever to have been presented.'

"By Board of Education policy, the principal of a high school has been almost like the captain of a ship. He and he alone is responsible for the good safety of his school. This man, through his 38-year career, has had this tradition inculcated in him . . . . an incident did occur and the principal who was on the firing line had to make an instant decision. . . .

"We are about to set a very important precedent. No principal, to my knowledge, has ever before received a monetary fine . . . . does the punishment fit the so-called crime? . . . . The trial examiner says it is to act as a deterrent. . . . I do not think so. . . . This principal has in the past been quite vocal in his criticism of the school system. But the criticism is not, and never should be punishable. . . . Remember that no system can long endure if it punishes or rids itself of every dissident. . . . I therefore move to amend the resolution to eliminate the fine of $3,500."

There was no second of the motion.

The next voice was that of Isaiah Robinson, the black member of the board. He expressed "surprise" that a "colleague . . . would go up in all kinds of superboly (sic)." He agreed with Barkan that the punishment did not fit the crime and moved that Dr. Hurwitz be dismissed from the school system.

The crowd quieted long enough to hear the board president say there was no second to Robinson's motion. He called a recess.

Robinson and I had clashed during the 36-day work stoppage of teachers and supervisors in 1968, long before he became a board member.

After he was appointed to the board, but six years before he moved for my dismissal, he was present when high school principals met with the board in that same auditorium. We hoped to win waning board support for the merit system. Robinson looked at the assembled principals and sneered, "I don't see any black faces out there."

None of my colleagues rose to respond. I stood up and denounced Robinson for his blatant bias. I defended the merit system of examinations that had made it possible for us to rise in the system. I emphasized that black principals were welcome to join us when they passed the stiff examinations to which we had been subjected.

During the recess before the final vote, some of the crowd emptied into the hall. Within three minutes, the doors were closed and the board quickly assembled for a vote. Its tactic was to empty the auditorium so that it could vote and leave, thereby heading off any demonstration.

For a moment, it looked like there might be a riot. I was near a group of policemen who were having coffee in the small cafeteria at the side of the hall. They quickly persuaded the board's security guards to open the doors and the crowd filed in and took seats.

The vote was 5 to 1 in favor of fining me $3,500.

Other than a cry of outrage, the crowd left peacefully. Many shook my hand on the way out—all waved to me. They left in the special buses and private cars. The next day's newspapers, radio and television reported on the meeting. The media were clearly with me.

We had 120 days to file an appeal of the board's decision in the State Supreme Court. On the 119th day we were in court with the appeal. The board had not moved to collect the fine. It waited until the final day of the school year, as I was about to deliver my commencement address in Colden Auditorium, Queens College, rented for the occasion. The front page of *The New York Times* (June 25, 1977) carried the headline, "Strict Queens Principal is Cheered As He Castigates Education Board." I was pictured before a battery of microphones with hand raised to make a point.

The letter ordering me to pay the fine was handed to me on the auditorium stage as a crew from "60 Minutes" was filming me. I exploded: "The typical bastards!" The CBS producer asked me to repeat the expletive for the cameras. I obliged. That comment did not appear in the segment in which I was interviewed by Mike Wallace. The "60 Minutes" crew had been following me for five days and took about 25 hours of film, skillfully edited to capture the essence of my stands on both discipline and bilingual education in the schools.

The appeal of the board's decision came up during the summer of '77, just after I had started my retirement leave. The board was represented by the New York City Corporation Counsel who argued that the trial should take place in Brooklyn, the borough in which the board has its offices. Frankle countered that it should remain in Queens County because I lived in Queens, the school was in Queens, and the suspension of the student that led to the charges against me had taken place in Queens. The board unsuccessfully appealed the decision to hold the trial in Queens.

The trial date was set for July 21. It was to be our chance for a fair trial on the issues. We were prepared to show how unfair the trial examiner had been in the hearing that had taken place more than a year earlier. We hoped to prove to the judge that I had been justified in disobeying an order that would have disrupted my school.

The board's attorney did not appear to defend the board's

decision to fine me and enter the suspension in my personal file. On July 28, 1977, Judge Alfred D. Lerner, in New York Supreme Court—Queens County, handed down a judgment "annulling and vacating" the resolution of the board. I had won. The court ordered that the sum of $3,500 be returned to me and that I be granted a new trial by the board.

Since the board had not collected the fine, no return was necessary. The board did not offer me a new trial and I did not seek one. I was already embarked on a new career, continuing as I type these lines, founded on my 40 years of school experience.

Only a month after our final victory in court, my wife and I visited Max Frankle in the Maimonides Hospital, in Brooklyn, where he lay dying from leukemia at age 72. He told us someone should write a magazine article on the "conspiracy of silence" surrounding my "conviction."

I was not clear for a moment about what he had in mind. He was recalling the superb brief he had written in response to the trial examiner's findings and how his brief had been ignored in the press. The final insult to Max was that the news reports of our victory in the State Supreme Court said not a word about Max.

I told Max that I would make it up to him in a book I hoped to write. He said he would like to see the manuscript, but for the fact that he was not sure of his future.

Max died a few days later, on September 6, 1977.

IV

A JEWISH PRINCIPAL CHARGED WITH GENOCIDE

I WAS ACCUSED OF GENOCIDE by government-financed poverty workers who had their office a minute-walk from our main entrance at Long Island City High School.

For a Jew to be accused of *genocide*—the planned extermination of an entire people—is monstrous. Jews were the people whose wipeout by Adolph Hitler was carried on with maniacal fury, advanced by gas-chamber technology in the years immediately preceding and during World War II. The era is inscribed in history as the Holocaust, a devastating epoch that must never be allowed to fade from the memory of mankind.

How was it possible for a Jewish high school principal in the City of New York to be the focus of so vile a libel? The irresponsibility of the charge reflects the nature and tactics of paid poverty workers who claim that they represent poor minorities.

I was not subjected to greater harassment by poverty workers than other school principals, but it was my resistance that won such huge public support. I had a friendly relationship with blacks in a community of 270,000 people in which blacks were less than 10 percent of the population. Ten of the 11 presidents of the Long Island City High School Parents' Association were black women. I consulted them regularly and they stood by me in all of the confrontations with poverty people and others who sought to disrupt what was widely and deservedly regarded as the most orderly school in the city.

Black students in the school knew that I was firm but fair. I did not discriminate against students on the basis of race, religion, national origin or sex. The black girl who was the center of the storm that led to my being barricaded in my office by the community was candid with a reporter when she told him—and he reported in a national magazine—that race had nothing to do with the disciplinary action I had taken.

Since my conscience was as clear as my record in race relations, I resented especially the efforts of the poverty workers to give a racial twist to our differences. Most of the poverty workers with whom I had dealings were white. Officials in the poverty corporation were almost all white.

I do not see poverty as a minority issue. Obviously the great majority of poor people in this country are white. The incidence of poverty among blacks and Hispanics is greater. It does not follow that poverty workers should see their roles as special protectors of blacks and Hispanics. It is my opinion that over the decades they have done a disservice rather than aided poor minorities. This is surely evident in my personal experiences with poverty workers who sought to take over the schools.

I know that without the support of whites, blacks, Hispanics, Asians, civic leaders, legislators, the teachers' and supervisors' unions, parents, teachers and students, I would have been smothered. What is more, I would not have had the incentive to fight back.

As I do the research for this book, I am given a lift by the hundreds of letters I reread from New Yorkers and sympathizers nationwide who supported me in my determination not to yield to those forces that would have destroyed discipline in the schools—the vital underpinning for learning.

I see poverty workers as subverters of the reasonable authority of school principals. They see schools as part of the Establishment and they are in the field to protect the poor from the Establishment. They see no contradiction between their anti-Establishment stance and their financial support by the Establishment—government, foundations, private enterprises—they seek to undermine.

Poverty workers are not necessarily recruited from among the poor—certainly not their lawyers. They are sometimes staffed by white graduates of the most prestigious colleges. I do not question the sincerity of these upper-class adjuncts. I question their judgment and tactics.

I can sympathize with poverty workers—indeed any citizens' group that seeks to gain the attention of the bureaucracy, such as the one at Livingston Street where the Board of Education, chancellor and his minions reside. Poverty workers lose my sympathy and my respect when they intimidate teachers and principals in individual schools. Individual schools are not bureaucracies. They house the flesh and blood on which the poor—and all others—must rely if they are to advance. For the poor, the schools are the catapult on which they must rely to propel them from the pit of poverty.

Schools are viewed by poverty workers as oppressors. Why else, they argue, are so many children of the poor doing so badly in the schools. Poverty workers are constantly on the prowl for children who have become school problems and can be used as a weapon with which to attack teachers and supervisors.

Poverty agencies are not indigenous to New York but are funded nationwide. No compassionate person would deny help to the poor, although we may differ over the best ways of helping them. The sage who suggested that the poor be given a fishing pole rather than a fish was in the right channel, if we are to judge by the existence of third-generation welfare families.

The poverty agencies, known also as community action corporations, offer the poor neither fish nor fishing tackle. The money they are allotted does not go to the poor. It goes to those who "serve" the poor. The City of New York in the mid-80's did a survey of the $14.8 billion that flows into the city to meet the needs of 1.2 million poor people—one-fifth of the city's population. It was found that 68 cents of every dollar goes not to the poor but to the social workers, counselors, lawyers and all who allegedly serve the poor. Poverty workers have an incentive to maintain people in poverty.

Poverty workers were not peculiar to Long Island City, a community of hard-working families in a semi-industrial part of the city. My colleagues citywide complained of the harassment to which they were subjected by poverty workers in the 25 community development agencies, allegedly acting for aggrieved children.

A junior high school principal in another part of the city wrote: "You know, of course, that you represent all professionals when you speak out against the harassment of principals by individuals and groups. All I can say is that no principal in the Soviet Union ever had problems like this. Do you think we ought to defect?"

The chairman of the teachers' union chapter in one school wrote: "New York City badly needs more people in supervisory positions who are willing to fight for the basic principles of education. It may be that your courageous stand will be the beginning of a restoration of courage to our schools.

"A number of young people go to school with fear because of the reign of terror in our schools, brought on by our inability to deal with disruptive elements. If your stand helps us to restore discipline in the schools, these young people will have less to fear and much to thank you for."

At LIC we never took the attitude that the parent was responsible for the child's behavior. While I do believe that there is no stronger force than parents in shaping a child's behavior, it is pointless to scold a parent when you invite him to school for a conference. We sought to enlist the parents' good will in an effort to bring about a change in the child's behavior. Poverty workers interfered with this approach. They would countenance no punishment for an erring student. There was no such thing as a bad kid, only bad teachers, bad principals, bad schools. This is the poverty workers' creed.

My credo, framed on the wall of my principal's office, and now a few feet to my right in my home office, is "Children have a right to go to a safe school in which they can learn to the best of their abilities." To the extent that a poverty group sought to interfere with this objective, I fought back. And I was not alone.

My first major confrontation with the local poverty workers followed from their effort to dictate the numbers enrolled in a citywide College-Bound Program. At LIC 200 of the school's 2,700 students were enrolled in the program. It was intended to provide special help for disadvantaged students so that they might gain admission to college.

The College-Bound Program, financed by the Board of Education, offered small-size classes to students—about half the regular class size of 34. Both paid and volunteer tutors were available to the students. To strengthen students in their reading, writing and speaking skills, double periods in English were part of the program. Students were encouraged to attend out-of-school activities as wide-ranging as basketball games and Shakespearean plays. The students were not a school apart from the regular program. More than half the teachers were involved in teaching them. They were mixed with other students in physical education, art, music and some other classes—and, of course, the lunch periods. They took part in the extensive extracurricular cultural and athletic programs.

College-Bound students had lower scholastic averages than those in the regular college-preparatory (academic) program. They were selected by guidance counselors on the basis of their perceived potential. While family income was not a measure of admission to the program, some of the students came from a low income housing project a few blocks from the school.

When a spokesman for a local poverty group asked to meet with me about the College-Bound Program, I readily agreed. Four poverty workers—two men and two women, white and black—met with me in my office on May 28, 1969. The chairman of the group, a black man in his thirties, was the director of a poverty group called Ravenswood Alert (Ravenswood being the name of the low-income housing project in Long Island City). The chairman brought with him two tots who slept through the one-hour meeting. I was to lose sleep in the years of trauma that followed the meeting.

The poverty committee asked me to increase the number of College-Bound students from 200 to 300. The additional 100 were to come from the entering 10th-year students the following September. I explained that the maximum number we could accommodate in the program was 200 and we would continue to have 200 in the program next September—100 in the 11th year and 100 in the 12th year. Any student in the incoming 10th year who wished to be in the program and eligible for it could be accommodated in other Queens high schools. I was to learn later that one of the committee members already had her teenage son enrolled in the College-Bound Program in a Queens high school where I had been an assistant principal.

I explained that the proposed 50 percent increase in the number of College-Bound Program students would mean the lengthening of our already long school day. The normal day of eight 40-minute periods had already been extended to 12 periods (and was soon to be extended to 13 periods) because we were the third most overcrowded high school in the city.

The 14-period day that would be required if we added 100 students meant that more students would be starting their school-day after the noon hour. It is axiomatic that learning falls off in the late afternoon. We had neither the teachers nor the class-rooms to allow for so great an expansion of the program.

Students would be leaving school in darkness during the winter months. Many would encounter homeward-bound rush-hour crowds. Supervision of students and teachers would be lacking in the final hours of the day because I could not mandate longer hours for the 10 assistant principals on whom we had to depend.

For all these reasons and others, explained patiently to the committee, the effect of their proposal if accepted would be to harm the program for those already enrolled.

The four poverty workers were silent when out of nowhere, it seemed to me, the chairman spoke out menacingly, "You got it too quiet here. We gonna make you some trouble."

I ended the meeting at that point.

Three weeks later, a Ravenswood poverty worker sought an interview with me about the College-Bound Program. I agreed to meet with him. A black man whom I did not recognize, he pretended that he had been part of the original committee of four and wanted more talk. I read to him the names of the four committee members who had been present, noted that his name was not among them, and observed that I could not forget a face under those circumstances.

The man's real reason for seeing me was to establish himself as a committee member so that he could deny any threat to good order in the school made by the committee chairman. Word had gotten out that I was seeking a government investigation of the poverty group's harassment of me.

The would-be imposter agreed after some further discussion that I was unable to expand the program. He added, "We must denounce you anyway." With those words he handed me a one-page, mimeographed, single-spaced flier. The opening line was in capital letters: "100 TEENAGERS IN LONG ISLAND CITY WILL DIE IN THE YEAR 1972 AND THAT NUMBER WILL INCREASE EACH ADDITIONAL YEAR! UNLESS. . . . . This Genocidal Process will begin in 1969 when Dr. Hurwitz, Principal of Long Island City High School, discontinues COLLEGE BOUND for the incoming Tenth Graders."

There followed an explanation of the benefits of the College-Bound Program, including mention of the provision that "Upon graduation the students that successfully complete the College Bound Program are guaranteed admission to any one of more than Eighty Colleges and Universities in the Metropolitan and adjoining areas. . . . The Elimination of this Program by Dr. Hurwitz at Long Island City High School in September will be a great disservice to the entire Long Island City-Astoria Community."

During June, July and August, the genocide circular was placed under thousands of doors in Long Island City. The attack on me was ignored by parents, teachers, students and the community, but the genocide canard moved me to further action.

My decision not to expand the program had been sustained by a superintendent whose purview included the College-Bound Program. She wrote in response to an appeal from the poverty committee, "It is not possible to accommodate a full cycle of three different years of College Bound Programs simultaneously unless the school register drops drastically. In other words, I concur with Dr. Hurwitz that he is not, at this time, in a position to make any commitment. . . ."

I reported the genocide attack to Congressman James Delaney, who represented the community. He made inquiry of the director of the Northeast Regional Office of the Office of Economic Opportunity (OEO), located in lower Manhattan.

The congressman sent me the report of the regional director, dated July 13, 1969, in which she denied "Dr. Hurwitz's allegation of intimidation" and wrote that the chairman of Ravenswood Alert had "commented to the effect that the school appeared 'too quiet' by comparison with other schools, and that 'seemingly the only way the communities got what they wanted was by demonstrations.' " The elegant language attributed to the Ravenswood Alert agitator must have afforded him great comfort. Subsequent government action did not.

The regional director of OEO had not so much as phoned me, or consulted anyone at Livingston Street about our continuing College-Bound Program. I refuted her report line by line in continued correspondence with Congressman Delaney. He agreed that her report "was more of a justification than an objective report." He pursued my complaint with Donald Rumsfeld, Director of OEO.

As an outcome of the congressman's intercession, a representative of OEO visited me during the summer of 1969 when the school was not in session. He spent several days investigating my complaint.

There followed the OEO director's report to Congressman Delaney (November 3, 1969) that my "description of the events was basically correct"; that the "Director of Ravenswood Alert used language at a meeting with Dr. Hurwitz on May 28 which could reasonably be interpreted as threatening disruption"; that "an employee of Ravenswood Alert entered the high school without permission on June 18, and that another employee prepared the circular referred to in Dr. Hurwitz' complaint."

The report concluded that "disruption of the schools or intimidation of school officials are not permissible activities for poverty program employees. . . . I trust no further incidents of this type will occur. We are sincerely sorry for any embarrassments or inconveniences which may have been suffered by Dr. Hurwitz."

The report was sincere enough, but the hopes expressed therein were unrealistic. The poverty dollars flow from Washington, but the line of communication becomes clogged as poverty workers do their own thing.

One communication affecting me did get through. Ravenswood Alert was dissolved by the OEO. Its cudgels were to be wielded by the education "arm" of another poverty corporation in the neighborhood, QUALICAP (acronym for Queens Astoria Long Island City Action Program). The other two arms of QUALICAP were appended to welfare and health programs.

The education arm of QUALICAP was tatooed Education Action Center, attached to the body of Amy Clodd (name changed), 40, a white woman whose girth and aura of hostility intimidated many of the teachers and principals in Long Island City where there were some 30 elementary and junior high schools.

In the same school years (1969–70) that I was assured by the OEO director that poverty workers would not interfere with school operations, we were confronted by Mrs. Clodd, who had been a member of the committee of four and the author of the genocide tract. At the head of a group of 15 poverty people, she sought to gain entrance to the school to distribute a circular they had been handing out on the school sidewalk all morning. It was part of the poverty program of agitation calculated to undermine the authority of the school principal.

I had expected a forced entrance and was ready with three physical education teachers to halt their march into the school corridor. Nose to nose with Clodd, I informed her that if she advanced another inch, I would charge her with assault. She retreated with her band, some of whom screamed that they had a right to enter the building.

Following this confrontation I notified all deans and guidance counselors that I was to be notified at once if Mrs. Clodd were ever again to enter the building for any purpose.

My notification did not fall on deaf ears. On November 18, 1970, the Dean of Boys phoned to tell me that Mrs. Clodd was in his office. At the moment, two detectives from the local precinct were in my office on some other business. I excused myself and walked down the main corridor to the dean's office. I identified myself to Clodd who of course knew me. She was in the company of the mother of a 16-year-old boy who was a discipline problem.

I told Clodd that I did not want her in the building and requested that she leave. I foresaw that she would hassle the dean in an effort to return the boy to a class from which he had been dropped for cutting. When Clodd refused to leave, I told her that if she did not leave I would ask for her arrest. She said, "Go ahead arrest me."

I asked the dean to have the detectives in my office come to me so that I might talk with them. I then told them that if they could persuade Mrs. Clodd to leave quietly, that would be all right; but, if she refused to leave the Dean of Boys' office that she be arrested. I asked that she be charged with "loitering" under Section 240.35 of the Penal Code.

The statute reads: "A person is guilty of loitering when he . . . . loiters or remains in or about a school, college or university building or grounds, not having any reason or relationship involving custody of or responsibility for a pupil or student, or any other specific, legitimate reason for being there, and not having written permission from anyone authorized to grant the same."

At the time of the arrest I understood the fragile ground on which the arrest would be made, but there was no other statute on which my case against the poverty worker might rest.

The detectives took Clodd to one side and made an effort to persuade her to leave. Detective Thomas McTigue, who made the arrest, was to testify in court that he asked her to leave three times. She refused, saying, "No, I am not going to leave the building. It's a public building." The detective said, "If you don't leave, I am going to be forced to arrest you." She said, "Well, then, arrest me. This is what I want. I want to make a test case of this."

The detective consulted me once again and I asked him to make the arrest. He was to testify at the trial that he went back to Mrs. Clodd "and I informed her she was under arrest."

V

COURT BATTLE: PRINCIPAL VERSUS POVERTY PANDERERS

A POVERTY WORKER is not without resources. The average citizen fears legal costs; not so with poverty people. QUALICAP, the local poverty corporation, had a full-time attorney. She may not have come forward to represent Amy Clodd, an employee of the poverty corporation, because Clodd was posing as a "friend" of a parent who had been asked to come to school about her son's misbehavior. A paid poverty worker representing a parent hardly constitutes a "friend."

In Clodd's case, Legal Aid Society attorneys volunteered their assistance. They withdrew when she changed her initial statement of salary—$6,500 a year—and admitted that she was being paid $10,000.

Within a half-hour of the arrest I phoned the Queens high school superintendent and informed him of the arrest and why I had requested it. He agreed that I had acted properly. I also phoned the Law Secretary of the Board of Education and was assured of legal counsel.

On the day of the arrest I wrote to the Law Secretary confirming the facts and adding, "It is my belief that Mrs. Clodd will seek to enlist the assistance of the Civil Liberties Union . . . in order to make this a test case. It is therefore especially important that we be prepared to win this case since, if we lose it, it will mean that any poverty worker will be able to enter our schools and remain with impunity despite the wishes and judgment of the principal of the school."

Two weeks after the arrest I appeared in the Queens

County Criminal Court with Detective McTigue and signed the complaint. I was represented by a Board of Education attorney. Clodd was parolled and the trial date was set for January 12, 1971.

On the day of the trial Judge John DiLeonardo listened to a Legal Aid Attorney explain that he could not defend Mrs. Clodd, but that she was entitled to an attorney. She was to be defended by attorneys for the New York Civil Liberties Union, an organization that has done much to harass school principals by assuring retention in schools of disruptive students.

The judge lectured Clodd for not leaving the building when the principal told her to do so and said, "Dr. Hurwitz is known to be the best principal in the City of New York and the whole city knows this." He postponed the case for a week, warned her to appear with an attorney, and stated that it was to be a "final" trial.

The judge did not know that earlier the same morning, as I talked with the District Attorney, he received a phone call from the attorney of schools Chancellor Harvey B. Scribner, who had taken office five months earlier. The chancellor's attorney sought to persuade the D.A. to drop the case. The D.A. explained that only Dr. Hurwitz, who was standing two feet away, could do that. He then placed me on the wire.

Scribner's attorney told me that I was acting contrary to the chancellor's policy. I told him that he was wasting his time talking to me that way; that I could conceive of no circumstances that would cause me to withdraw the charges against the person whom I regarded as a disrupter who had refused to leave the building when I told her to do so. I said goodbye, and the D.A. and I proceeded to the courtroom.

I realized what was happening. The poverty people and the New York Civil Liberties Union had reached the chancellor. He was new on the job and had come to New York from Vermont where he had been State Commissioner of Education; before that he had been Superintendent of Schools in Teaneck, New Jersey and had no big city experience. Scribner had succumbed to pressures of the two most disruptive elements in the schools—

poverty corporations and the NYCLU; neither spoke for the vast majority of New Yorkers and both were anathema in Long Island City.

The pressure became explicit a week after the postponed trial. On January 18, 1971, I received a telegram from the Queens superintendent, who had initially agreed that I acted properly in ordering the arrest. This was the day of the trial. The telegram had been read to me over the phone on the previous Friday. The Monday telegram read: "It is necessary in view of the hearing before the court scheduled for Monday, January 18, 1971 that this method of communication with you be used.

"In the light of all the facts reported to this office relative to the arrest of Amy Clodd at Long Island City High School and in accordance with the policy stated by the president of the board of education at the public meeting on December 15, 1970 it is apparent that your continuing to press charges against Amy Clodd is contrary to stated policy of the board of education. I have reviewed the matter and I conclude that since there was no actual disruption of the school nor danger to safety and welfare of students resulting from Mrs. Clodd's refusal to leave the school the arrest was an overreaction to the incident especially since it occurred in the context of previous similar incidents. The policy of the board of education concerning accompaniment is clear following the president's statement of December 15. I therefore strongly suggest to you and following instructions from the office of the chancellor direct that you discontinue charges against Amy Clodd brought by you in your capacity as principal of Long Island City High School."

I was not dissuaded and proceeded to court where I was to learn that Clodd's NYCLU attorney had placed before Judge Di-Leonardo papers filed with the Federal District Court, seeking removal of the case from the Queens County Criminal Court. The judge was prepared to proceed anyway, but was advised by the D.A. that he must await determination by the Federal District Court whether it would hear the case or refer it back to the Queens County Criminal Court.

The judge set a trial date four months later, but at that time the Federal District Court had not yet made its decision. Although eventually the case was returned to Queens, 18 months were to elapse between the arrest and the start of the trial in the summer of '72. I had heard that the wheels of justice grind slowly, and I would have been ground down by the process had not the citywide support for my stand been so inspiring.

I had responded to the superintendent's telegram the day after the aborted court appearance. I wrote: ". . . I am informing you, once again, that I am determined to pursue vigorously my complaint against the defendant. To do otherwise would be to open Long Island City High School to the outside agitators who have disrupted other schools in our city.

"You have agreed with me that Long Island City High School is one of the best administered high schools in the city. We have had no disruption in the five years that I have headed the school. We have carried on an effective learning program . . . in a school that by your own statistics is the most heavily over-utilized building in Queens (constructed 1902, 1928).

"I am a principal who enjoys the support and cooperation of students, teachers, supervisors and the community. My reputation is based on school, citywide and national professional activity. . . ."

I called the superintendent's attention to the chancellor's circular which happened to be issued two days after the arrest of Clodd, which stated ". . . the principal has the responsibility and the authority to limit admission to the building . . . . any adult who violates the law either inside or immediately adjacent to a school building should be dealt with by law enforcement officials following a complaint by school authorities. . . ."

The letter continued: "I am not a litigious person. The defendant was the first adult I found it necessary to have arrested in my 32 years in the school system (18 as an assistant principal and principal). I dissent from the belated assessment of the arrest in your telegram. . . . Now, at the direction of the Chancellor, you fault me for my 'over-reaction to the incident.' If I have over-reacted, why is the Chancellor and the Civil Liberties Union so determined to prevent the case from coming to trial? It is you who have under-reacted to the implications of an outsider (with the defendant's record of disruptive behavior) refusing to leave the building when a police officer directed her to do so. . . .

"I have acted responsibly to secure the safety of the students and teachers entrusted to me. I am, therefore, asking you, and the Chancellor at whose direction you have proceeded, to cease what I must regard as your harassment of me. I am asking, also, that you reconsider your actions in the Clodd case."

I sent copies of the letter to the Board of Education, chancellor, other superintendents and the heads of professional associations who were supporting our cause. From the first, I involved the teachers' union, supervisors' union, legislators, community leaders, parents' associations, the clergy, and colleagues.

In interviews with reporters, I made known my resentment of the chancellor's harassment of me. In response, he denied that he had ordered me to drop the loitering charge, but had "merely questioned whether Mrs. Clodd had been within her rights being within the school." I then released to the press the direct quote from the telegram from the superintendent sent to me at the direction of the chancellor.

As the controversy grew heated, the chancellor was moved to say on TV: "Dr. Hurwitz feels apparently that I am harassing him. I feel of course that I am merely asking him some questions. I think he's an excellent administrator. I hear great reports. He's got a fan club that's really impressive."

So gross was the harassment that one board attorney phoned my home repeatedly during the summer. He would tell my wife, "I want to help your husband." He wanted me to drop the complaint and I did not return his calls.

The harassment also continued when Clodd sought to enter the building, again on the pretext that she was a "friend." To buttress the poverty worker's contention that she was a friend, the high school division director sent a letter to all high school principals, February 5, 1970, ten weeks after the arrest, stating: "It has been the practice in the high schools for the principal and staff to offer a parent maximum opportunities to discuss the schooling of his child including being accompanied by a friend when the parent has felt the need. Recently, the Board of Education and the Chancellor have formally endorsed this practice.

"Please allow a parent to have a friend accompany him if he makes such a request."

Emboldened by this statement, Mrs. Clodd again sought entrance to the building. I had conferred with the District Attorney in anticipation of just such an eventuality. Since Judge Di-Leonardo had at one of the postponements warned her to stay away from Long Island City High School, the D.A. told me to tell Clodd that she would be in contempt of court if she entered the building. I did so—and it worked.

I had on at least two occasions, prior to her arrest but subsequent to her genocide involvement, admitted Clodd to my office on suspension hearings. The state law explicitly allowed parents to be accompanied by an adviser of their own choosing. I abided by the state law.

It was one thing for Clodd to be in my office while I conducted a hearing and quite another when she confronted subordinates. She knew better than to hassle me.

The singling out of "friend," as I have noted, was not made until after the Clodd arrest. I would surely have undertaken the contempt proceeding if she had not left the building. Otherwise, Clodd would have continued to test my determination from the time of her arrest to the trial—18 months.

It was not my battle alone. The people in the city, state and nation—then and now—want effective, orderly schools. LIC was such a school. The chancellor should have been encouraging, not undermining principals who had demonstrated their capacity to work with teachers, students and community to maintain safe schools in a city wracked by fear. His departure, after three years, was hastened by demands for his resignation. His stand in the Clodd case did him no good, despite his astounding testimony. We'll touch upon it, shortly.

State Senator Martin J. Knorr wrote to Scribner: "It is incredible to me that you should not be warmly encouraging Dr. Hurwitz rather than seeking to unnerve him. . . . I shall be glad to talk with you and to discuss in detail what we can do to reassure Dr. Hurwitz of the esteem in which we hold him as a strong leader in these very troubled times. I know that Dr. Hurwitz has the complete support of his faculty, staff, parents, and community leadership. And I count myself among them."

Our battle with Scribner was covered in the press with such headlines as "School Union Hits Scribner, Backs LI Principal in Fight" (*Long Island Press*). The New York *Sunday News* took editorial note of "the arrest of an antipoverty worker," recorded my support by "B'nai B'rith, the YMCA, American Legion, parent organizations, civic associations, etc." and concluded: "In other words Queens is making it loud and clear that its schools be used to educate not agitate. And no one's ever too old to learn—not even a chancellor."

I was to write to the president of the High School Principals Association of "political activity so necessary these days, if a principal is to remain alive. . . . I have no fear that Scribner is going to get me. He understands political support. And I have that from Senator [James] Buckley through the Rotary Club of Queens and the Queens Federation of Parents' Clubs. Walter Degnan [president of the Council of Supervisors and Administrators] has been with me a hundred percent—staff, legal aid, etc. In addition, my teachers, supervisors, staff, parents, students and community are united with me in the fight. My only opposition is Scribner and the New York Civil Liberties Union."

I must not have lost my sense of humor because I concluded: "A note of hope: I have reason to believe that my prefiled bill extending the 24-hour day to 36 will be passed at the next session. I, therefore, continue as your representative on the negotiating committee." (I acted for the HSPA on the CSA committee that negotiated agreements with the Board of Education.)

The chancellor testified at the trial. He had been subpoenaed by the NYCLU attorney who fully expected him to take the opportunity of scuttling me. To the NYCLU's consternation the chancellor affirmed my right to determine whether the defendant should have been permitted to remain in the school.

There follows an excerpt from the trial transcript (*People of the State of New York-vs-Amy Clodd*, Queens County Criminal Court, July 26, 27, 28, 1972). The questions are by the District

Attorney and the answers are by Chancellor Scribner:

"Q. But the person in the end who makes the decision is the principal; is that correct?

"A. Yes.

"Q. And his decision would prevail at the time of his making the decision; is that correct?

"A. That is correct.

"Q. He doesn't have to call you and say, Dr. Scribner, may I have permission to exclude so and so in my office?

"A. Your first statement was correct.

"Q. I see. Then a principal excluding a person at a particular time had the authority at that time to do so?

"A. Based upon proper cause. He had the authority, yes."

The thrust of the NYCLU defense of Clodd was that she had the right to act as a "friend" of any student or parent and that the principal had no discretion in the matter.

The substance of the state's case was that the proper administration of the schools can only be maintained if the educators are given reasonable discretion to determine which individuals seeking admission to school property have a legitimate reason for being in the school. The schools would cease to function if the discretion were vested in the interloper, not the educator.

Clodd contended in court that she had the right to enter a public high school since it was open to the public. This mistaken notion continues to threaten schools. Outsiders should have no more right to represent themselves as "friends" than they have to use a school toilet as a matter of public right.

Clodd's role as a "friend" of the Hispanic parent whose son was being disciplined was further undermined. It was alleged that the mother could not speak English. Clodd, however, neither spoke nor understood Spanish. Our attendance coordinator, however, spoke Spanish fluently and had carried on previous interviews with the parent in Spanish. When the parent testified on behalf of Clodd, she understood the questions asked of her in English and responded in English.

Judge Harold Mayer (in a non-jury trial) found Clodd guilty of "loitering" under the New York Penal Code. She was neither fined nor imprisoned, but was discharged "conditionally." The condition was that she not seek to enter Long Island City High School without first obtaining the principal's permission. He resolved the case in the state's favor when he decided that the defendant had no legitimate reason for remaining in the school when the principal told her to leave.

A year later the NYCLU was successful in having the decision reversed in a one-sentence statement by the Appellate Term of the Brooklyn Supreme Court. Three judges agreed that the People had failed to establish that the defendant committed the violation of loitering in or about a school without "a specific, legitimate reason for being there." A month later, the Appellate Court found the loitering law itself to be unconstitutional as "too vague."

The reversal was not unexpected. I reflected on the insulation of judges from the reality of the school world. By undercutting so simple a principle as the right of a principal to order a person whom he believed to be disruptive from the school, the tribunal further impaired the capacity of the principal to keep order at a time when discipline was—and continues to be—the Number 1 problem in the schools. The situation is made worse when superintendents and boards of education weaken the authority of the principal.

VI

PEACE STRIKERS DECLARE
WAR ON SCHOOLS

THE VIETNAM WAR years—late 1960's and early
1970's—were the most turbulent in the history of American education. The carnage in colleges and high schools was spread
from coast to coast. Student activists occupied offices and buildings, school authorities were defied, demonstrations disrupted
school and college life, students clashed with law enforcement
agencies.

Administrators spent much of their time negotiating over
"non-negotiable demands," put forward by anti-war militants.
Some students had their heads bashed by police; four were killed
by the National Guard; others blew themselves up making
bombs; more were fined, imprisoned, expelled.

All—activists and moderates—suffered severe interruptions
of their school programs. Scarcely anyone from nursery to graduate school escaped the turmoil of the times.

At Long Island City High School we enjoyed comparative
peace. *Comparative* is the key word. We had our share of excitement. There was scarcely a day that I did not meet with students,
teachers, supervisors, parents and community leaders. From
time to time, as "peace strike" days loomed, I conferred with
officers of the 108th Police Precinct in Long Island City with
whom I had established a close relationship.

I made it clear to students from the first that they had the
right to protest, provided their actions did not interfere with
class instruction. Students sent me petitions, conferred with me
in my office, talked with me as I moved about the building and
streets bordering the school.

THE LAST ANGRY PRINCIPAL

Some of my decisions were modified when I was persuaded that a principled position would not be compromised. I would not assent to any change that might interrupt continuity of instruction. LIC students and teachers knew that they had plenty of opportunity to be heard, and my open-door policy was well-known.

Early in the escalation of anti-war protests, a committee of students requested permission to meet with me about formation of a Peace Club. Five of them assembled in my office. I perceived that the proposed name of the club held special significance for those most opposed to the government's mounting efforts to defeat the Viet Cong and North Vietnam.

I told the group that I would approve formation of their club, but suggested a title other than Peace Club. Such a name, I said, would by implication exclude students who favored the war aims of our government. I suggested forming a Current Affairs Club or History Club. Since there was already a Human Relations Club, I thought that it might lend itself to their purpose.

Above all, the students wanted Mr. Marmelfarb (name changed) to be their faculty adviser. I approved. In my early days as a classroom history teacher—the late 1930's—I took pride in being asked to be a faculty adviser of clubs. By the 1960's, it had become difficult to cajole a teacher into undertaking unpaid, after-school club advising. Mr. Marmelfarb, I had reason to believe, implanted in students the idea for a Peace Club.

The Peace Club committee left, convinced that I approved of their club, albeit with a different name. Late in the day Mr. Marmelfarb, a soft-spoken gentleman in his mid-thirties, thanked me for my attitude and asked whether Vietnam Discussion Club would be a satisfactory title. I agreed.

The same students soon requested permission to advertise their opposition to the ROTC (Reserve Officers Training Corps) in the school newspaper. I proposed a letter to the editor. They persisted. I yielded.

The lines were drawn at LIC and in the nation's schools on April 16, 1968, proclaimed by anti-war protesters as the day for a "Peace Strike." Two days before the strike day, I placed a memorandum below the time clock used by teachers informing those who planned to be absent to see me.

As expected, the two Marmelfarbs showed up. They were a married couple (later divorced) whom I knew to be good teachers with deep political convictions. In evaluating teachers I did not permit political convictions to affect my appreciation of their teaching talents. If there is anything more important to the schools than good teachers in the classroom, I have yet to learn about it.

Mr. & Mrs. Marmelfarb told me that they would be absent and on the picket line.

I advised: "If you are absent but *not* on the picket line, it will not be necessary to report your absence to the superintendent." I had the feeling that I was talking to Christian martyrs who would face lions with the same equanimimity.

I added: "I did not expect to dissuade you from participating in the peace strike, but I should like to count on you to keep the line orderly. You will be permitted to walk in front of our main entrance since students use the side entrance. There is to be no singing or shouting or any effort to dissuade students from entering the school."

The Marmelfarbs nodded assent.

Although I had cautioned the Marmelfarbs, I was reasonably sure that LIC would not experience an upheaval that was to mark the peace strike in schools and colleges nationwide. I had been principal of LIC for two years and the peace strike was not the first threatened disruption of the school. Students and teachers had learned that I countered with no threats. If I said I was going to take action to prevent disruption, I would take it.

I had taken a number of precautions as soon as I learned about the peace strike. I had met with my cabinet (10 assistant principals in charge of departments) and conferred with the police. In addition to the regular police officer assigned to the school, there would be a squad car at the front of the building and other officers would be available as needed.

I used our public address system to inform students that we would have a regular school day; that any student who molested a picketer would be suspended; that if any outsiders created a

THE LAST ANGRY PRINCIPAL

disturbance they would be arrested by police assigned to the school. I would deal personally with any student who misbehaved.

I had arranged with key supervisors and teachers to arrive early on the day of the strike. By 8 a.m., there were 23 youths and the two Marmelfarbs walking in front of the building in an orderly manner. They carried signs protesting the Vietnam War and racism.

A police squad car arrived at 8:30 a.m. and I left the building to talk to the officers. I noted that the picketers were orderly and expressed concern that outsiders might molest them. One of the officers interjected harshly, "You're too concerned about the picketers. We do the arresting."

I calmed him down. He was new to the precinct and did not know me. I replied: "I know what your responsibilities are and I know mine. We're running a full school day and I appreciate your help."

Before the strike day I had reminded teachers that April 26 was a Friday, a day on which quizzes were often given, and that scheduled quizzes were not to be postponed.

Early on the strike day I followed this up:

"Re: Quizzes. . . .

"Our attendance today is excellent and I would not want any student to interpret a quiz as a means of assuring better attendance. Please understand that giving a quiz is purely voluntary and if it will not further the educational process at this time, you may feel free to dispense with it."

There was an incident connected with the quiz precaution that I shall never forget.

I met one of our varsity basketball players in the hall. Since I thought he might have come in from the picket line, I asked him where he had come from. He handed me a note: "Please excuse James for lateness to school, today. His mother passed away."

James had come to school on the day of his mother's death because he did not want to miss the quizzes which had been announced in most classes.

PEACE STRIKERS DECLARE WAR ON SCHOOLS

I expressed my sympathy for his loss and wrote on the note, "Excuse James from all classes on Friday, April 26."

I sent James home.

I am chilled by this memory. How could I have put into effect a plan that would bring a boy to school on the day of his mother's death?

I have written a half-dozen history books, so I can only summon to my defense, sorely needed at this point, historical perspective. I was seeking to prevent my school from being disrupted by anti-war protesters. Yes, *my* school. Students refer to their schools as "my school"; so, too, do teachers. I feel the same way. I did not own the school, but I surely was responsible for everyone in it. I was responsible for teachers teaching and students learning.

The media had reported widescale school disruptions during the year preceding the peace strike. My school had been scarcely touched by earlier demonstrations. The media had noted the unique order at LIC. I was determined with the help of teachers, supportive parents, students and the police to retain our reputation as a school in which learning went on no matter what.

Was there egotism in all this? Of course.

I had to contrive ways of maintaining order and this included causing students to fear the consequences of disruptive behavior. Fear generated for a good end can be a healthy corrective.

I wish there might have been easier ways. Most of my colleagues took easier ways and we are still paying the price.

I derived some consolation for the pressure I had placed on James. A year later I was visited by a man representing Dartmouth College. He asked my opinion of James as a student. The Ivy League college was considering offering him an athletic scholarship.

"James is an average student, but a hard worker," I said. "If you must grant athletic scholarships, I would certainly offer one to James. If you arrange for tutoring, he should make it."

Four years later, in 1973, James visited LIC and I talked

with him. He had been graduated from Dartmouth. As a black man, he had been lonely at Dartmouth, in bucolic New Hampshire, far from any big city. While in his senior year, his sweetheart in Long Island City came to him and they married. She obtained a job in nearby Manchester.

James told me that he wanted to go to law school but did not have the money. The last I heard was that he got a job in the physical education department of Columbia University where he was the assistant basketball coach for a time.

Back to the day of the peace strike: It was peaceful at LIC. A program honoring Arista students, scheduled months earlier, was carried on in a dignified way with some 50 parents attending. The assembly was followed by a collation in the library, attended by the honor students, parents and teachers who did not have a class to teach at the time. These occasional social get-togethers gave me some relief in tense times.

Did LIC's approach to the peace strike mean that students and teachers did not care about the war? Their concern was evident. For a month before the peace strike, teachers and students talked about how they should act on the strike day. Parents phoned, anxious to know whether their children would be in danger if they came to school. I assured them that there would be a regular school day, but could offer no guarantees. I asked them to remember our record up to that point. Evidently they were persuaded.

After the strike I interviewed each student who was on the picket line—no group interview. They told me that this was their way of showing a commitment to peace in Vietnam; that by striking on a school day, they were dramatizing their cause; that the strike was part of their education.

I did not demean their arguments. I reiterated my rationale for opposing their actions. They were youths who needed an education. They could not get it if schools were to be disrupted repeatedly during the war. There would be time enough for them to be active after graduation. The issues could be studied in school and discussed freely. Adults were free to be anti-war protesters during the school day. They were not yet adults. Their responsibility was to attend school, not to destroy it for themselves and others. They might legally protest after school. By absenting themselves they had broken the state compulsory education law. This might be a small potato in their diet, but I was noting it on each permanent record card. Yes, it would be a factor in any employment or college recommendation, but I would be persuaded to overlook the notation if they were graduated without further incident.

Pressure? You betcha.

The strike day in 1969 was part of an emerging pattern of protest in which schools were to be used as a lever to prod the president into pulling our troops out of Vietnam. I did not accept student action as an instrument of foreign policy.

Our students' conduct on the day of the peace strike was approved enthusiastically by parents and community leaders.

As an example of my continued willingness to encourage debate on the Vietnam War, I agreed to a teach-in shortly before the peace strike.

I was friendly to the teach-in from the first. I am disposed to encourage the widest expression of opinion on controversial issues. I believe that freedom of expression, provided it does not interfere with the freedom of others, is the heart of the democratic process. It is a belief that I sought to instil in teachers whom I supervised at St. John's University (Queens, New York) where I was an adjunct professor for 10 years (1956–66). I gave a course in "Methods of Teaching Social Studies in the Secondary Schools." I emphasized that controversy is not only characteristic of current affairs but is marked in the study of history from the earliest times. A critical examination of issues—past and present—can lend excitement and reason to the teaching of history, often a badly taught subject in our schools.

It was easy for me to go along with teachers and students who asked my permission to hold a teach-in. What I did not go along with was their initial proposal to invite students from other high schools. I wanted the teach-in for our students and teachers only and was not going to risk disorder by students over whom I had no control. I could count on my students to behave decently no matter how inflammatory the issue.

As things turned out I was happy with the teach-in. Some

THE LAST ANGRY PRINCIPAL

200 of our students and many faculty members were present at various times in the late afternoon and early evening of January 8, 1969. We had six speakers on various sides of the question. Students lined up at the microphone to ask questions or make comments directed to the speakers on the auditorium stage. The student chairman did a creditable job in introducing the speakers and keeping the discussion moving.

Later, a student remarked to me, "But it didn't settle anything."

I answered: "We didn't expect to settle the war at the teach-in. We offered students and teachers an opportunity to express themselves on a highly controversial issue and to react to adult-informed opinion.

"Communist leaders," I added, "don't have to worry about public opinion. In our country political leaders do worry about public opinion and often act on it. At the teach-in you were being helped to form an opinion." The impact of public opinion was undeniable when President Lyndon B. Johnson, on March 31, 1968, announced that he would not seek reelection.

Two decades later former Secretary of State Henry Kissinger, meeting with Vietnamese emigres in Paris, admitted that he had misunderstood the motives of the anti-war movement. "I thought," he reflected, "that those opposed to the war wanted a reasonable settlement, but now I see that many organizers [of the anti-war demonstrations] wanted us to lose in order to show that the United States could not support its allies" (*New York City Tribune*, Dec. 8, 1987).

Three days after the Kent killing I arrived in school at 7:30 a.m. The front and sides of the building had been defaced with large red letters—"STRIKE." Our custodial staff was engaged in scrubbing out the front of the building and painting over the sides of the building in accordance with my standing request of our custodian.

Few students were in the building because it was Ascension Day. Outsiders and some students were gathered a half-block away from the school. They carried a red flag and strike signs.

During the morning of May 12, 1970, about 50 of them

picketed across the street from the school, chanting, "Fuck Hurwitz."

My dean of boys and girls and a few teachers identified each of our students who was picketing. I was to be occupied with them for the next three weeks.

On the same morning as the picketing, I wrote to the parents of each of the students: "This is to advise you that your child, _____, participated in a picketing demonstration across the street from the front of this high school, on Tuesday morning, May 12, 1970, during school hours.

"I believe that your child's place is in school and not outside where he contributed to the disruption of the school day. Please do not mistake this reproduced letter as anything other than a very serious matter. I have not written individual letters only because some twenty students are involved, each of whom I am disciplining.

"I shall welcome discussing this matter with you, if you wish to phone my office for an appointment."

I held separate interviews with 19 of the 20 students and their parents. Each of the 19 was required to write an apology. I was to wish as I read each apology that I might have been content with an oral apology. The spelling and grammar in many of the notes were disheartening. They documented in my mind Justice Hugo Black's dissenting opinion in the Tinker free speech legacy left by the United States Supreme Court in *Tinker v. Des Moines Independent Community School District* (1969). The court majority protected the right of the Tinker children to wear black anti-Vietnam War armbands to their schools, although the principals thought it disruptive. Justice Black wrote: "Turned loose with lawsuits . . . against their teachers . . . it is nothing but wishful thinking to imagine the young, immature students will not soon believe it is their right to control the schools. . . . This case . . . subjects all the public schools in the country to the whims and caprices of their loudest-mouthed, but maybe not their brightest students."

I saw that I was dealing with loud-mouthed but considerably chastened teenagers as they sat opposite me with one or both of their parents. Each was permitted to say anything he had to say in defense or extenuation of conduct I regarded as unacceptable. No parent defended the conduct of his child. Apart from an entry on the student's permanent record card, I wanted an apology.

One boy wrote, amidst a sprinkling of heavy crossouts, "I was just walk by to go uptown. I was not protesting. I don't believe in protest. I amd very sorry."

A more gifted lad wrote, "You have my word that I will not take part in a demonstration during school time in front of LIC. Furthermore, I assure you that I did not use any obscene language against you while I was on the picket line."

A girl wrote, "I am sorry for being part of a dirty mouth demonstration, and I promise never to be part of any demonstration in or around Long Island City High School."

Another girl, who wrote well but whose grades did not reflect any close attention to school work, stated: "Though I don't think it necessary to apologize for our peaceful demonstration, I request your permission to do so in regard to the language used against you during this period. Though I deny the fact of participating in that specific action, it seems there is nothing I can do to prove me innocent in your eyes. Therefore, I apologize and hope that one day, you will see my point of view."

The only student who refused to apologize turned out to be the stepdaughter of a notorious agitator. She had somehow contrived to be admitted to LIC although she lived in Harlem. This was not unusual since parents were using strategems to gain admission to LIC, widely known as a "safe" school in a city in which public schools were becoming a shambles.

The girl's mother phoned in mid-June and her threat to "have your police ready" was relayed to me by my secretary. I had decided not to sign the girl's diploma under any circumstances, apart from the fact that she was failing most of her subjects.

I wrote to Mrs. "X": Your threat "is unconscionable. I have never submitted to intimidation of any kind and I have no intention of yielding to it now."

In late June the stepfather arrived sans wife, but accompanied by one of his henchmen. My secretary was visibly alarmed. I told her to send them in.

As was often the case in my experience, confrontations that I anticipated were deflated to routine exchanges. In response to my inquiry, "What can I do for you ?" he asked not for the girl's diploma for which I had a ready reply but for a record of her marks since she would be going to another school. I told him that would be no problem and to wait for a transcript in my outer office. He was given the transcript and I never heard from the "X's" again. I could have told Mr. "X" that the transcript would not be accepted at another school. The school would send for an official transcript that did not pass through the hands of parent or child. But there was no sense in complicating "X's" life.

I was to hear shortly from the lawyer for the poverty group around the corner. I agreed to see her about the apology I had required from each student following the foul-mouthed demonstration. Once in my office she took no more than a moment to let me know with certitude that the word "fuck" was within the First Amendment rights of students.

Now, I'm a Brooklyn boy who served over three years in the Army Air Force in World War II. I am also a Ph.D. in political science from Columbia University, who has written many a piece on the First Amendment. I was not in the mood for listening to a disquisition on the alleged constitutionality of obscenity by a poverty pimp living off the poor.

I responded: "I am exercising my First Amendment right to tell you, 'Get up and leave my office, now.' "

She did.

Subsequently, my requirement of an apology and the entry on students' records were sustained by higher authorities.

The anti-war protests not only undermined school discipline, but bred disloyalty. From time to time, outsiders distributed near the school fliers denouncing the war. There was one mimeographed sheet, "IS THIS YOUR FUTURE?" It featured a cartoon of a stripped, except for a military cap, obese, squatting two-star general, stuffing naked boys into his mouth and excreting them in the shape of rifle-bearing soldiers.

The typed message below the cartoon read in part: "The

war in Vietnam affects all of us. Some think we must fight to 'serve the country'. Many others now realize that the people who run this country are making us fight against the Vietnamese people so that the rich can get even richer.

"Guys will be affected because the draft is waiting for you. Girls will see their boyfriends, husbands, and brothers taken away from them.

". . . But more and more young people are saying 'NO!' to the draft and the war. . . .

"On Monday, October 6, At Long Island City High School, And on Wednesday, October 8th, at Bryant High School, A GI STATIONED AT FORT DIX, N.J. WILL TELL US WHAT THE ARMY AND THE WAR ARE *REALLY* LIKE. He'll Tell US About the Hundreds of GI's AT Fort Dix Who Have Said No, and 38 Of Them Who Are Facing Court Martials and Up to 43 Years In the Stockade. . . ."

The flier concluded with a call for a rally "to start when school lets out outside main entrance."

It was nice to learn that the rally was to be *after* school. What the organizers—no name was affixed to the flier—did not know was that LIC students left at various times in the afternoon (overlapping sessions) because of the overcrowding, with the older students leaving two hours before the scheduled start of their rally. I observed that almost none of our students lingered to hear the speaker.

As part of the ongoing agitation I received a "delegation" of three students who asked me to cancel a scheduled military guidance assembly. I gave them as much time as they desired to justify their request. (No "demands" were made of me by students at LIC.) When cancellation proved to be out of the question, they asked for equal time to present the position of those students who favor "conscientious objection" to service in the armed forces.

I explained that the military guidance assembly was an annual event in the New York City high schools; that the uniformed enlisted Army, Navy, Air Force and Marine corps representatives spoke about career opportunities and the possibility of learning a trade in the service. They would say not a word about the war.

I declined to place on equal footing "conscientious objection" with the need to inform high school students of their obligations under the Selective Service Act. I suggested that "objectors" might meet after school, as we did when we held a teach-in to discuss varied positions on the war. I refused to permit a "sharing" of the auditorium stage with the armed forces representatives and "conscientious objectors."

A possibility I offered was to permit boys who felt strongly about not entering the armed forces to meet in the cafeteria during the assembly period which was limited to seniors (approximately one-third of a student body too large to fit into the auditorium for a single assembly). I would not excuse senior girls from the auditorium, not because women were not subject to the draft, but because I did not know how large the group in the cafeteria might be.

Later in the day one of the "delegation" asked whether I would permit an outside speaker from the American Friends Society to address students in the cafeteria. I agreed.

On the day of the military guidance assembly only 80 boys exercised their option to report to the cafeteria where they listened to an American Friends Society speaker. I dropped in to welcome the speaker.

In the auditorium the armed forces' speakers were politely applauded as each finished his presentation. Quite a few boys and girls remained for an additional period (40 minutes) to ask more questions.

In my regular column, "Principal's Views," in the school newspaper, *Skyline*, I reviewed our experience with the military assembly and concluded with the hope that "by next year, the division in the country over the Vietnam War will be ended—by peace." This was 1968.

The war did not end until 1975. Almost 9,000,000 men and women had served in the armed forces during the war; about 50,000 died in battle; there were another 11,000 deaths from other causes, 153,000 wounded; in all, 211,000 casualties. This compares with about 1,000,000 casualties in World War II.

The Vietnam War was not a little war. And it is not a forgotten war. It had the impact of a tidal wave on our schools and colleges, where we continue to feel the undertow.

The schools were a battlefield during the war years. And while there are few dissenters from General William Tecumseh Sherman's pronouncement, "War is hell," there are light moments.

In the midst of the demonstrations, I received a petition from 25 students: "We the undersigned students of Long Island City High School must protest the operation of the lawn mower during school hours. It has interfered with our educational process." The kids may have been pulling my leg, but I did halt the operation of the lawn mower.

Another touch was a bomb threat, four days after the lawn mower petition. Hand-lettered, it read: "To whom it may concine. This school will be blown up on friday May 29 at 12:00 During school which I do not attend I go to Bryant and am being transferred to Queens Voc. Good luch student threat Browned Paper."

I filed the bomb threat with others accumulated over the years. Although I was nominally required to empty the building and call the police for a search, I learned very early in my experience that if I had done so the bomb threats would have been as regular as the morning mail. The effect of my noncompliance was that bomb threats became few and far between.

So, too, were threats to shoot and kill me as I left the building. These notes were placed in the bomb file. My secretary knew about them. My wife, who edits everything I write, will learn about these threats for the first time, a decade after my retirement from the schools.

My rationale for ignoring written or phoned threats was that someone out there was kind enough to warn me of impending doom. A real "perpetrator"—a word that fascinates the police—would be less considerate. A further consideration was that if ever I showed fear, I would be finished.

The bomber had mentioned Bryant High School in nearby Sunnyside, Queens. The principal was my good friend, Donald

PEACE STRIKERS DECLARE WAR ON SCHOOLS

Ryan, whom I described as 10 feet tall when I was asked to say a few words at his retirement party in 1972. At the time I received the bomb threat, I had occasion to write Don: "I received your message in which you advised me that Morris Gans (name changed), a student at Long Island City High School, gave a stimulating address to the students of Bryant, in which he urged them to march on Long Island City High School. The fact that they did not march on Long Island City High School I attribute to the holding power of Bryant. How do you do it?"

I then told Don that "In a skillfully structured interview with Morris Gans and his mother I was able to convert him from demonstration to arson and dynamite."

My kibitz about "holding power" was a reference to the high dropout rate of students, already a problem in the early 70's. In the late 80's, the dropout rate is cited as proof that our schools are failing.

Another casualty of the Vietnam War was the Pledge of Allegiance to the flag of the United States. While the Pledge does not go back to the early days of the Republic, it quickly became a respected symbol of patriotism. The Pledge was first published in the September 8, 1892, issue of *Youth's Companion*, a weekly magazine published in Boston.

The Pledge, once widely adhered to in the nation's schools, became controversial in 1954 when the words "under God" were added by act of Congress. Atheists, abetted by the American Civil Liberties Union, rushed to the barricades screaming that the wall separating church and state had fallen. The wall is in excellent repair, but the Pledge has been snipped at by almost every anti-patriotic element in the nation.

Patriotism itself has fallen under suspicion among those who equate it with a curb on freedom to criticize the government. They are quick to quote Dr. Johnson's aspersion of "patriotism as the last refuge of a scoundrel." They omit Boswell's successful effort to get the great man to modify his views. "But let it be considered," Boswell wrote in 1791, "that he did not mean a real and generous love of our country, but that pretended patriotism which so many, in all ages and countries, have made a cloak for self-interest." The English biographer of Samuel Johnson added, "I maintained that certainly all patriots were not scoundrels."

In the United States from the 1890's to the 1940's, the public schools transmitted through history and civics courses our national traditions and patriotic sentiments. This role of the public schools was especially vital as we absorbed the greatest flow of immigrants in our history.

Those were the years in which children were familiar with such trumpet calls as: "Liberty and union, now and forever, one and inseparable"; "We have met the enemy, and they are ours"; "Millions for defense, but not one cent for tribute."

No student in my American history classes during the 1930's, 1940's and 1950's, before I became an administrator, could say that these famous phrases were not weighed in their historical context. And I was not alone in this approach to our nation's past. Nor did it follow that we failed to stimulate criticism of governmental actions, past and present. The development of critical mindedness was a fundamental aim of history teachers. History, since those years, has been diluted by what is called "social studies." Although I have used the term hundreds of times, it remains hard for me to swallow.

Beginning with the Vietnam War years, many students and teachers renounced the Pledge of Allegiance. We are not including those who see the Pledge as an oath and will not honor the flag for deeply held religious reasons. Their right not to pledge was affirmed by the U.S. Supreme Court in 1943 (*West Virginia State Board of Education v. Barnette*).

I have in mind the 16-year-old New Jersey girl, hailed by the American Civil Liberties Union for her refusal to stand in class when the Pledge was recited. Huzzahs from sympathizers were evoked when she declaimed, "I look around me and see every day that blacks, poor people, women, American Indians, atheists and countless other minorities do not have equal rights under the law."

Had she and her followers been less myopic, they would also have noted laws that are fiercely protective of minority rights and welfare programs that mark this nation as the most generous in world history.

PEACE STRIKERS DECLARE WAR ON SCHOOLS

In recent decades judges have come down on the side of the child or teacher who refuses to participate in the Pledge. In 1973, the Second Circuit Court of Appeals (New York, Connecticut and Vermont) unanimously reversed a U.S. District Court ruling which upheld the dismissal of a high school teacher for refusing to participate in the daily Pledge, required by New York State law. The appeals court ruled that the teacher's conduct was protected by the First Amendment.

Among other court decisions that supported the resolve of some students to abstain from the Pledge was one which followed the suspension of two students at Junior High School 217, Briarwood, Queens, New York. The school is a half-mile from where I have resided for over 30 years. My son, Donald, had graduated from Van Wyck J.H.S. a decade earlier.

The two children had been suspended by the principal for refusing to recite the Pledge and for refusing to stand or leave the room when ordered to do so. They were back in school two days later (Oct. 9, 1969) on the ruling of a federal court order. The U.S. District Court temporarily enjoined the New York City Board of Education from ordering the students to leave the classroom, stating that the students had a constitutional right to remain seated during the Pledge until the school could prove that the students' action materially infringed on other students' rights or caused any disruption. Thereupon, the New York City High School Principals Association of which I was a member urged that the Pledge ceremony be suspended at the beginning of the new term.

On January 29, 1970, I released a statement in my "L.I.C. Newsletter," which I used frequently to let the community and media know of my stand on school issues.

I wrote: "The Executive Board of the High School Principals Association has given up the fight too quickly. While opposing Judge Judd's Federal District Court decision, which decreed that two 12-year-olds and a venerable high school senior could sit down during the flag salute, the Executive Board has given up the ship and the flag at the same time.

"I respect the practicality of my colleagues' recommendation, but I believe that they have succumbed to the inflamed civil libertarians who have, in a sense, forced them to haul down the flag and, incidentally, to break the law.

"The law of New York State and the regulation of the Superintendent of Schools still require salute to the flag. I have in the past been able to persuade youngsters, who balked at saluting, that they are being too literal-minded in interpreting the 'liberty and justice for all' clause. It is a goal for which critical-minded Americans continue to strive and which we have reached in this country to a greater extent than elsewhere in the world.

"I am not impressed with the wisdom of Judge Judd and other justices who have extended the First Amendment rights to children in the schools. Lower court rulings have been reversed before. . . .

"At Long Island City, we are going to wait for legislative action, or the specific directive of the Superintendent of Schools. If it is decided that the flag salute is not worth upholding in the high school classrooms of the city, we'll be saddened. We do not anticipate, however, any speedy retreat. It may even be that in our lifetime, respect for authority, tradition and a wee bit of patriotism, will become general once again. The 'Pledge of Allegiance' will not then be viewed as defacement of the civil liberties of overly critical youngsters and some of their older but quite sick mentors."

A few days later, the HSPA reversed its earlier decision and urged the New York City high schools to continue the daily recitation of the Pledge "for the time being." It was not my demurrer alone that elicited the reversal. The Association had not met and the Executive Board had gone off the deep end. Colleagues whom I phoned joined me in producing the about-face.

During my 11 years as principal of LIC, students and teachers continued with the daily Pledge. I did not receive any order from the superintendent to desist and the New York legislature has not to this day repealed the Pledge law.

My defense of the Pledge invited an outpouring of support in the Long Island City community and press comment. A parent in eastern Queens wrote: "It is refreshing . . . to read about an educator who is not afraid to speak out. Too many sit back and remain silent.

"I can't understand how some parents and principals go along with the children's refusal to say the Pledge of Allegiance. What next? . . . ."

A few days after the HSPA changed its mind about the Pledge, I was visited by State Senator Martin Knorr (Republican-Conservative) of Ridgewood, Queens, where my column, "Inside Education," has appeared in the community newspaper, *Ridgewood Times*, continuously since January 1977.

Senator Knorr arrived in my office carrying an American flag that had flown over the State Capitol. At the moment he was making his presentation, outsiders marched in front of the school carrying placards, "Free the Black Panthers." Twenty-one Panthers had been indicted for trying to blow up a department store. One of the Panthers was a LIC student (of whom more later).

The senator in his formal remarks to a small group in my office said: "Forces are seeking to bring street corner anti-Americanism into the classroom, so this flag presentation today dramatically symbolizes what the action is all about. . . . I believe tribute should be paid Dr. Hurwitz for taking his strong stand in defense of the flag Pledge when he did. . . . I only hope the Board of Education will be inspired by his example to take a strong stand for the flag and the fight for the Pledge of Allegiance through the courts" ("Principal Gets Star Spangled Salute," *Long Island Press*, Feb. 7, 1970).

The Board of Education was not inspired.

Two weeks after the flag presentation, I joined Senator Knorr at an outdoor meeting calling for the appeal of a court decision allowing students to remain seated during flag ceremonies in schools.

It was an icy cold Washington's Birthday (Feb. 23, 1970) when my wife and I took the subway to Federal Hall where a statue of Washington abuts Wall Street. There were only ten of us assembled, including representatives of veterans' organizations.

THE LAST ANGRY PRINCIPAL

Although television crews from CBS, NBC and WOR were present for about 45 minutes, not a single second of film was shown that evening. There was sparse coverage in the print media.

Had Washington's statue and the senator been splattered with red paint, or if we had been attacked by the Black Panthers, our meeting would have been covered. A mere statement by a state senator and a high school principal, at a time when the flag was being besmirched by kids and courts, merited no comment.

I have been something of a newsman for a half-century when you include my years with Scholastic Magazines as its teacher-editor (1946–62). There is mounted to my left, as I type these words, a letter dated, July 6, 1962 signed by the president and publisher, the late M.R. Robinson, and Jack Lippert, executive editor.

"Dear Howard:

"Word of your resignation as teacher-editor has jolted us out of a 17-year dream world to which we had become accustomed through a happy and profitable association with you. We now wake up to the realization that this was not a world without end. However much we regret it, we understand the reasonableness of your decision. Who would be better qualified to understand a man's desire for relief from the weekly copy deadline? We say this without diminution of our high regard for your ability and appreciation for what you have done to keep Senior Scholastic moving with the times.

"Besides the professional competence you brought to the job, your many sacrifices in adapting to sudden changes in our schedule (how often had we asked you to do two issues in one week?) and your perfect record of meeting weekly deadlines have done so much to lighten the load of the editors with whom you worked.

"For these gifts and the opportunity to know and work with you we shall always be grateful. It is characteristic of you to carry your thoughtfulness through by offering to stay on during the period of transition. This makes us feel a bit more secure than we otherwise would at this stage of our planning.

"Howard: Ken Gould is in the hospital (chest surgery) and

Roy Hemming and Eric Berger are on vacation, which explains the absence of their signatures."

Apart from the pride I feel in receiving such a letter from "Robbie," as the publisher was known and signed himself, it suggests that I have compassion for editors.

I have had my share of radio, television and print media coverage so the media slighting of the flag episode is forgiven. What is less easy to forgive or forget—the reason for this book— is the undermining of our schools. It has brought us, as we edge into the 21st century, to the lowest point in the history of education in America.

VII

STUDENTS' RIGHTS AND WRONGS

IF THERE IS any truly new development in the history of American education, it is the students' rights movement that was fueled by the anti-Vietnam War protesters. Never before in the history of our schools and colleges had students sought to gain for themselves decision-making powers in education.

Students most certainly had rights prior to the movement of the 1960's and 1970's. They were not repressed by principals or teachers. Political activists among them seized upon the U.S. involvement in the Far East as the focus of their anti-Establishment animus. On the college-level they were the products of the post-World War II baby boom. They were part of an affluent society and had experienced none of the trauma of their parents who had survived the Great Depression and great war. They wanted for nothing and were impatient of restraints imposed in school and college. Their parents were for the most part permissive and indulged their tastes. They did not see that the national interest was involved in a country that they could scarcely locate on a world map, and they had no desire to risk dying in a war that they opposed.

Students' rights were not detailed in any document and most certainly did not include unfettered agitation on campus or school grounds. Primarily, students had the right to obtain the best possible education for citizenship that their abilities allowed. They had the right to attend a safe school. They had the right to ask questions of teachers and school administrators and to be informed of their progress at regular intervals. They had the right to criticize aspects of the school. It went without saying that such criticism could be expressed firmly, if politely. They had the right to a diploma or degree once they satisfied the requirements for graduation.

Since students were minors, parents acted for them in the comparatively few cases brought before the courts. These were largely for injuries sustained by students where school authorities were being charged with negligence.

As a consequence of the antiwar protests that expanded to include empowerment of students in areas traditionally regarded as powers of the school authorities, the relationship between students and school authorities has changed radically.

Although my focus is on students' rights in New York City, school systems in the nation were similarly affected. Often the language in students' rights codes were so similar that you might conclude that the New York City experience was being replicated in other parts of the nation. The similarity of language may be explained in large part by the activity of the American Civil Liberties Union. Students nationwide received the New York Civil Liberties Union *Student Rights Handbook* which counseled students to defy school authorities and to rely on the courts for actions against principal and teachers.

Most culpable in the surrender to students' demands in New York City were the Board of Education and a succession of weak superintendents. As early as 1969, a board draft of students' rights was circulated among high school principals. Principals saw at once that students' responsibilities were frozen out owing to the climate of the times. Their reaction was to draft a paper that emphasized students' responsibilities. I saw that the compromise would merely encourage the board to believe, as proved to be the case, that students' rights were the order of the day. It was to assure disorder for many years.

There was a fruitless meeting of a committee of three principals with Seymour Lachman, the board member who had drafted a statement of students' rights. Following the meeting, the three wrote to Lachman on October, 6, 1969: "At our meeting in your office on September 26, you must have sensed our concern with the form and tone of your draft statement entitled 'Bill of Rights and Responsibilities for Senior High School Students.' We were disturbed that as presently written it would seriously undermine our efforts to assure an effective school program. . . . You can appreciate our professional apprehension at the unpleasant possibilities of an official statement from the Board of Education that implies criticism, no matter how subtle. . . . We call to your attention the fact that we have endorsed an unequivocal statement of responsibility and accountability."

The board ignored the principals' pleading and printed 250,000 copies of its booklet, "Rights and Responsibilities of High School Students," mandating its distribution to all students.

The board was impervious to the principals' warning that student militants would read no further than rights. One realistic principal, Louis A. Schuker, Jamaica High School, wrote to Lachman (November 3, 1969): "Most high school principals feel that their schools are in a state of tension and instability edging towards disruption. . . . The majority of high school students today need psychological and sometimes even physical protection against the small minority of aggressive, dogmatic, negative and loudly assertive adolescents who dominate the scene. . . ."

Lou Schuker sent me copies of his correspondence until his retirement in 1971. He has been my good friend for thirty-five years. I understood the invidious pressures which caused him to retire at age 65. He was a brilliant leader and we sorely missed him as the violence of the students' right movement escalated. I had been his assistant principal at Manual Training High School (1953–55) and Jamaica High School (1956–66) and could not have had better preparation for my stint as principal of LIC.

Efforts of principals to dissuade the board from codifying students' rights had failed. Apart from piddling modification, ignored by students in the ensuing years, the code stated:

"Official school publications shall reflect the policy and judgment of the student editors. . . .

"Students may exercise their constitutionally protected right of free speech and assembly. . . .

"Students have a right to wear political buttons, arm bands and other badges of symbolic expression. . . .

"Students may distribute political leaflets, newspapers and other literature at locations adjacent to the school.

"Students shall be allowed to distribute literature on school property at specified locations and times designated. . . .

"Students may form political and social organizations, including those that champion unpopular causes. . . .

"Faculty advisers shall be appointed by the principal after consultation with the student group.

"Students have the right to determine their own dress. . . . This right may not be restricted even by a dress code arrived at by a majority vote of students. . . ."

This down payment on students' demands was to be expanded by further curbs on the principals' decision-making powers. As issued in 1970, the board's codification of students' rights provided that "The student government shall be involved in the process of developing curriculum and of establishing disciplinary policies."

Principals were directed to establish "A parent-student-faculty consultative council . . . to consider matters of school-wide concern submitted by individual students." Principals were required to report to the chancellor [new title for the Superintendent of Schools] on the "structure and operating procedures" of the consultative council.

My colleagues saw as clearly as I the dangers of the board's capitulation to students' demands. The difference between my colleagues and me was that they kept their criticisms "in house." They wrote to each other and to board members. When they issued a release, it was a collective effort.

I saw early in the struggle that principals would be crushed by the board. I had the support of the Long Island City community and determined to go it alone. I could not imagine myself listening to students' "demands." No student was ever to make one of me. It was easy enough to talk to me—I like talking with students. LIC students had the good sense to know that I was not the kind of man of whom you made demands.

As board member Joseph Barkan remarked in 1976, when

he was the only board member to oppose the fine against me, I was known to the board as "a dissident." This dissidence had been expressed in my "L.I.C. Newsletter," distributed to the community and media. My criticisms of wrong directions that the board was taking in other areas preceded my opposition to students' rights and followed it.

On February 11, 1970, two weeks before the board was to convene for the purpose of adopting its students' rights code, I released a statement that invoked a resounding public response.

The text follows, except for references I made to paragraph and page in the board's document.

"J'ACCUSE"
HIGH SCHOOL PRINCIPAL RAPS BOARD OF EDUCATION FOR "CHAMBER OF FOOLISH HORRORS"

"I am accepting the invitation of the Board of Education to submit written comments on the 'resolutions stating rights and responsibilities of senior high school students (amended),' that is to be considered for adoption by the Board at hearings on February 26.

"I am writing because I cannot bring myself to appear at a Board meeting where the vilest elements in the city have appeared in the past to spew forth their venomous hatred of all authority and especially that of the high school principal. Their disruptive behavior has been largely unrestrained by the Board, except on those occasions when even the Board terminated meetings which were spiraling toward the violent confrontations which the present resolutions are likely to produce.

"It is my recommendation that the proposed resolutions be buried in some chamber of foolish horrors, which a well-intentioned Board, but one oblivious of the realities of running a high school, seems determined to plunge us. Ironically, the resolutions will also be rejected by the sick militants who will say that it does not go far enough. That the principal is hemmed in by resolutions and the threat of reversal by higher headquarters (e.g., "Appeals from the decisions of the head of the school must first be lodged with the assistant superintendent in charge of the high schools, then the Chancellor and finally the Central

Board of Education") will not satisfy the elements bent on disruptions of the high schools.

"It is laborious to take apart the spurious document that purports to 'foster an atmosphere of trust' when it is so patently based on the assumption that principals are tyrants and innocent children are being violated on the altar of civil rights. The resolutions have been conceived in the heated political atmosphere which has so distorted the Bill of Rights that some judges are being entangled in their robes as they rush to cover children in the protective blanket of the First Amendment.

"Seemingly, we have lost our sanity. What has happened to the traditional, court-supported 'in loco parentis' concept which enabled teachers and principals to act as mature guides for the children who are our responsibility in the schools? By what magical turn do we now draw upon the wisdom of high school pupils in 'making decisions in certain areas, including curriculum and disciplinary policies'?'

"Why is it now necessary to establish by ukase that 'representatives chosen by the student government shall meet at least monthly with the principal to exchange views. . . .'? Is there a principal who does not recognize the need for meeting regularly with students on the exciting problems which confront us daily in the schools?'

"What ill-concealed distrust of the principal motivates such caveats as the clause which mandates a 'parent-student-faculty consultative council . . . to insure implementation of agreed upon innovations'?

"What special gifts have high school writers inherited that in the full flower of their teen years 'Official school publications shall reflect the policy and judgment of the student editors'?'

"How far removed is the Board from realities of the high schools, where it is virtually impossible to dragoon a faculty adviser for a club, when it proposes: 'Faculty advisers *shall* (my emphasis) be selected by the student groups and recommended to the administration for appointment'?

"Why is it necessary to exacerbate the tensions in our high schools by distributing the manna of the *Tinker v. Des Moines* decision, thus inviting students to 'wear political buttons, arm bands and other badges of symbolic expression, as long as these do not advocate racial or religious prejudice'?

"Has the Board inured itself to the filth which hides under the cover of a free press so that it now proclaims that 'Students may distribute political leaflets, newspapers, and other literature, without prior authorization, at locations *adjacent* (Board's emphasis) to the school'?

"Has the Board made itself oblivious to irresponsible dissent so that it now seeks to inflict misanthropes on the schools? This it promotes with the provision: 'Students may form political and social organizations, including those that champion unpopular causes providing they are open to all students. . . .'

"Of the Board's policy toward dress, we have heard enough. Weird costumes are de rigeur. Sanctimoniously added is the caution that such dress must not be 'clearly dangerous.' All is then leavened by the reminder: 'This right may not be restricted even by a dress code arrived at by a majority vote of students as Dr. Ewald Nyquist, Acting State Commissioner of Education held this year. . . .'

"The pièce de résistance of the Board's indigestible fare states: 'Students have the right to receive annually upon the opening of school a publication setting forth all the rules and regulations to which students are subject. This publication shall also include a statement of the rights granted to students. It shall be distributed to parents as well.' Woe betide the principal who fails to enumerate among the dont's: 'Thou shalt not stick thy finger in thy neighbor's eye, or knock his incisors out with a poorly directed blow.'

"Determined not to open any avenue that might permit an ingenious principal to maintain order, the Board emphasizes the adversary nature of any meeting between student, parents and principal by stating: 'Students shall have the right to a fair hearing, as provided for in the State Education Law, which includes representation by counsel, with the right to question witnesses against such pupils, *prior* (Board's emphasis) to any disciplinary action whch could result in suspension from classes for *more than five days.'* (Board's emphasis). This amendment to the State

Education Law, quietly enacted in April, 1969, has contributed greatly to the disruption of the high schools. Its elimination is now being sought in the State Legislature.

"The effect of the questioning by counsel of witnesses in suspension hearings means that teachers, deans, etc. are summoned from their classrooms by the lawyer for the disruptive student, since the principal is presumed to be devoid of any judgment in assessing complaints by teachers that he does not personally witness. No principal can undertake suspensions with this kind of harassment built into the proceedings. Students are now challenging principals: 'Go ahead! Suspend me!' They are being deluged by civil libertarians and anti-poverty agency pap that the lawyers will set them free, no matter what their depredations.

"The net effect of the Board resolutions on students' rights will be to make it increasingly difficult for a principal to exercise sufficient authority to insure a learning atmosphere for the great majority of students.

"It is up to the all too silent majority to rise up and be heard."

The "silent majority" roared its approval of my "J'Accuse," but before I tell you about that response, let me remark on some of the conditions which I touched upon.

The board meeting was almost riotous. It was terminated by the vice-president of the board because of the disruptive behavior of students present. A searchlight battery was thrown and struck the head of a board aide. When it was announced that the board president, Joseph Monserrat, could not be present because he was ill with pneumonia, many in the crowd jeered and laughed.

As I predicted, militant students, presuming to speak for the great majority that longed for a little quiet, were not content with the board's statement of their rights.

The City G.O. [General Organization] Council, guided by a faculty adviser appointed by the chancellor, published its own demands about two weeks before the board meeting. The three-page, mimeographed, single-spaced, $8^1/_2 \times 14$ document, was sent to me by a fellow principal. I noted at once the expanded sponsorship of the demands. The "as proposed by," instead of reading "City G.O. Council," was ascribed to "The continuing committee of City Council with the addition of representatives from: Third World Committee; Student Mobilization Committee." There followed a list of students by name and affiliation. Among the bonafide high school representatives, whose schools were named, there appeared the names of City College students, who had added their affiliations with the "Third World Committee" and "Student Mobilization Committee."

I shall quote only a few of the 75 demands set forth:

"the student government shall be independent of the administration and the faculty adviser. . . .

"the student government shall have free access to all school facilities without interference from the administration or faculty adviser. . . .

"no less than eight assembly programs per term shall be available to the student government without interference from the administration. . . .

"There shall be a student member of the Board of Education with full voting privileges. . . .

"Students shall have the right to distribute political leaflets, newspapers and other literature, without censorship and without fear that the ideas expressed will be recorded for future use against him. . . .

"School publications shall reflect the policy and judgment of the student editors, without censorship by the school administration. All student groups shall be allowed access to the newspaper to advertise their activities and ideas. . . .

"Students shall have the right to wear buttons, armbands or other badges of symbolic expression. . . .

"All flag salutes, pledges of allegiance and other ceremonies of political loyalty are optional for both students and teachers. . . .

"Students shall have the right to choose their own dress, conduct and personal appearance. . . .

"Students . . . shall have the power to govern themselves according to their own system. . . . Their organizations shall have access to school facilities, with the ability to distribute its publications and propagandize its point of view. . . .

"these organizations may lobby for the purpose of changes in curriculum and school policy. . . .

"there shall be no suspension hearing unless deemed necessary by the School Liaison Board. . . .

"students shall have upon request, a hearing before a judicial body composed soley (sic) of his fellow students. . . .

"Students and their parents shall have the right to file complaints against school officials before an independent panel. . . .

"Any use of police shall be subject to review by the School Liaison Board. . . .

"Students shall be free from the use of anecdotal files as a method of student evaluation. . . .

"Schools shall be open daily to parental observation. . . .

"All students shall have the right to receive information on abortion and contraception. . . .

"There shall be a complete examination of all books and educational supplies upon request of the student body. . . ."

Since I have nowhere suggested that student militants were representative of the student body, it is appropriate to note that the G.O. President of Lafayette High School (Brooklyn, N.Y.) wrote to a board member with copies to several superintendents and the faculty adviser of the City G.O. Council, on February 20, 1970, calling attention to the fact that "unauthorized people had been admitted" to the meeting; that "the subject under discussion was supposed to be the committee report by members of the City G.O. Council not a coalition of radical groups. The impracticality of the final document and the improperly drawn committee were never discussed by the membership of the council and none of its recommendations were properly passed. Our efforts to bring these matters up in discussion were not recognized by the chairman."

The youth from Lafayette observed also that "despite repeated requests" of the faculty adviser "to help restore order and decorum, proper procedures were not instituted so that the meeting could function properly."

He concluded, "Because of the above, Lafayette High

THE LAST ANGRY PRINCIPAL

School will find it necessary to withdraw its membership from the City G.O. Council unless remedial action is taken immediately."

The oft-repeated plea by student militants for the unrestricted rights to "propagandize" "unpopular causes" caused me to reflect on the Black Panthers, the alleged department store bombers. A flier, "Free the Panther 21!", distributed outside of LIC by the High School Student Union, singled out the one Panther whom we knew to be a LIC student from press reports of his arrest. The flier stated: "As high school students we know what it means to be treated like shit. Ronnie Botts (name changed) was organizing a Black Student Union chapter at L.I.C. HS to try and change that. NOW HE'S IN JAIL. AS HIGH SCHOOL STUDENTS WE HAVE TO SUPPORT HIM."

I have changed names frequently in this book. This time I have changed it because I do not want the one Panther I met to be embarrassed.

When Ronnie was let out on bail, he returned to LIC. My instructions were to send him to me before admission to any classes. Ronnie sat down beside me.

"Ronnie, you've been out of school for several weeks. Please explain your absence."

Ronnie started to say, "I was in jail . . . . ," when I interrupted.

"Ronnie, you're chewing gum. Please deposit the gum in this basket before you continue talking."

I held out the basket for Ronnie. He wrapped the gum in the proffered scrap paper and placed it in the basket.

Ronnie then continued: "I'm out on bail, but I didn't do anything. I never had anything to do with a plan to blow up department stores. We have a lawyer and he's going to get us off."

"Right, Ronnie, you're innocent until proven guilty. You haven't given us any trouble in school up to now and I want you to keep your record clean on that score. I am readmitting you to all classes."

Readmitting Ronnie had its danger. An anti-hero syndrome had developed among youths and they were likely to look upon a

90

classmate returned from jail as a hero. Ronnie had been in the newspapers as one of the 21 Panthers and could be looked upon as a celebrity. There would be the temptation to talk to him in the halls; others would crowd around. Students would be late to class. The halls might become bedlam.

I laid out some conditions for Ronnie's return:

"It is probable that students will meet you in the hall and ask for a first-hand account of your experience. You are to say nothing. Excuse yourself and walk directly to class. I am tightening your program—no study period—so that you can leave early. Go directly home.

"If I find that your presence in the building is disturbing, I shall dismiss you immediately.

"Do you agree to these conditions for your readmission?"

"Yes, Dr. Hurwitz."

Ronnie stayed in school for the few months until the end of the term. I never saw or heard from him again.

The High School Student Union was mistaken in attributing to Ronnie efforts to organize a chapter at LIC prior to his arrest. Neither before nor after his jailing and subsequent acquittal, along with the other Panthers, did Ronnie cause us a bit of trouble.

Getting back to the reception of "J'Accuse": It reached far beyond New York City. Some months later I was to address the annual meeting of the National Association of Secondary School Principals in Houston on "Constitutional Rights of Students and the Law and Order Issue." As previously mentioned I wrote a booklet, *The Principal, School Discipline and the Law*, published by the Council of Supervisors and Administrators. My reason for writing it was that I believed that principals nationwide needed some reinforcement. They had been led to believe by the NASSP in its reports on the law that the courts had surrendered completely to student militants. The surrender was only partial. The booklet was given an excellent review in the *Christian Science Monitor* and attracted attention among educators.

Several principals wrote to me. Edward I. Phillips, principal of Jane Addams Vocational High School (Bronx, N.Y.), wrote: "Your J'Accuse newsletter has described succinctly and cogently not so much the plight of the principal, not the inanity of the present Board of Education (and its predecessors), not the fanatical self-serving of the civil rights lawyers, not the self-aggrandizing of the marginal lunatics, but the end, or at least the well-defined beginning of the end of public education in New York City.

"Your warning should be spread upon the pages of our papers, sent to the networks, and brought to the attention of our 'liberal' Mayor [John Lindsay]. I suspect that your acute judgments will have the effect of Cassandra's predictions.

"I, however, enjoyed reading them and agreed from start to finish. I fear that the effect will be that of an Open School Night, when we see only the parents of our good pupils. Those who would profit most from your clarion call, and who need it, are deaf!'"

Parents of LIC students presented me with a framed account of my "J'Accuse," headlined in the *Long Island Press* (Feb. 12, 1970) as "High School Principal Opposes More Rights," enlivened with a photo of me smiling. In part, the *Press* account read: "Hurwitz, a serious-minded educator who also retains a keen sense of humor, said 'There is very little now in our New York City school system to be humorous about.' "

A sense of humor was required for survival and mine was tickled early in those dog days by Arthur Chappell, an administrator at board headquarters and a good friend. I had requested appointment of a Secretarial Studies chairman of department. Arthur replied that I had done all that I could to bring about the appointment. He added: "My advice at this stage is to become friendly with as many students as possible so that when they take over, you will have some contacts that may enable you to get help or the students in charge may let you help in running the school."

Humor was in thin supply among high school and college faculty and administrators. So depressed were campuses that at the end of the spring term, May 1970, after the board released its students' rights statement, New York University announce that it had to cancel its administration of advanced placement examinations for high school seniors "because of the inability of the university to insure stability and security on the NYU campus due to student action."

Six months later the High School Principals Association issued a white paper, "To Save Our Schools." In three solid pages the HSPA documented the "violence in our high schools . . . reaching the point where soon there may be no safety for any child."

In part, the paper reported: "The riot that overflows into the subways commands newspaper headlines, the attention of the entire public and of officialdom. The insubordination, disruption and crime that are now commonplace in our schools are ignored. Worse, our highest officials have shown by their actions that they are willing to tolerate lawlessness in the determination of policy."

The HSPA cited two high schools, Benjamin Franklin and George Washington, in Manhattan, "among a number of the recent cases of violence and destruction. A score of others have had confrontations, riots, and burnings. These have been the dramatic situations that have commanded the headlines and been publicized over television and radio. What does not seem to be general knowledge is that, with few exceptions, all of the high schools of the city are being destroyed, although some more slowly and without publicity."

At LIC we were having no picnic. I figured that in the war going on, if I lost a single battle, no matter how small, my defeat would be total. Here again, I am personalizing a war in which I was aided immeasurably by those who supported my every maneuver.

Principals were taking a beating. There was the example of an esteemed colleague, who was told when he cautioned a girl to behave in the auditorium, "Kiss my ass, you mother-fucker." He was compelled by the superintendent to retain the girl in his school. He had to remove a notation on her record. He retired soon after and the system lost a giant.

There was the LIC student who walked the halls briefly with a political button, "Fuck the State." He was brought to my office by the Dean of Boys. I listened to the boy explain that he was within his rights as set forth in the Board of Education's statement of students' rights. I did not interrupt as he expounded the First Amendment.

"Have you anything else to say?" I asked.

"No, Dr. Hurwitz."

"Now, listen carefully to me. I'm going to count to 10. If you have not removed that button and handed it to me when I reach 10, I'm going to take you to the door and put you through it. You will never again enter this school as a student. If you give me the button, I shall nevertheless take you to the door. You will return tomorrow with your mother or father or both. We will then discuss your First Amendment rights."

It was not necessary for me to start counting. The boy handed me the button.

The next day the boy appeared with his parents. I showed them the button and talked about the implication of their son's behavior on good order in the schools. They could not understand why their son would do such a thing. These parents were not alone in expressing dismay with their children's acts.

The boy said he was sorry and that he would not ever wear such a button again. He liked the school and wanted to stay.

I felt from the first that there was no basis for students' agitation for their rights at LIC. True, I could not bring the Vietnam War to an end; but I sure could make them feel that I was interested in their views and would go along with anything I thought reasonable.

In 1967, a year after I became principal, I formed a Student Cabinet. It was headline news in the student newspaper. Soon after the word got around that we were meeting twice a month "by the dawn's early light" (7:45 a.m. to be exact), I received a delegation from our Pre-Technical (Medical) program. It was their feeling that in selecting the cabinet I had overloaded it with "those who get high marks."

I explained that I had not chosen the Student Cabinet on the basis of high marks. I had selected student leaders who were representative of the student body—the president of the G.O., the president of the Senior Class, the president of Arista, the president of the Business Honor Society, the editor-in-chief of

Skyline and a varsity athlete recommended by the chairman of the Physical Education Department.

I was glad that the Pre-Tech students had come in to see me and invited them to choose one of their number. They did.

I also received a letter signed by the S.T.E.P. class (School to Employment Program) approving the cabinet idea but requesting that students other than "leaders" be included in the cabinet. I invited them to sent a representative. They did.

Our discussions over the years extended beyond students' immediate concerns. I wanted the cabinet to help me understand young people. One of the early questions I asked of them was: "Why do some young people rebel against their parents and run away to the East Village?"

LIC students were the children of working class parents. They did not see themselves running away from home, although they thought their parents were too strict and behind the times. The rebels had a cause, as they saw it. They wanted more freedom from control by their parents. The rebels didn't like school. Many of them lived in small communities where there wasn't much to do. The East Village had an easy lifestyle. Sex and drugs were easier to come by. "We understand, but we're not going for it," one LIC senior concluded.

Sociologists have a field day attributing motives to youth for one dereliction or another. They take polls; they interview; they read each other's articles and books. They have not brought about any change; neither have workers in other disciplines. Children flee to the East Village in fewer numbers these days, but many of them have shifted their focus to Times Square where some end up working for pimps.

There was scarcely a day that students, other than cabinet members, did not come to me with suggestions that were adopted or considered. These ranged from a change in the hour at which we ended evening dances to the introduction of civil rights law in the business law course we offered. In the extracurricular field they included change of the name of the Human Relations Council to RAP (Reaction Action Program) and establishment of the Afro-American Culture Club.

In addition to the cabinet, we soon established a Leadership Class that met daily with a faculty adviser during one of the lunch periods. The class was never at a loss for ideas and I found that they were meeting with me, rather than in the cafeteria about once a week. They ate before coming to my office.

Although the war was raging, these youngsters could heat up over a change of title for our annual show, "Festival of the Arts," in which the Music and Art departments combined their talents for an evening performance.

The Leadership Class had decided that it wanted a fashion show. They were soon persuaded that fashion alone could not fill a two-hour performance. It was then suggested that fashion be part of a show that would include the chorus, band and orchestra.

The Leadership Class wanted to change the title of the show from "Festival of the Arts" to "Style and Sound." While I conceded that the new title sounded good, the traditional name for the show had won an audience over the years. I explained that there was an element of goodwill involved in the title, much as a business often retains its name when it is sold to new owners. The purchaser pays for the goodwill, apart from any inventory or equipment that might be purchased. Goodwill, I concluded, is built up over a period of years in which a good relationship with customers is established.

The kids were not buying my explanation. They were almost unanimous in favoring "Style and Sound" as the new title. I agreed to the new title.

But the matter was not closed. I learned from the faculty adviser that the Choral Class, a major participant in the "Festival of the Arts," in past years, felt slighted by the change in title. It had not been consulted by the Leadership Class and wanted to be heard.

Representatives of the Choral Class came to me after they were turned down by the Leadership Class. I reviewed the issue with them and agreed that it would have been wise, if we had thought of it, to have consulted them in advance of any change in title.

The Choral Class accepted the situation gracefully. History

shows that they performed beautifully on the evening of the show.

I met again with the Leadership Class. This time my concern was its role when students' interests were involved—the importance of consultation. I admitted that I had not thought of consulting the Chorus, or for that matter the instrumental groups and Fine Arts Department, about a change of title. As an outcome of that meeting, the necessity of a fair hearing was affirmed freely by the Leadership Class.

I am recalling only a fraction of the concerns of students that I dealt with as a principal. They may seem trivial to adults, but they were not trivial to the kids. I respected their interests.

There was the student who asked me to let him use the public address system for an announcement he wished to make about a meeting on students' rights during school hours to be held elsewhere in the city. I refused.

"You're a dictator, Dr. Hurwitz.!"

Before refusing I had explained to him that I did not wish to suggest by use of the P.A. system that I approved of students leaving school to attend the afternoon meeting; that our P.A. system was not intended for such announcements; that the Board of Education meeting he wished to publicize had received publicity in daily newspapers; that anyone who had a genuine interest in going already knew about the meeting.

The dictator charge followed. I told the student to return to class. He did so, remarking as he went, "That's what it's all about."

I agree. That's what it was all about. In my "Principal's Views" (*Skyline*, May 4, 1970), I reported the incident and wrote: "If the time comes when a student can use the P.A. system because he wants to, despite the decision of the principal, you will not want to come to such a school.

"Of course the principal should listen to students. But it does not follow that the student must have his way. The principal is legally responsible for everything that happens to you in the school. He cannot abdicate this responsibility to teen-agers entrusted to him by parents.

THE LAST ANGRY PRINCIPAL

"As principal of LIC I listen to students. There have been many times that I have changed my attitude toward student proposals. Most recently I modified my views on drug assemblies, cheerleading at away-games, the admission charge for the senior-faculty basketball game, and students working together in the study hall. There have been other instances when I did not accept a student proposal. I have always taken the time to explain why.

"Certainly high school students have rights—most assuredly the right to be heard. It is a fiction, however, to suggest that students have the same rights as adults. They are not adults. Youth are given special protection under the law as juveniles. In most states youth are considered 'infants' for the purpose of property law and inheritance until they are 21 [changed to 18 with passage of the 26th Amendment in 1971]. They are under the care of their parents until that age. In school there has been the long and valuable tradition that teachers are *in loco parentis* (in the relationship of parents) to the pupils.

"Too often we forget that youth do not have adult responsibilities, nor do they face the adult penalties which are part of adult rights in our society. . . .

"It is not the job of high school students to change the social order—to understand and criticize it, yes. But the criticism must be orderly. The violence which has characterized some student reactions to the problems of our time can only undermine the very institutions on which all of us must depend, if we are to improve the society in which we live."

My pronouncements on the state of the school were not unanimously appreciated by students. At the first meeting with the *Skyline* staff, at the beginning of the school year following the views just quoted, one of the writers said, "Since there's so little space in the paper, we should leave out the 'Principal's Views.' He has other ways in which to let us know what he's thinking—the public address system, assemblies, etc."

The student was not seeking to bait me. He was polite and sincere. Others present at the meeting were astonished by his proposal. I replied: "*Skyline* is an important way of reaching students, parents, and teachers. Since the principal's views often

98

determine the direction in which the school moves, it is always helpful to know what the principal is thinking."

Only a few minutes later, my view was illustrated when the editors asked for my opinion on the "Statement of Rights and Responsibilities of Senior High School Students." I shall not at this point reiterate my views expressed in "J'accuse." I did use the next issue of *Skyline* to respond to an earlier request of the editors.

"Student demonstrations? I shall be *happy* to give you my views on them. . . .

"Actually, *happy* is the most inept word I would have used to describe my feelings about student demonstrations. *Sad* is the word I should have used. In the past four years I have come to believe that student demonstrations are *bad* for the students who participate. They violate the right to an education of those who do *not* demonstrate; and they are a dangerous threat to the nation. Student demonstrations have reached not only the point of diminishing returns, they have reached *the point of no return*.

"The effect of student demonstrations is to destroy the schools on which we must depend to carry forward knowledge of the past and to develop insights into the present that will permit us to move forward. Student demonstrations have included book burning and defecating in the office of the president of Columbia University.

"There is no such thing as a peaceful student demonstration. Even when violence is specifically abjured, the effect is violent. The 'peaceful picketing' of the high schools by anti-war demonstrators in May 1970 disrupted a week's education for most students in the city. Most of our 2,600 students at LIC did not come to school for one reason or another on May 12 ("Ma, they're rioting!" or "Nobody's gonna be there anyway"). Those who came were disturbed by the loud filthy chanting, the feeling of unrest generated by screamed slogans and police summoned to keep order outside the school.

" 'Peaceful' demonstrations at LIC have included defacement of our building by painted signs. Chanting has included threats to the principal. This principal, however, is not deterred by threats. When seven outsiders entered our cafeteria on May

12, I had them arrested *before* they could do any harm—not afterwards. The deans assisted me. I *have* punished and *will* punish any student whose actions disrupt the education of other students. There is no civil right that permits students to disrupt the school which they attend or to vilify the principal.

"No student should imagine that he can march on a picket line outside this building and chant the filth I have heard, or disturb classes, without being disciplined. He mistakes his rights—and totally misjudges me. I shall not sign a diploma for such a student or permit him to demean our commencement exercises with his presence. Furthermore, I shall not permit any student to remain in this school whose foul mouth or disruptive behavior prevents *you* from getting a full day's instruction every day that the school is open.

"The great majority of students at LIC and parents to whom I have written agree with me. They want school to be carried on in a peaceful atmosphere.

"Innocent dupes are now being manipulated by revolutionaries who seek to rock and overthrow 'The Establishment.' I have listened to dissidents, and I shall continue to listen. But make no mistake about it. I am determined that at LIC, at least, there will be no yielding to the few who would destroy the rights of the many by their disruptive actions. I shall continue to count on the goodwill and understanding of LIC students, their parents, the police of the 108th Precinct, and the teachers and supervisors who have stood with me these past four years.

"The school bell shall continue to ring at LIC."

VIII

FREE PRESS: STUDENT STYLE

ON JUNE 23, 1975, for the first and only time in the history of schools anywhere, a school newspaper was printed by a board of education and forcibly distributed in a high school.

The Queens High School Superintendent entered Long Island City High School at 9 a.m. with seven assistants (three assistant principals and four security guards). They carried walkie-talkies and fanned out through the five floors of the 3,000-student school with a two-page (not the usual four) "Special Edition," carrying the traditional masthead, "Skyline," with the headline, "An Issue of Free Press."

The "Special Edition" contained without change a student's article on students' rights that I had allegedly censored. It also contained a second article by the same student that was not a rewrite of the original article, as it was supposed to be, but an update on developments following my refusal to permit publication of her article that I held to be irresponsibly written.

Anita Cauza (name changed), a 16-year-old average student who wrote the article, was one of 14 students in the journalism class that produced the school newspaper. The teacher of the class was the faculty adviser of the newspaper and the students received course credit towards graduation.

Anita's article was given to me by the faculty adviser who did not believe that it should be published because of numerous misstatements. The journalism students agreed with his opinion that it should not be published. Anita, however, was insistent that it be published as written.

When I read the article, I saw that it was badly written—

poor spelling, incorrect punctuation, lack of paragraph structure. These deficiencies, however, could be overcome. The weak writing skill of students was the reason we established a journalism class rather than leave the school newspaper to student editors with minimal teacher assistance in getting out the paper.

I called Anita to my office to talk with her about the article—not the poor writing, but the contents. She told me that she had attended a summer camp since the last time we had spoken and that she had learned about students' rights. The camp seemed to be something of a commune sponsored by civil libertarians.

Before writing the article Anita had visited the New York Civil Liberties Union (NYCLU). Her original article, after grammatical corrections, started: "The other day, I took a trip to the New York Civil Liberties Union. There I acquired a little paper called 'Statement of Rights and Responsibilities of Senior High School Students.' It is valid for all New York City high school students. *It is the law* (emphasis in original).

"What struck me as being strange," Anita continued in the article, "was the fact that I had to go to the N.Y. Civil Liberties Union to get this paper in the first place."

Anita then went on to state that at LIC students and teachers were not permitted to talk about the NYCLU "without prior permission from Dr. Hurwitz"; that there was no "parent-student-faculty consultative council" in the school, as required by the Board of Education; that students were not allowed to "distribute political leaflets, newspapers and other literature at locations adjacent to the school"; that there was a dress code at the school, although such a code is prohibited by the Board of Education; that students were required to buy gym suits; that "what concerns me personally the most" is that "Official school publications shall reflect the policy and judgment of *student editors*" (emphasis in original); that "we can't print a picture of a pregnant teacher because Dr. Hurwitz thinks it is in 'poor taste.' "

Anita's article concluded: "Students arise and demand your rights, because that's the only way you're going to get them!"

I was not taken aback by Anita's paraphrase of the *Communist Manifesto* in her final peroration. At no time did I regard the original article as so devastating that LIC would burn to the ground if the piece appeared in print. It was simply that I objected as a matter of principle to publication in a student newspaper of half-truths and outright lies.

After giving Anita full opportunity to state her case, I explained to her why the article could not be published. I made clear that the statement of students' rights she had seen in the office of the NYCLU had been printed in 1970 and that I had most certainly opposed its distribution at that time (Chapter VII). I pointed out that the statement had been out of print for years; that if she had read the "Directory of Public Schools," given to her when she was in junior high school, just before entering LIC, she would have found the students' rights statement contained therein.

I then took up each of Anita's allegations and told her why they were false:

First, that although I have been a keen critic of the NYCLU and regarded as despicable its incitement of students to defy school authority, at no time did I suggest or imply that teachers or students could not discuss the NYCLU, or any controversial subject.

Second, that I met regularly with parents, students and faculty in the consultative council that she charged was non-existent.

Third, that I had not sought to prevent the distribution of leaflets adjacent to or inside the school; that I had not interfered with such distribution for years prior to her entering LIC and that she could not name a single student or point to any organization that would support her charge that I was currently preventing such distribution; that I was continuing, up to the moment we were speaking, the right of students to distribute "outsider's" literature in Demarest Hall (the corridor outside the auditorium, named after LIC's first principal); and that consistent with the Board of Education regulations that specific times be indicated, distribution was limited to the first period of the school day and the end of the day.

Fourth, that while students were requested to buy gym uniforms, a citywide practice, no student was "penalized" as she charged for refusal to buy a uniform; that no student had refused to buy such a uniform, including herself, and that students who might not be able to afford a uniform (almost none at LIC) were given uniforms without charge.

Fifth, that we do not have student editors because the level of writing at LIC required that a class be established if we were to have any school newspaper; that students in the journalism class did determine what was to be published, except in rare cases. "Anita," I told her, "Yours is one of those rare cases. The students in the class agree that your charges are false."

Sixth, that there is no dress code in the school, nor could she specify what kind of clothing must be worn by students. There is a wide variety of dress in our school, unlike most parochial schools where students are uniformly dressed; that my objection to "bare midriffs," espoused by Anita in the article, did not constitute a dress code.

Seventh, that no issue had been made of printing the picture of a pregnant teacher; that the teacher herself had requested a head and shoulders picture go with the story about her, and that matters of taste did indeed enter into publication of a student newspaper.

Finally, that it would be a sad day for LIC when her judgment prevailed over mine as to what constituted "responsible reporting" by students.

In the "Special Edition" in which Anita's article was printed, the superintendent appended an italicized statement, immediately following Anita's call for students to "arise and demand. . . ." *"It is to be noted that there have been meetings of the Consultative Council at Long Island City H.S., that there is no dress code at the school, that students are not required to buy gym uniforms, and that controversial literature can be distributed."*

In a letter to Anita dated October 31, 1974, the superintendent had at first sustained my decision not to publish her article. He rejected it as "unpublishable" and urged Anita to rewrite it. The NYCLU, however, threatened court action unless the article was published without change.

At Chancellor Irving Anker's direction, the superintendent visited me with two of his aides and placed one of them in charge of the journalism class for the purpose of getting out the fifth and final issue of the school year. I permitted this unprecedented takeover "under protest" on advice of counsel.

The journalism class refused to cooperate with the "outsider." He inferred that the students' attitude was an outcome of the principal's influence on them and proposed a secret ballot to determine the real feelings of the 14 students in the class. All the students except one (Anita was present and voting) voted against producing a final issue that contained Anita's article on students' rights. The superintendent's representative did not return to the class.

When the officers of the General Organization (elected student council) learned the results of the ballot, they sent a letter to Chancellor Anker, dated June 3 , 1975. It concluded: "We oppose the action of the superintendent and support our principal, Dr. Howard Hurwitz. . . We have, therefore, voted to disapprove payment for the printing of any future issue of 'Skyline' until such time as you make it clear that Dr. Hurwitz is restored to full authority in all aspects of heading our high school."

I had nothing to do with suggesting or preparing the letter. The first I knew of it was when the G.O. president handed me a copy. I have never solicited student support for any of the actions I defended.

I concluded that the departure from the journalism class of the superintendent's representative, the vote of the students in the journalism class and the letter of the elected student officers, ended the possibility of any issue of *Skyline*. I was wrong this time and at other times in expecting my kind of logic to prevail among the higher-ups in the New York City public school system.

Chancellor Irving Anker handled the issue of responsibility by getting Anita to rewrite after corresponding with the NYCLU, and promising that the original article would be published along with a second article by Anita. The latter, headed "Students' Rights Revisited," was a summary of the developments during the year in which I resisted publication of the original article. It noted that the board's statement on students' rights had been distributed at LIC, as an outcome of Anita's demands supported by the NYCLU. Anita reported that I had appeared on television in support of my position; that I had used my column in *Skyline* to advance my position; that the "issue reached a climax at a rally held for Dr. Hurwitz. . . . Many parents were there to support Dr. Hurwitz." She concluded: "This issue of the paper is the final result of these changes. What happens now is largely up to students of L.I.C."

The students of LIC had stuffed the "Special Edition" in trash baskets. The distribution had taken place on a day that the school was not in regular session. The special task force handed copies to students leaving their homerooms to which they had returned for their end-of-year report cards. Also in the building in late June were 640 seniors, lined up outside the auditorium for a graduation rehearsal. The "practice processional" was disrupted by the forced distribution of the paper over the protests of the teachers supervising the rehearsal.

The superintendent in "An Open Letter to Students, Staff and Community From the High School division," boxed on the first page of the spurious *Skyline*, explained the reason for the "Special Edition." "We believe," he wrote, "that denial of publication in a school newspaper on grounds other than those spelled out in the statement of Students' Rights and Responsibilities is undemocratic and dangerous." He also stated: "Students must learn to respect the standards of responsible journalism. . . ."

It was precisely because the student writer expressed herself irresponsibly that I had asked her to rewrite. I did not see as "undemocratic and dangerous" my requirement that students write responsibly.

As an outcome of Anita's enlistment of the NYCLU, the Board of Education's 1970 statement of students' rights was scheduled for reprinting without change for distribution in the high schools. I had urged substantial revision of the statement with emphasis on students' responsibilities. At the very least, I called for a vote by the newly constituted Board of Education, since only two of the original seven members had voted for the original document. My appeal was not answered by the chancellor.

There followed the prospect of a repeat of my "J'accuse" (see pages 84–87). I was ordered to comply with the distribution of a pamphlet objectionable to me, that I had resisted successfully four years earlier in 1970. I had made no distribution in subsequent years. I satisfied the chancellor by making copies of the unchanged leaflet available in the school library. At no time had I feared that the leaflet would induce LIC students to behave disruptively. I had opposed it on principle. This resolution of the renewed conflict over the students' rights leaflet allowed for full concentration on the censorship battle.

At the beginning of the new school year, a 16-year-old boy sought to replace Anita as the instrument whereby the NYCLU might continue its pressure on the chancellor to keep up his pressure on me. Robert Gomberg (name changed) wrote to the Queens high school superintendent accusing me of preventing him from joining the journalism class and of blocking publication of one of his articles on students' rights. The NYCLU vowed its support of Gomberg.

The chancellor and superintendent knew that they could count on my resistance to Gomberg's accusations. During the furor of the previous school year, I had enlisted parents, community leaders, legislators and citizens citywide in my determination to require responsible reporting in students' newspapers. The struggle had been reported in the press and I had made several appearances on television and radio. The Council of Supervisors and Administrators supported my stand fully.

Peter O'Brien, president of the CSA, in an open letter to Chancellor Irving Anker, wrote: "It is clear that you are serving the NYCLU. The NYCLU has been censured by the CSA for its continuing efforts to disrupt discipline in the schools and to undermine the exercise of reasonable authority by principals and teachers. . . . Most recently, the NYCLU was taken aback by the favorable national comment on our booklet, "The Principal,

THE LAST ANGRY PRINCIPAL

School Discipline and the Law," [by Howard Hurwitz] emphasizing students' responsibilities. There is no contradiction between this emphasis and students' rights.

"In contrast to the CSA booklet, the NYCLU published its 'Student Rights Handbook for New York City.' It offers countless ways of challenging the authority of principals and teachers. It has become a bible for paranoids who equate authority with tyranny. As a single example of its judgment, it would have school children believe that 'the use of the word f—[spelled out in the Handbook on page 10] could not be prohibited in a high school newspaper since it also appeared in magazines and books in the school library.'

"Militants do not see that the NYCLU mission is destruction of school authority, thereby diminishing drastically the possibility of education in an orderly atmosphere for the vast majority of our children. In brief, the NYCLU whose positions you buttress has corrupted civil liberty and rejected simple civility as a reasonable requirement in school discipline.

"In embracing the meretricious counsel of the NYCLU, you are undermining discipline in the schools."

The NYCLU, however, could not resurrect Anita in the image of Robert. The superintendent wrote to Robert: "On the basis of the information before me, I do not find it necessary to overrule the principal . . . . the school newspaper is not required to accept an article on a subject of your own choosing simply because you desire it."

The fact is that I rarely saw an issue of *Skyline* until it was distributed. I relied on the faculty adviser (three different ones during my 11 years at LIC) to call to my attention any article about which he was in doubt. No faculty adviser gave up the journalism class because of any differences with me. It was simply that teaching the class was a tough assignment during turbulent years. It required time far beyond the 40 minutes given regular classes during the school day.

Until Anita enlisted the NYCLU in the "censorship" charge, the newspaper had never been embroiled in a controversy. I met occasionally with the journalism class and with the seven designated editors after the Anita episode. When the students could not agree with the faculty adviser, they came to me directly. I did not decide immediately, but arranged a meeting with them and the faculty adviser. Together we reached a decision. The disagreement and its resolution were typical of my relationship with the student newspaper. For example, in one issue prior to the free press furor that culminated in the "Special Edition," the faculty adviser disapproved of a headline.

The headline in dispute, "Is Paper A Puppet?" was opposed by the adviser who thought that it might be offensive to the principal. I approved the headline and the story that followed:

"What is a school newspaper? Is it a tool of the administration, a puppet of the principal? Or, is it a voice for the students? The school newspaper is funded, written, edited and distributed by the students of the school. It can be censored by the administration. Often, a principal has a free hand in manipulating the newspaper to his advantages. We are not saying this is being done with *Skyline* (we are not saying that it isn't either), but certainly the practice does exist. It is our feeling that the school newspaper, as all newspapers, should be an objective vehicle of student expression, even when it must criticize the administration.

"With whom should ultimate responsibility lie for the content of the paper? It is the students who should be held personally responsible for everything printed. Rarely will a student write something that he cannot substantiate. More specifically, the editors should be trusted enough to use their discretion in passing judgment on all articles. With such responsibility, we are certain that it would not be abused.

"*Skyline* feels that it and other school newspapers must be objective components of the news media, independent of administrative control. Otherwise, the school newspaper is nothing more than a puppet.

"If the administration feels that it cannot grant students such freedom, then it should, in our opinion, fund, write, edit and distribute the paper itself—independent of student manpower."

The foregoing article in *Skyline* was published at a time

when student militants were riding high on the crest of the rights movement. It did not reflect my view of a student newspaper, a view widely shared by my colleagues who had long experience in the schools. It did, however, mirror the view of the Board of Education, the Chancellor and the NYCLU.

Skyline was *not* censored. The very term "censorship" has no place in the context of a high school publication. Student writers are not responsible for its contents in the sense that adult writers or owners of a daily newspaper are responsible for what appears in their publication. If school policy is misrepresented or a malicious story were to be written about a teacher, the young writers would not have to pay the cost—either in cash or in loss of reputation. The principal and the Board of Education would be responsible. There is not even the possibility that a correction might appear the next day because weeks elapse between the issues of most student newspapers.

It is a mistaken notion to think of a high school newspaper as an organ of opinion that can exist independent of any judgment which the principal might make of its contents. The principal is obligated to develop in students who write for a school newspaper a sense of responsibility while encouraging them to be as resourceful as their abilities permit. It makes sense for the faculty adviser of student publications to bring questionable articles to the principal's attention *before* he sees them in print.

I have emphasized *before* because it raises the charge of prior restraint. It was raised not with me, but with the principal of Sheepshead Bay High School (Brooklyn, N.Y.), again at the height of the students' rights clamor.

A junior at Sheepshead Bay H.S. appealed to the chancellor on the alleged prior censorship of his speech as a candidate for president of the Student Government Organization. The chancellor ruled that there could be no prior review of speech. "A rule which requires prior review of all speeches," the chancellor stated, "would mean that the student who chose to speak extemporaneously could not run for student office. The student who deviated from a prepared text during delivery would do so at the risk of punishment for not following the sanctioned speech. To carry such a procedure to its extreme, the student could not answer questions unless he submitted his answers for reviews in advance.

"While the school has the right to explain to student speakers, that obscenity, defamation, and advocacy of racial or religious prejudice are to be avoided, the Statement of Rights and Responsibilities does not require or authorize that speeches be approved in advance. . . ."

As principal of LIC I did not require candidates for student office to submit their speeches in advance. I listened to all of them in the school auditorium during student election assemblies. Invariably, the candidates promised students that if elected there would a smoking room, a student lounge, freedom to leave the school during lunch periods, weekly dances ending at 2 a.m., hard rock music in the cafeteria to aid digestion of the greatly changed menu they could assure. That none of these promises were kept did not dissuade candidates year after year from making the same promises. The student body changed each year and fresh ears were attuned to the election platforms. In microcosm, I reflected, the youths were not all that different from candidates on national platforms whose promises are largely unkept as the platforms are speedily forgotten.

The speeches of the valedictorian and salutatorian at commencement exercises, however, were previewed, but not for content so much as they were for correctness of expression. I entrusted this responsibility to the chairman of the English Department. There was not a single occasion on which the chairman took exception to the content of these addresses to an audience of parents, relatives and friends of the graduates. I do believe, however, that a principal would be mindless and gutless to allow such an audience to be assaulted by irresponsible utterances of a teen-ager who attributed none of his growth to the school that nurtured him but used the platform as a podium for attacking principal, teachers, the government and anything that sounded like respectability.

Such students claim the right on the podium and in the school press to speak and write as they please. Invariably, they are abetted by civil libertarians, and court cases weighing their words could fill volumes.

THE LAST ANGRY PRINCIPAL

Illustrative of the volumes of student writing that could fill court reports if included verbatim in decisions is the language that appeared in *Corn Cob Curtain*, a publication of Indianapolis high school students. It was deemed "Obscene, indecent, vulgar, and profane" by school authorities. The "underground" paper was being sold on school premises by students who maintained that their writing is protected by the First and Fourteenth Amendments.

The *Corn Cob Curtain* case bounced around lower federal courts for years in the 1970's, but fell short of the highest court in the land. In 1974, the majority of the Seventh Circuit Court of Appeals held that "the issues of the *Corn Cob Curtain* in the record are far from obscene in the legal sense. A few earthy words relating to bodily functions and sexual intercourse are used in the copies of the newspaper in the record. Usually they appear as expletives or at some similar level. One cartoon depicts a sequence of incidents in a bathroom. . . . These issues contain no material which is in any significant way erotic, sexually explicit, or which could plausibly be said to appeal to the prurient interest of adult or minor."

A dissenting justice found the foregoing hard to take. "The euphemisms employed to describe contents of the publication," he wrote, "do not fully describe the type of language and the imagery that are given rein."

The judges in the *Corn Cob Curtain* and too many other cases have become inordinately fond of a widely used four-letter expletive. They are impatient with school authorities who demur when children use the word as verb or noun to express discontent with their teachers or the state of the world.

Principals badgered by the "underground" press are concerned also with the aboveground press. It has only been since the onset of the students' rights movement in the late 60's that the freedom of the press, enjoyed by the adult community, is thought to be a constitutional right of schoolchildren.

In the educational community, brainwashing has produced a climate in which it might seem that four-letter words are the *lingua franca* of the student press. Yet, here too, it is far from certain that students carry with them the full panoply of constitutional rights. In the landmark *Tinker v. Des Moines Independent Community School District* (1969), Justice Abe Fortas saw the wearing of armbands protesting by schoolchildren the Vietnam War as an exercise of First Amendment rights of free speech.

It is not, however, to be inferred from *Tinker* that the principal may not anticipate disruption and act to prevent it. Even Justice Fortas affirmed "the comprehensive authority of the States and of school officials, consistent with fundamental constitutional safeguards, to prescribe and control conduct in the schools."

We have already quoted Justice Hugo Black's spirited dissent in which he lashed the "loudest-mouthed" to whom First Amendment rights had been extended by the court majority. In a separate concurring opinion in *Tinker*, Justice Potter Stewart added that he "cannot share the Court's uncritical assumption that, school discipline aside, the First Amendment rights of children are co-extensive with those of adults. . . . [A] State may permissibly determine that at least in some precisely delineated area, a child—like someone in a captive audience—is not possessed of that full capacity for individual choice which is the presupposition of First Amendment guarantees."

In the realm of school publications, New York State commissioners of education have been overly zealous in protecting students' rights. In one case, Commissioner Ewald B. Nyquist ruled that the only circumstances under which a board may censor free expression by students is where it is necessary to prevent substantial disruption or material interference with school activities. The commissioner added that students working on a publication must bear their measure of responsibility. A student's request that he be allowed to remain anonymous is not consistent with the requirements of responsible journalism.

Elsewhere in the nation, courts have divided over what is permissible in students' publications. In an Illinois case the high school's literary journal editors charged the school administration with being "utterly idiotic" and "asinine"; the senior dean had a "sick mind"; an editorial urged students to ignore all "propaganda" that the school administrators published. A lower federal district court sustained the school board's decision to expel the students involved. The federal appeals court looked benignly on the students' "freedom of expression" and did not see that it contributed to "substantial disruption of school activity. . . ."

In the East, the prestigious Second Circuit (New York, Connecticut and Vermont) in *Eisner v. Stamford Board of Education* (1971), took a critical look at how far the school officials may go in controlling student distribution on school grounds of material that the school board viewed as interfering with the discipline of the school. The court upheld the lower federal district court's finding that the board's policy was "fatally defective for lack of 'procedural safeguards' " to protect the students' right to freedom of expression. However, the Second Circuit held that "prior restraint" by school officials of written and printed materials by students is constitutional if a board sets forth its policy clearly.

The court saw that "it would be highly disruptive to the educational process if a secondary school principal were required to take a school newspaper to court every time the principal reasonably anticipates disruption and sought to restrain its cause." In brief, the Second Circuit held that "reasonable and fair regulations" by a school board determined to restrain students from abusing First Amendment rights would be looked upon favorably by the court.

The federal courts have been heavily involved in students' rights cases arising from student writing and speech that are seen to be offensive by principals and boards of education. A needed corrective of the widely held belief that anything goes in student publications was handed down in 1986 by the U.S. Supreme Court in the *Fraser* case.

Matthew Fraser, a senior at Bethel High School, Pierce County, Washington, delivered a nominating speech for a fellow student in which he used sexual metaphors that caused the assembled students to hoot approvingly and demonstrate their recognition of the sexual qualities of the candidate being nominated.

Fraser's behavior was held to be in violation of school rules. He was suspended for three days and removed from the list of students eligible to speak at the commencement ceremonies.

Fraser first resorted to the school district's grievance procedure. The hearing officer found that the boy's speech was "indecent, lewd and offensive to the modesty and decency of many of the students and faculty in attendance. . . ."

Fraser next entered the federal courts for a three-year bout that reached the highest court in the land. At the federal district court level, the judges found that Fraser's First Amendment rights had been violated. The court awarded Fraser $278 in damages, $12,750 in costs and attorney's fees, and enjoined the district from preventing him from speaking at commencement ceremonies.

The U.S. Court of Appeals for the 9th Circuit affirmed the lower court decision. It found no reason to distinguish Fraser's speech from Mary Beth Tinker's wearing of a black armband as a protest against the Vietnam War.

By a 7 to 2 vote the U.S. Supreme Court reversed the lower courts. It held that the school district had not violated Fraser's First Amendment rights and that its action was justified because the speech was "offensively lewd and indecent."

Chief Justice Warren Burger, writing for the majority, made clear in his opinion that the scope of freedom of speech for public school students is not necessarily the same as that for adults in the society at large; that simply because the use of an offensive form of expression may be permitted an adult, it does not follow that the same latitude must be extended to children in a public school. It was one thing to wear Tinker's armband and another to spout Fraser's filth, the court observed.

The high court saw nothing vague or too broad in the school's rules about speech and publications. "Vague and broad" are court favorites in striking down a rule or law. The lower courts had alleged just such vagueness and broadness in exculpating Fraser. The high court majority held that the school's restrictions were clear enough to Fraser and that he willfully chose to ignore them.

The high court further reflected: "The process of educating

our youth for citizenship in public schools is not confined to books, the curriculum, and the civics class; schools must teach by example the shared value of a civilized social order. Consciously or otherwise, teachers—and indeed older students—demonstrate the appropriate form of civil discourse and political expression by their conduct and deportment in and out of class. Inescapably, like parents, they are role models. The schools, as instruments of the state, may determine that the essential lessons of civil, mature conduct cannot be conveyed in a school that tolerates lewd, indecent, or offensive speech and conduct as that indulged in by this confused boy. . . ."

As I write, two years after *Fraser*, still suffused by the glow of sanity spread by Chief Justice Warren Burger (now retired), I am lifted to the highlands by Justice Byron White. In a 5 to 3 majority vote (one vacancy on the nine-member court) the Supreme Court held ". . . educators do not offend the First Amendment by exercising editorial control over the style and content of student speech in school-sponsored expressive activities so long as their actions are reasonably related to legitimate pedagogical grounds." The court held further that "a school may refuse to lend its name and resources to the dissemination of student expression."

The controversy resolved by the high court arose when the principal of Hazelwood East High School directed deletion of two articles in *Spectrum*, the student newspaper produced in a journalism class. The practice was for the teacher to submit page proofs to the principal for his review prior to publication.

The principal objected to one article describing three Hazelwood East students' pregnancies because he believed that the identity of the girls could be deduced despite the writer's effort to conceal the names of the girls. He objected to a second article in the same issue that reported a girl's hostility to her father in a divorce case. Here, too, identification of the persons involved was perceived by the principal.

The 1988 Hazelwood East decision sustaining the judgment of the principal was the latest in a series of court decisions that have restricted students' rights.

Although I did not shrink from combating board, chancellor, superintendent and NYCLU when they sought to reverse my judgment of what constituted responsible writing by students, I preferred working peacefully with students to resolve differences.

There was the time when two poems were submitted by black students to our literary magazine, *Phoenix*. One of the poems was submitted by Danny Dade (name changed). Danny was highly regarded at LIC. Although the black proportion in the school was 10 percent, he had been elected president of the General Organization.

My relations with Danny were good. I saw him almost every day and either greeted or chatted with him. He was in my office frequently, representing the G.O.

Nevertheless, Danny's poem reflected his hostility to his country. He wrote of blacks being "castrated" and "raped" in America. The black girl wrote about "stinking liberty."

I was told by the chairman of the English Department that if a single word in the poems were changed, the poems would be withdrawn and that Danny might seek to prevent publication of the magazine.

I held a meeting in my office with the two students, the English Department chairman and the faculty adviser of *Phoenix*. I congratulated the youths on the quality of their poems, but said that I did not agree with their point of view. However, the magazine contained other contributions which balanced their views. Therefore, I hoped that their poems would appear in the issue of *Phoenix* that was ready for publication.

I suggested that while I did not wish to interfere unduly with their freedom of expression, two or three words they had used would give offense needlessly and might diminish the effectiveness of their message. There was the further consideration that the inflammatory words might discredit *Phoenix* and the school. It was my responsibility to prevent this from happening.

I proposed that the word "defiled" be substituted for "rape"; "emasculate" for "castrate"; and that "miscalled liberty" replace "stinking liberty."

The students accepted my proposed changes. The magazine was published and there were no repercussions.

THE LAST ANGRY PRINCIPAL

While I welcome any court turnaround that would encourage principals to use their own judgment and not let it go by default to irresponsible youths, it may be that students' rights, especially in students' publications, have been embedded in the school system.

The high school experience in the past two decades has emboldened college youths to the abuse of the student press. Perhaps the most flagrant desecration of freedom of the press was committed by editors of the student newspaper at the City College of the City of New York (CCNY). In *The Observation Post* (May 4, 1979) there appeared the photograph of a former student posing as a half-clad nun masturbating with a crucifix.

Concern was expressed by City University Chancellor Robert J. Kibbee, whose apology to Terence Cardinal Cooke made clear that he saw the obscenity made more foul by abasement of religion. Kibbee did not proceed against the student editors. I would have given them due process and door process within a week of the violence they did to common decency on campus.

Kibbee sought intervention by New York District Attorney Robert M. Morgenthau. Morgenthau, too, found "the photographs of sexual conduct in that edition of 'The Observation Post' . . . very offensive. However," he added, "the obscenity decisions of the United States Supreme Court now prevent us from prosecuting an individual for obscenity, in connection with a published work, unless the publication considered 'as a whole' both appeals to the prurient interest and lacks serious literary, artistic, political or scientific value."

Morgenthau went on to cite parts of *Miller v. California* (1973), the landmark decision that is cited in all subsequent obscenity cases. His reading of *Miller* would seem to still any voices that might cry out against the depravity allegedly protected by the Constitution.

Obscenity in American communities. including the college community, Morgenthau notwithstanding, is *not* cradled by courts. There is a part of *Miller*, not cited by Morgenthau, which holds: "This much has been settled by the Court, that obscene material is unprotected by the First Amendment. The

First and Fourteenth Amendments have never been treated as absolutes. . . ."

In effect Morgenthau sustained the right of college editors to indulge the most sordid tastes. He was leaving society in a hole.

Are we to conclude from the Kibbe-Morgenthau correspondence that college editors can do precisely what Kibbee predicted? Kibbee admitted that the college newspaper might publish obscenity in the future and there was nothing he could do about it.

This kind of helplessness is an admission of defeat so complete that if it were to prevail our society must be judged decadent and disgraced.

College youths contend that between June and September they become adults and that the college grounds confer upon them a maturity that might be denied to high school students. While I agree that the contents of a school or college newspaper must take into account the age level of readers, there should be no license for obscenity or irresponsibility at any school level.

High school and college editors are not liable for their utterances. The adult authorities must pay the price for students' irresponsibility. And it is not price in the sense of dollars and cents that should be our concern. Students are in schools and colleges to learn. They are learning little if they acquire the sense of complete freedom that anything goes in student publications and utterances on campus.

The argument that if students are curbed by adult authorities they will not be prepared for citizenship in a democracy is sophomoric. There is time enough for students, after they complete their formal education, to exercise freedom of expression. They will find out soon enough that while there is wide freedom of expression in the United States, the exercise of absolute freedom—too often perceived as students' rights—incurs real penalties.

IX

DISCIPLINE: UNDERPINNING OF LEARNING

"**WHAT DO YOU** think of my proposal that principals give students a receipt for a weapon at the time it is taken from them?" The question was asked of me by New York Assemblyman Leonard Stavisky, chairman of the Assembly Education Committee.

With TV cameras grinding, I replied: "You will never see the day that I give a kid a receipt for a knife or gun or any weapon. I have taken my share of deadly weapons from kids. On occasion, I have told the boy or girl to have a parent come in for the weapon. I have yet to meet the parent who seeks to reclaim a deadly weapon for his child."

The foregoing exchange took place at an Assembly Education Committee hearing in 1977, held in the library of Long Island City High School. Stavisky had persuaded me that LIC would be a great place to hold the hearing because of our reputation as a safe school.

Although hearings by legislative bodies are intended to produce legislation, it is often the case that there is no positive outcome. Reduction in school crime did not follow the Stavisky hearings, nor was there any legislation that might bring about such a desirable outcome.

There are principals who can show you cabinet files filled with chains, brass knuckles, blackjacks, knives, mace, cherry bombs, guns, clubs, etc. My collection was small, but my memory was long. I learned a long time ago that if you do not deal quickly, firmly, fairly and without fear with the would-be criminal element in your school, you would do better to close the doors. In fact, this is what has happened. We have closed the door to learning in many of the schools in the once-great New York City public school system.

In the 1987–88 school year *The New York Times* (Dec. 10, 1987) reported, "Knives and Guns in the Book Bags Strike Fear in a West Side High School." The story stated that at Park West High School in Manhattan, "students have assaulted and robbed each other, stealing jewelry, coats and radios, since the start of the school year."

Nancy Casey, a guidance counselor at Park West, who was selected in 1986 as "guidance counselor of the year" by the Board of Education, said, "In 18 years in public education, I've never seen anything like this on a daily basis—where girls get robbed, kids get knifed out of school and bring their knives in school."

Edward Morris, principal of Park West High School, told *The Times* reporter that the school is safe and the level of violence is nothing new. "We're dealing with all the malaise of society and 3,000 individuals," said Mr. Morris. "The school is a microcosm of society." Shortly after making the statement, Morris was relieved of duty and assigned to board headquarters where several principals languish.

Morris had uttered the precise cop-out that I could not live with in the turbulent 70's. It remains a bleak outlook in the late 80's. The schools, rather than being dragged down to society's lowest common denominator, must be a mirror of a better society or they will be justly described as "the blackboard jungle."

Morris's defense of grotesque behavior in his school was no different from the defense I encountered from the chancellor, board of education and Livingston Street lackies, who attributed the crime rise in schools to socio-economic factors. This is a fancy way of saying that blacks and Puerto Ricans, who comprised almost 70 percent of the 1.1 million students in the New York City public schools in 1977 (almost 80 percent of the 965,000 pupils in 1988), cannot behave decently.

In my experience blacks and Puerto Ricans want to learn as much as any other group. I never met a black or Hispanic parent who condoned misbehavior on the part of his child. It is more difficult to teach children who come from homes where there are no books, but it does not follow that such children are uneducable. Where the black or Hispanic home holds to middle-class values, there is no racial or ethnic barrier to learning at the highest level the child can reach.

A great obstacle to learning in schools where minorities are the majorities is misguided board of education policy, implemented by servile superintendents and principals, to retain in schools the incorrigible. Simple civility so essential to fostering a climate of learning has been destroyed on an altar of civil liberties designed by American Civil Liberties Union zealots.

In my determination to preserve LIC as an oasis of learning, I had to deal with delinquents who more often than not were sent to me by the superintendent as part of the game of musical chairs we played.

No matter how severe the discipline case, even when the youth's short fuse and propensity for violence had been manifested repeatedly, he was never expelled from the schools. He was transferred to another high school as an outcome of a superintendent's suspension hearing or by agreement with the parent.

As principal of LIC I suspended few students. Since suspension procedures under New York law are so much like a criminal court proceeding (true, also, in other states), I avoided invoking the time-consuming and complicated suspension law. I talked with the student and parent, explaining to them their options. It was with reluctance that I offered the possibility of a transfer to another high school, for the game of musical chairs was more like Russian roulette in my experience. When the student was over 16 and way behind in meeting requirements for a diploma, I urged attendance at night school (available in New York City) or getting a job or both. We had previously exhausted all possibilities of bringing about reasonable behavior in the boy or girl.

When a transfer was in order, particularly for students under 16, the superintendent invariably made the arrangement when I told him the parent had agreed. I was expected to admit a comparable case from another school. This sharing of the wealth is possible in cities where there are several high schools. The practice continues in New York City where there are 116 high schools, allowing this pawning of disruptive teenagers.

I shall not soon forget the case of Lee Rouay (name changed), for it illustrates the futility of retaining in our schools youths who are vicious and destroy the right of other students to be educated in a safe school. Lee, a 16-year-old, had been transferred to LIC after suspension from another high school. He had assaulted the principal, started a fire, engaged in extortion, used profanity and in other ways merited expulsion rather than transfer to another school.

Under the existing regulations (still in force), I would not have known about Lee's behavior because of the federal Family Education Rights of Privacy Act of 1974 (the Buckley Amendment), whereby the confidentiality of all school records is assured. Parents and students have the right to inspect and copy student grades, clinical, guidance, health and test records and to challenge school records believed to be misleading or derogatory. They have the right to enter explanatory statements concerning these records and also to prevent others from seeing records without parental consent.

On the face of it the Buckley Amendment (introduced by former Senator James Buckley of New York, now a U.S. Court of Appeals judge in Washington, D.C.) seems reasonable. The effect of it, however, has been to intimidate principals who fear being challenged by litigious parents and civil libertarians. Consequently, they water down or omit writing up disciplinary cases.

In the case of Lee, a colleague gave me background information over the phone. I sought such information from a fellow principal whenever a discipline case was transferred to our school. Just as the police must know the M.O. (method of operation) of criminals so that the list of suspects can be narrowed in the event of a crime, principals must now be competent detectives if they are to assure a safe place for learning.

When I learned about Lee, I gave the information to our Dean of Boys. Soon thereafter he would meet Lee, or any similarly circumstanced student, and let him know that we were aware that he had had some difficulty in his last school. The dean had been trained by me to take a tone that would encourage the student to believe that he was being given a fresh start and, at the same time, inject a note of firmness to suggest that we were not going to be soft touches for future depredations.

Soon after Lee's arrival, we learned that students were being robbed in the toilets. We were able to persuade one slightly built 14-year-old, weighing about 100 pounds, to identify his assailant, who proved to be Lee, standing six feet tall and weighing about 175 pounds.

When Lee was brought to my office, I asked him why he had punched a student in the mouth and taken a quarter from him. Lee soon explained that he had accidentally hit a boy in the mouth with his elbow as he was combing his hair and had merely borrowed the money from the boy. It is not always so easy to extract confessions from youths accused of crimes, but Lee was not particularly sharp and my interrogation was not so simple as it might appear above.

On the basis of the evidence I decided to suspend Lee and set in motion the appropriate procedures under Section 3214 of the New York State Education Law and school circulars relevant to the statute. The suspension law was enacted in 1969 and exists virtually unchanged today. It has been copied in most other states pursuant to the students' rights movement of the 1970's.

In brief, suspension laws invariably provide that parents of the accused be informed by certified mail, following a phone call, of the precise offense and time of the hearing. The parents must be advised in the initial letter of their right to be accompanied by two representatives, one of whom may be a lawyer. Parents, representatives and the accused have the right to question the complainant who is required to be at the hearing. The parents are further advised that they have the right to appeal if they are not satisfied with the principal's decision. All of the foregoing must be completed within five days.

I had reason to believe from what my colleague (who himself had been assaulted by Lee) told me that I might have difficulty at a suspension hearing. Therefore, in preparation for the hearing I arranged for one of the school's security guards to be outside my office and for the police officer assigned to the vicinity of the school to be available for call.

Lee arrived with his parents and two representatives from a local poverty agency. I greeted them cordially and explained the seriousness of the suspension. In a matter of moments one of the "poverticians" interrupted to tell me that he wanted to question the complainant. In a hostile tone he went on to explain the suspension law to me, especially as to the requirement that the accused or his representative had the right to question the complainant and witnesses.

I assured the poverty worker that I knew the law, but that I had no intention of producing the complainant. I was satisfied that the charge was well-founded. I would no more produce the complainant than I would my own son under the circumstances. While I could safeguard a student in the school, I could not safeguard him outside of the school. I doubted whether any complainant would be safe with Lee. Furthermore, under state law I was entrusted with the health and safety of the students and teachers in the school. It was my firm belief that this was a higher law than the narrow suspension regulations.

The "povertician" shouted, "You're a fascist dictator!" I responded quietly, "This hearing is over." I directed the group to leave the building immediately and followed them into the hall. In passing, they reviled the security guard as a "mother-fucking Uncle Tom." I told them if I heard one more abusive word, I would order their arrest by the police officer who was walking towards us.

There followed the superintendent's arrangement for the transfer of Lee to yet another high school. This failure to expel offenders with long records of violent misbehavior is typical of the breakdown of discipline that prevails in many schools.

In another case—rare because I was the complainant—a student new to the school shoved a security guard who had told him to remain in the auditorium until the passing bell. When I came to her assistance, Joe Doak (name changed) took a swing at me. Embedded in a stream of filth, he declaimed plans for removing security guard and principal from this world.

Our Dean of Boys, Stuart Weiss (who added years to my life by handling cases that never reached my desk), appeared miraculously as I was parrying Doak's blows. My experience on the Boys High boxing team served me well so long as karate kicks were eschewed in combat. Together we subdued Doak and brought him to the dean's office. The dean phoned the boy's mother, who was asked to come to school to take her son home, as required under the regulations, since it is not permissible for a principal to send a child home prior to the end of the school day. I then phoned the superintendent who knew there was no way that Doak could remain in my school after such an incident.

There followed the hours of preparation necessary for presenting the case to the superintendent. I was incredulous when I looked at Doak's elementary and junior high school record and found nothing in the previous nine years to suggest that he had been in any difficulty. I have never known a serious discipline case in which the action precipitating a suspension had not been preceded by a considerable record of misbehavior.

Therefore, I asked my assistant principal in charge of guidance to phone the "feeding school" from which Doak had come to us a few months earlier. In about 15 minutes she reported that Doak has a "volatile temper . . . if he were crossed he would react with hostility." He had assaulted students, security guards and members of the faculty and had been suspended several times.

I surmised that in the case of Doak the junior high school principal had followed the regulations on "confidentiality of records" and saw them as a bar to sending forward derogatory comments about a student. We gained from the principal the promise that he would send us promptly a copy of Doak's record.

What I received was a worthless unsigned statement in which the principal wrote that Doak was "an outstanding athlete" with "adjustment problems which manifested themselves in occasional altercations with his peers, security guards, cafeteria workers and the faculty. On three occasions he was kept out of class by the superintendent until conferences could be arranged with his parents."

I advised my superintendent of the paucity of documentation available from the junior high school and rested my case on the boy's behavior that had caused me to request a superintendent's suspension in the first place. The superintendent transferred Doak to another high school

In contrast to Doak's principal, I had continued to make all entries in students' records as explicitly as possible and if they were less than complimentary so be it. I permitted any parent to read the record and add to it if he questioned its accuracy. Unfortunately, many insecure administrators who fear confrontations with parents, the American Civil Liberties Union and "poverticians" have been muzzled. This has had a chilling effect on the freedom of principals to act in a principled way.

Principals are now faced with students whose past disciplinary records are unknown. We cannot obtain them, except on an informal basis, as backgrounds for suspensions. The destruction or concealment of records by principals is widespread, especially in New York, where the directives from Livingston Street exude concern for the civil rights of uncivil youths.

As the legislative representative of the High School Principals Association and as an officer of the Council of Supervisors and Administrators, I drafted amendments to the suspension law almost every year during the 1970's. We sought among other changes an increase from five to 10 or 20 days the time that a student could be kept out of school; elimination of the requirement that a complainant be present at the hearing; amelioration of the adversary nature of the hearing by removal of an attorney to represent the accused. We dropped the last proposed amendment when we perceived that lawyers in the legislature interpreted the recommended change as an insult to their professionalism.

When the New York State Temporary Commission on Child Welfare met in 1977 on proposed changes in the suspension law and other legislation affecting children, I testified as an "expert witness" for one and one-half hours before some 20 commission members. Although the conference room was perched high in the World Trade Center, I had the encouraging feeling from questions that were asked that the legislators had their feet on the ground.

Their sympathy, however, was not enough to bring about changes in the suspension law. One state senator wrote to me : "I want you to know that we are under great pressure to vote against [your amendments] by the New York Times and the Civil Liberties Union. However I have made an independent investigation and believe this legislation . . . to be in the best interests of education in New York City."

Whatever the senator believed, and no matter the number of hearings, the results have been the same. The suspension law is intact. Over the years I had met with city councilmen, state legislators, district attorneys, parents' associations, political clubs and community leaders, all in unsuccessful efforts to inject a note of sanity in suspension regulations.

Reflecting on the state of discipline in the schools in the 1987–88 school year, I compared it with the 1970's when I became a symbol for discipline. The nation has been aroused by the fighting stance of Joe Clark, the black principal of the 3,000 student, almost all-black Eastside High School in Paterson, New Jersey. Clark had expelled 66 students at one swoop without the due process detailed in the New Jersey suspension law. The Paterson Board of Education forced the immediate return of the students and charged Clark with insubordination for having ignored regulations. A few days later it lifted the insubordination charge alleging that it was unaffected by the public outcry in defense of Clark. It turned the case over to the Paterson superintendent of schools who had indicated his sympathy for Clark.

Clark is the voice of desperation that echoes the sentiments of principals during decades in which schools have been menaced by the drug problem. It is part of the ugly discipline picture—especially in city schools. In 1987 drugs replaced discipline as the Number 1 school problem in the Gallup poll.

At LIC there was no second chance with me when we apprehended a drug user or pusher. There was little point in arresting the user because the district attorney was overloaded with serious cases and advised me not to waste my time in court.

The user I turned over to the superintendent for transfer to another high school. Parents did not impose any objection when I talked with them because the alternative was arrest. We did not have to go through the laborious suspension procedures.

In one case our Dean of Boys apprehended a 17-year-old pusher and the dean had him empty his pockets. Refusal to cooperate in such a search meant that we would call in the police and have the student arrested. The boy's pockets yielded five "nickel bags" ($5 a bag) of marijuana. I decided to have the boy arrested because a check of our records showed a previous juvenile arrest for loitering with intent to sell drugs.

In court the judge listened to the policeman, a security guard, the Dean of Boys, the boy and the Legal Aid Society lawyer who represented the accused. The judge concluded that this was the youth's first offense (that is, the first offense that the judge had knowledge of since juvenile offenses adjudicated in Family Court are not made available to other courts). The Court decided on an ACD (adjourned contemplating dismissal) for one year. The boy left the court a free man.

At the time of the arrest I instituted a superintendent's suspension for the boy. This was to make sure that he would not return to LIC. As customary, he was transferred to another school.

Efforts to combat drug abuse in schools have taken on some of the aspects of crime prevention in the community at large. There is the undercover operation that I encountered firsthand when I was a teacher at Seward Park High school in lower Manhattan.

At Seward Park, I was a history teacher and chairman of the program committee (1949–53). In the latter capacity I scheduled classes for the entire school. When a special program was required, the principal would send the student to me. I thought nothing of programming a young man who was sent to me after the beginning of the school year. I was to think quite a bit about it a couple of weeks later.

It turned out that two of the youths whom I had programmed at different times were undercover cops, both of whom could pass for teenagers. They were not known to each other, so careful were the police to keep the operation secret. Soon after I programmed them, they arrested each other in the boys' toilet.

That was the end of the undercover operation at Seward Park. We had a good laugh. It was then early in the drug epidemic and we could still joke about the Keystone Cops.

Many years later when I was a high school principal, I was approached by the police who asked whether I would permit an undercover operation in my school. Although I invariably accommodated the police, I declined. The problem at LIC was not severe enough to warrant the operation, and I had not forgotten Seward Park. Also, implicit in such an operation is the entrapment of students who might not otherwise have been disposed to engage in the sale of drugs in the school.

The undercover operation in high schools is being continued in the late 80's. The New Jersey drug law contains penalties that are not so severe as to make the law unenforceable. Especially intriguing is the penalty for school kids who are found guilty of puffing a marijuana cigarette. The youth loses his driver's license or the prospect of getting one. This has struck terror in the hearts of New Jersey schoolchildren. No doubt the American Civil Liberties Union will seek to challenge the constitutionality of such cruel and unusual punishment the very first time the penalty is invoked.

On the more stringent side there is the three-year mandatory sentence for anyone caught selling drugs within 1,000 feet of a school. There are also mandatory sentences for anyone selling drugs to a minor under 18 years of age or using such a minor in the sale of drugs.

In addition to ingenious state laws and stepped-up activities in and around schools, there is a usual drug curriculum. This adds up to telling kids in Health Education classes that drugs can kill you. The drugs are identified and the horrors of abuse detailed. These programs, now being pushed vigorously by the U.S. Department of Education, have been going on for decades. Ironically, the more widespread the drug program in the schools, the more widespread the incidence of drug abuse.

Despite the national, state and local government emphasis on drug programs in the schools, including updated syllabi, peer group and individual counseling, talks by ex-addicts, etc., I do not believe that drug abuse in the schools will be significantly abated by these means. We cannot effectively curb drug abuse in schools until law and order are recognized as the indispensable underpinning of learning and implemented consistently throughout the school system. Unlike most disciplinary infractions, drug possession, use and sale are criminal acts. Although the practical school administrator will try to treat drug abuse as a school offense and not involve police and courts, the possibility of invoking the law must become increasingly available to school authorities.

There are few schools free from crime. Without getting into the numbers game, our schools are being ravaged by student misbehavior that would be crimes if committed by adults outside the school (this, apart from drug crimes). Boards of education, teachers' unions and police departments are seldom at a loss for the most recent figures. What they are at a loss for is the means of reducing the incidence of robberies, assaults on teachers and students, vandalism, rapes and even murders.

We had the answer at LIC. We used due process as a prelude to door process for putting through the door the so-called student who thought that his mission was to hassle other students, disrupt classes and destroy the rights of others to learn. The occasional intruder who invaded our building was arrested or harassed to a point of no return. Bums in the neighborhood knew that LIC was off-limits. We established a learning climate and we had close to the highest average daily attendance in the city.

The courts have been heavily involved in school discipline cases for the past three decades. Although I wish the courts might leave to school authorities the settlement of such cases, the courts cannot be held responsible for the state of discipline in the public schools. In suspension cases, the U.S. Supreme Court offered a rule that might have saved us much grief. The high court did not see that criminal and civil court procedures were necessary to assure fairness in a hearing. "Due process," the court held, "is an almost elusive concept. Its exact boundaries are indefinable, and its context varies according to specific factual contexts . . . . as a generalization, it can be said that due process embodies the differing rules of fair play, which through the years have become associated with differing types of proceedings." (*Hannah v. Lorche*, 1960).

Basically, due process is meant to ensure what the courts call "fundamental fairness." It is embodied in the Fifth and Fourteenth Amendments to the Constitution, which provide that neither the United States nor any local government may deprive a person of "Life, Liberty or Property without due process of law."

Recent efforts to impose upon school discipline tortuous procedures in the name of due process have bogged school principals in a morass. The bitterness of some attacks upon school principals and boards of education who have attempted to remove from the schools the most dangerous disrupters is almost psychopathic in its intensity.

No principal questions the desirability of a fair hearing in a disciplinary case. The mandate of common decency would dictate as much. What has happened, however, is that in a desire to apply an inapposite type of due process to the schools, the common sense relationship between teachers and children has been obscured. Critics assume unfairly that the principal is an adversary in disciplinary proceedings and that his powers must be curbed by lawyers acting on behalf of parents who are uninformed and students who are too young and helpless to defend themselves.

The role of the teacher in discipline has a long history rooted in the doctrine of *in loco parentis* set forth in Blackstone's *Commentaries on the Law of England* (1765–69) where it is said of the parent: "He may also delegate part of his parental authority, during his life, to the tutor or school master of his child, who is then *in loco parentis*, and has such a portion of the power of the parent committed to his charge, *viz*, that of restraint and correction, as may be necessary to answer the purposes for which he is employed."

If there is any doubt about the U.S. Supreme Court's view of due process in the schools, it was resolved by *Goss v. Lopez* (1975). The court stated that lawyers were not required to satisfy due process in cases involving suspensions. It would be enough for parent and student to be interviewed by the principal.

Although the anti-Vietnam War armbands in *Tinker* are programmed in the principals' memory bank, there has been considerable printout since 1969. There is the eloquent opinion voiced by the Fifth Circuit Court of Appeals (Alabama, Canal Zone, Florida, Georgia, Louisiana, Mississippi and Texas) in *Shanley* (1972):

"*Tinker's* dam to school board absolutism does not leave dry the fields of school discipline. This court has gone a considerable distance with the school board to uphold its disciplinary fiats where reasonable. . . . *Tinker's* simply irrigates, rather than floods, the fields of school discipline. It sets channels through which school discipline might flow with the least possible damage to the nation's priceless topsoil of the First Amendment."

It seems clear as we move into the last decade of the 20th century that the courts are disposed to sustain the principal who acts to prevent high school students from using the First Amendment as a club to pummel those who seek to educate young people in an atmosphere conducive to learning.

The *Tinker* bell was so loud that subsequent court messages moderating students' rights to say and publish what they please have been muffled. Professional associations, too, in their publications in the 70's—and right up to the present—cautioned administrators to be careful in matters of students' constitutional rights. The cautions have been adopted uncritically by principals, superintendents and boards of education. If their energies had been applied to enforcement of reasonable authority in the schools, the precipitous decline of the schools might have been averted.

As a throwback to earlier days when students' rights were not a preoccupation of courts, there continues to exist in 41 states provision for corporal punishment. While there is no precise definition of what constitutes corporal punishment, it is *not* a case of a teacher lashing out at a misbehaving child. It is intended to be punishment promptly administered by a school administrator who uses a paddle—not a four by four or clenched fist. The school authority is acting *in loco parentis*. There is no requirement that the parent be notified in advance of the punishment, but it is a good idea to advise the parent of the action taken and the reason for it. It is wise, too, for corporal punishment to be administered in the presence of a second person—a teacher or administrator. The practice is understandably confined to elementary schoolchildren.

The U.S. Supreme Court looked at corporal punishment in *Ingraham v. Wright* (1977) and did not find it unconstitutional under the Eighth or Fourteenth Amendments. It was neither "cruel and unusual punishments inflicted" nor "denial of due process." According to the court, the "prevalent" rule in the nation is the principle derived from the common law that teachers may impose "reasonable but not excessive" force to discipline children. To the extent that the force is "unreasonable" or "excessive," the court said, school officials almost everywhere are subject to possible criminal or civil liability. The majority seemed confident that the current law provided enough civil and criminal sanctions to deal with cases of abuse by teachers and other officials of their disciplinary power.

Even where corporal punishment has been abolished, as in New York in 1985, the changed law allows for the use of reasonable force "to protect oneself from physical injury; to protect another pupil or teacher . . . to protect the property of the school . . . to restrain or remove a pupil whose behavior is interfering with the orderly exercise and performance of school district function . . . if that pupil has refused to comply with a request to refrain from further disruptive acts."

It is estimated that there are some three million applications of corporal punishment a year, chiefly in the South and Midwest. I have no confidence in the statistics and even less confidence in the efficacy of paddling as a corrective for misbehavior. Yet, I would not abolish corporal punishment where school administrators believe that it works and it is honored by custom. We need no additional signals to youth that misbehavior goes unpunished.

The current spate of child abuse cases includes severe beating of tots resulting in their death, and incest that caused a Long

Island teenager to arrange for the murder of her father. In contrast, corporal punishment was never intended to do anything but bruise the feelings—not the body—of an offending child. In the few cases in which teachers have acted brutally, they have been charged with assault and been punished by the courts.

In the late 80's corporal punishment was given a racial twist when a white mother opened a gash over a black principal's eye in Pell City, Alabama. The principal's paddling of a seven-year-old white boy was legal. What was *not* legal was the mother's assault on the school administrator. The mother was sentenced to five years in prison and is expected, pending appeal, to serve at least six months.

On my last visit to Alabama, I talked to an elementary school principal about her use of corporal punishment. She said it was distasteful but helpful. The Pell City case will make it more distasteful.

In the Pell City case the white parent lived in a rural area and the very idea of her son being beaten by a black woman contributed to the assault. The woman denied racial motivation for the attack on the black woman administrator, but the judge did not believe her.

There are millions of survivors of corporal punishment, including the 31-year-old daddy in the Deep South who reacted to Pell by giving voice to the awesome dictum: "If the student needs a paddling he ought to get butt-busting." That daddy did not see corporal punishment as a racial issue.

Punishment for misbehavior is as old as schools. The range of punishment has remained limited while misbehavior has expanded to the point where learning is impaired. The media are quick to give attention to heinous behavior in the schools, as when a teacher is robbed at gunpoint by an intruder who enters the classroom, or a student is murdered by another student after a mad chase through the building. Little attention, however, is paid to the commonplace misbehavior that has caused teacher "burnout," a term that has been given currency in recent years.

A student does not have to slash at a teacher with a knife to induce havoc. There is an inexhaustible range of antics that exhaust teachers. There is the kid who uses the windowpole to joust with an imaginary knight; there is the child who leads the class in a coughing spell; there is the run on the pass to the bathroom; there is clamor as kids enter or leave a room.

My letter to one LIC teacher, after we had exhausted efforts to improve her, will suggest that it is not murder in the classroom but horseplay that can wreck a class.

"Dear Miss Franey (name changed),

"On April 12, at approximately 4:05 p.m., the sound of hysterical screams reached my office. I quickly found the source of the screaming a considerable distance from my office—Room 119. You are the English teacher in charge of this 12th period class.

"I determined that a girl had with her an old style fur (fox) which women used to wear years ago. I attribute the outburst of the class, not to the fox skin but to your inability to maintain order or command the respect of your students.

"When I arrived at the scene, the boys' dean . . . was already there, along with the security aide, Miss. . . .

"Even after I spoke with you, outside the room, and also to the student involved, I was not halfway down the hall when I again heard disorder in your room. It was necessary for me to scold the students and to change your room from 119 to 102 so that you might be close to the dean's office. I have no doubt that you are unable to maintain reasonable discipline."

I regretted having to put in writing my reprimand of the teacher, but the requirement of supportive data for a recommendation that a probationary teacher be terminated made it necessary. I wrote very few such letters. While it is difficult to terminate a teacher who is on probation, it requires a monumental effort to obtain dismissal of an unsatisfactory tenured teacher. Teachers' unions are hugely protective and unions see themselves as under the obligation to defend the most unsatisfactory teacher. They do so ingeniously. Although union leaders allege that they seek to persuade unsatisfactory teachers to resign, they scarcely dent the numbers who should never have been appointed as teachers, many of whom remain for decades. To the extent that any unsatisfactory teachers remain in a system, it hurts the children, their fellow teachers and the perception of the schools.

Fortunately, there remains a core of teachers who would establish good order if they had the assurance of firm backing from the higher-ups. This core of older teachers may soon disappear as early retirements deplete faculties. Their flight from the classroom is dismaying.

Teachers would be encouraged to remain in the schools if only they could be assured of sufficient orderliness so that they could teach. There are a few teachers who can maintain order through careful lesson preparation and a personal demeanor that brooks no antics from the kids. Some teachers can walk into a classroom and with a first word command respect. This teacher need not be imposing physically. It is the tone and manner that children can sense. Such a teacher who prepares lessons carefully has it made even in a difficult school. Other teachers require additional support if they are to make it through the day.

The ultimate source of strength is the classroom teacher. To the extent that a poorer type of teacher is entering the schools, it will be increasingly difficult to maintain order. While I always sought to protect the weakest teacher in the school, I acted to remove a teacher when I believed that the teacher was not cut out for the classroom and that no amount of support would be warranted. Before reaching such a decision I would direct a department chairman to observe the teacher frequently and offer constructive suggestions for improving classroom control. I would urge the teacher to observe other effective teachers during unassigned periods. I would observe the teacher myself and have what we called post-observational conferences. These and other efforts to assist a weak teacher might be continued for a year or more.

There has been and continues to be a good deal of buck-passing in matters affecting school discipline. The classroom teacher, who is on the front line, complains that he has not been supported by the principal. The principal complains that there's no backing by the superintendent. The superintendent complains that the board of education is unsupportive. The board of education complains that it is not supported by the citizenry, the state commissioner of education, the courts, etc. The result has been that many students feel that nothing serious can happen to them no matter how they behave. The loosening of parental control of kids adds to the difficulty of maintaining discipline as the underpinning of learning.

The public schools cannot carry on effective programs where the defiance of a single student goes unpunished. The public schools are going to remain the institution responsible for educating some 90 percent of all children in the nation. If they are to regain public confidence, firm discipline must be established in every school at once.

X

TEACHERS' STRIKES: A SWORD THAT CUTS TWO WAYS

THE DOWNWARD SPIRAL of the New York City public schools started with the strike of 1968 when almost 85 percent of the 900 schools were closed for seven weeks, beginning with the opening day of school on September 9. Unlike other strikes in which the teachers' union engaged, the strike of '68 had nothing to do with wages. It was forced on the union when white teachers were dismissed without due process by a black administrator in the Ocean Hill-Brownsville experimental school district.

The Ocean Hill-Brownsville demonstration district (hereinafter referred to as Brownsville) was one of three experimental school districts established by the Board of Education and funded in part by the Ford Foundation. The experimental nature of the district was perceived as a prelude to a decentralization plan for the city being considered by the New York State legislature. It was thought by proponents of decentralization that the single district was too huge and unwieldy to allow for parents to play a role in the schools their children attended.

The Brownsville people involved in the experiment interpreted decentralization to mean community control of the schools. This was very different from the kind of control over community school boards that was envisioned by most supporters of the incomplete decentralization plan.

Brownsville is an enclave in Brooklyn, New York. In 1968 it was (as it continues to be) almost entirely black and Puerto Rican. The experiment called for the election of a governing board to administer the eight elementary and junior high schools in the 9,000-pupil district. The board of 24 was elected by parents of school children in the district with only about one-fourth of the 4,000 eligible voters participating in the election.

The governing board chose Rhody McCoy, a black, to be the unit administrator. McCoy had entered the school system 18 years earlier as a shower attendant and, at the time of his selection, was the acting principal of a small school for emotionally disturbed children.

In the spring of '68, less than a year after the establishment of the experimental district, McCoy, at the direction of the governing board, dismissed 19 teachers and supervisors on alleged charges of insubordination and defaming the experiment. There was not so much as a nod in the direction of required procedures. The governing board proclaimed its determination to keep the dismissed 19 out of its schools. "As usual," it declared, "we were told this was against the law. We were told that we as Black and Puerto Rican parents cannot get rid of people who were messing up our children by their racism. We were told we had to write up charges and submit them for a hearing to Shanker and Donovan. No one understands—but they really do understand—that the game is over. Decentralization means that *we* decide who will teach our children—NO DONOVAN, NO SHANKER, NO LINDSAY, NO 500 COPS—WE DECIDE!!!!" (Brownsville Governing Board, "Fact Sheet: To the People of Our Community," May 1968).

The persons challenged by the governing board were Albert Shanker, president of the United Federation of Teachers, AFL-CIO, the largest local in the United States; Bernard Donovan, Superintendent of Schools; and John V. Lindsay, Mayor of the City of New York.

McCoy, who was to defy Donovan during the strike, announced, "Not one of these teachers will be allowed to teach anywhere in this city. The black community will see to that" (*The New York Times*, May 9, 1968).

Ten of the 19 teachers and supervisors were given a hearing during the summer of '68 by a Board of Education appointee, retired Civil Court Judge Francis E. Rivers, who was black. Of the other nine, only one teacher was black and he had been returned to his school. The other eight had requested assignment to schools outside the district. Rivers found the 10 innocent of all charges. Their reinstatement was ordered by Superintendent Donovan and resisted by McCoy, who did not assign them to classes.

The dismissal of the 19 and the threatened dismissal of another 150 teachers in the Brownsville district came at a time when teachers were being threatened with violence, and racial overtones were becoming clear. The tensions were generated by the race riots in Newark and Detroit, following the assassination of the Reverend Martin Luther King, Jr. during the same period.

When conditions became unbearable for the unionized teachers, over 150 of them walked out of the Brownsville schools near the end of the spring '68 term. The UFT hoped at the time to confine the boycott to the demonstration district and avoid a citywide strike.

Eruptions in Brownsville, however, contributed to unrest in other parts of the city. Vigilantes elsewhere had ousted some 30 white principals accused of failing to educate black children. Locked out of their offices, the principals sought restoration to their jobs by the central board of education. Vigilantes also intimidated hundreds of teachers into accepting transfers. Superintendent Donovan and the Board of Education, meanwhile, failed to offer the UFT the protection for its teachers that was seen to be imperative.

Although the schools were not in session during the summer, the simmering continued and the UFT made plans for a citywide strike. The goal was to assure due process for all teachers, not only in Brownsville but in other districts as well. In a letter to parents of Long Island City High School pupils, the teachers and supervisors wrote that they "must be free from fear if they are to teach effectively. We believe that a teacher can lose his job, but only after he has been given a fair trial ('due process')." They asked parents to help open the schools by writing, phoning or telegraphing Mayor Lindsay: "URGE HIM TO SETTLE THE STRIKE BY ASSURING TEACHERS 'DUE PROCESS' AND ASK HIM TO ANNOUNCE THAT HE WILL CLOSE ANY SCHOOL WHERE TEACHERS CANNOT EN

THE LAST ANGRY PRINCIPAL

TER BECAUSE OF VIOLENCE OR THE THREAT OF VIO-
LENCE."

I was supportive of the strike from the first in sharp contrast to my opposition to all previous (and subsequent) teachers'
strikes. In fact, so firm was my opposition to participation in
work stoppages for wages that I refused to close LIC when my
own union, the Council of Supervisors and Administrators
(AFL-CIO), joined the UFT in the 1975 strike. My principled
opposition to strikes was recognized by my colleagues when they
re-elected me as a vice president of the CSA soon after the strike
settlement.

How is it, then, that I struck for every day—36 in all? I
struck because I was convinced that if teachers and supervisors
were to be denied a fair hearing and subjected to violence and
the threat of violence, as was the case in Brownsville, no teacher
would be safe anywhere in the city. It would not be possible for
me, as head of a school, to make a decision without fearing
reprisals by some virulent, disaffected element in the community.

I struck because racial hatred was being taught to children
in Brownsville and other heavily black districts in the city. Classroom walls were decorated with pictures of Negroes who had
preached black supremacy and advocacy of an independent national state for Negroes.

And I struck because apart from racial slurs against white
teachers in Brownsville, there was evidence of anti-Semitism.
One of the black teachers in the district, Leslie Campbell, recited a poem written by a 15-year-old-girl in one of his junior
high school classes. The poem, dedicated to Albert Shanker and
heard on a Pacifica radio station (WBAI-FM), began, "Hey, Jew
boy with that yarmulka on your head/ You pale-faced Jew boy—I
wish you were dead." A few weeks later a student from the same
junior high school was interviewed on WBAI and declared that
"Hitler should have made more Jews into lampshades."

Anti-Semitic fliers also began to appear in Brownsville. An
irate UFT reproduced and circulated them citywide with the intention of making known the depravity of certain elements in the
district. At the same time the UFT was spreading a virus and

was criticized for doing a job that the Brownsville anti-Semites could not have done.

The Brownsville unit administrator himself had made racist statements. Allegedly representing "black educators," McCoy had written: "The tokenism which we now endure must develop into a rampaging conflagration that will ultimately mean control. The policy-makers and first-line implementors of educational process for black and Puerto Rican children must be black and Puerto Rican . . . educators" (*Phi Delta Kappan*, April 1968).

The Reverend C. Herbert Oliver, head of the Brownsville governing board, shared that racist position. While denying that he was anti-white and anti-Jewish—70 percent of the Brownsville teachers were white and of these 50 percent were Jewish—he said that it would take 10 years before they could be replaced by blacks. His prediction was not unrealistic, for in 1988 there are school districts, such as the one in Harlem, where 70 percent of the teachers and supervisors are black and Puerto Rican. In the city as a whole, 18 percent of the staff is black and 8 percent Hispanic. The one black member of the central board, Gwendolyn Baker, said, in 1988 the hiring patterns represent "systematic racism." It had not occurred to her that considerations of merit might have entered into the licensing of faculty.

Although there were teachers' strikes in which school supervisors did not participate, support of the '68 strike by supervisors was nearly unanimous. There were 3,500 members of the CSA, which I had helped to establish in 1962, compared with 50,000 in the UFT.

I was elected by the school district that encompassed LIC to be representative to the CSA Executive Board. The district supervisors were unanimous, with four abstentions, in affirming the CSA resolution to close the schools. In discussing the resolution one of the abstainers said that he would open his school for black teachers and others who wanted to come in. He argued that the strike would alienate black people in Brownsville who were ready to oust the governing board.

I rose to reply that it was exactly his kind of advice—a counsel of weakness—that had brought the system to the brink of chaos. We had been intimidated by black militants long enough.

THE LAST ANGRY PRINCIPAL

The physical safety and job security of teachers and supervisors were at stake. We could do no less than stand with the UFT in an effort to halt rampant racism that was destroying a system built on merit examinations for teachers and supervisors. Blacks, I said, were welcome to join us in larger numbers when they passed the objective examinations that the Board of Examiners administered.

I closed LIC on September 9, 1968, the first strike day, and the only keys to the building were held by me and the custodian who cooperated with me fully. On that first day I arrived early and spoke with the 30 teachers already picketing. I then entered the building to keep an appointment with the captain of the local police precinct who talked with me for some 20 minutes about keeping order during the strike. We predicted that both parents and students would support the school closing. We proved to be right.

About 9:30 a.m., I went out again into the street and moved about among some 200 students telling them that I could not open the school until the strike was over because there were no teachers or supervisors available. We had kept the school open during the teachers' strike of 1967 with the help of supervisors who had not struck the schools and a few teachers who were not members of the UFT. The students were orderly and respectful. The one student who was smoking extinguished his cigarette immediately when I reminded him of school regulations about smoking on the sidewalks surrounding the school.

At LIC, only two teachers—one black, the other white—asked me to open the school. The black teacher, Andrew Meyers, taught biology and was the Dean of Boys. I explained that the building was closed because there could be no instruction without teachers; that unlike the strike of 1967, no supervisors were available to assist in carrying on any kind of school program; that the superintendent would make provision for his pay.

On that first day of the strike, after speaking to teachers, the police captain and students, I left for Manhattan Center where the CSA had scheduled a meeting. A turnout of over 3,000 supervisors filled the auditorium and street. Speakers were unanimous in supporting the teachers. Walter Degnan, the

CSA president, denounced Mayor Lindsay for his "stupidity" in announcing that schools would be open.

Lindsay was not stupid but sympathetic to blacks and fearful that the rioting in other cities would engulf New York. Early in the strike his failure to keep promises to the union and support of the experiment in community control incurred the everlasting enmity of the UFT. In a city with strong labor unions, Lindsay's political demise was guaranteed.

After the mass meeting I joined the CSA Executive Board for a meeting on the stage of the Manhattan Center. Concern was expressed that the CSA would run afoul of penalties provided in the Taylor Law, effective September 1, 1967 (still in effect), by which the state legislature prohibits strikes by public employees. A year before the 1968 strike, the UFT had struck for two weeks for higher wages among other demands, and had been subjected by the court to a $150,000 fine and a 15-day prison sentence for Shanker. Less drastic action was to follow the '68 strike.

At the CSA Executive Board meeting I was appointed to a committee to write an advertisement for the newspapers stating the CSA position in what we described as a "walkout." The media scarcely ever used any term but "strike" to describe our action.

Also, at this time, I represented the High School Principals Association on the CSA committee that was negotiating an agreement with Board of Education. I left Manhattan Center for the Hotel New Yorker where I reported to the HSPA on the progress of negotiations.

During the strike I also spoke at public meetings and to supervisors in widely separated parts of the city. I concentrated on holding Queens supervisors together. As the days wore on, fears as to the eventual outcome mounted. By keeping my fellow supervisors up to the minute on CSA and teachers' union relations with the Board of Education, they at least felt they were not in the dark. Defections were few and the district superintendent, Mary Halleron (now in her nineties and with whom I exchange holiday greetings and notes) was supportive. Nominally, she was required by Superintendent Donovan to keep the schools open.

At one meeting in Miss Halleron's office, the ninth day of

145

the strike, there were about 100 parents, teachers, three local school board members and about 15 black parents assembled for an exchange of views on the strike. Some of the black parents said they were willing to see only the Brownsville schools closed by the strike, if it could get their schools opened. This idea for limiting the strike had been considered by the union during the summer along with other failed proposals.

I reminded the speaker that Abraham Lincoln had addressed himself to a similar problem and had concluded, "A nation half-free and half-slave cannot exist." It seemed to me that if we sacrificed the teachers and supervisors of Brownsville, a few miles away, we would experience the same treatment they were suffering. "Liberty," I remarked, "is not divisible." Prior to voicing the Lincoln analogy, I had reviewed the abuses by McCoy and the community-control fanatics on the Brownsville governing board that had caused the strike.

At the conclusion of my talk the applause was great, but not unanimous. A huge, well-dressed black, about 30 years of age, got the floor. He pointed to me and said, "I'm glad I caught up with you. I've been trying to find you for years. This man, who spoke about good education [I had mentioned this in my talk] . . . . Why, I can name teachers—I won't name them in public, but they are in his school—and they told me that he has in his school kids who read on the third-grade level."

His concern was genuine and he was undeservedly booed by the audience. When the meeting was over, I asked the man to phone me after the strike and I would be glad to discuss reading retardation with him.

In the course of the strike many a reputation was ruined. Bernie Donovan, a consummate politician who had never headed a school or passed a supervisory license exam, had become Superintendent of Schools. He had appointed me to my first supervisory post—teacher-in-charge of a summer high school—in 1946, when he headed the summer school program. In 1966, when he was superintendent, he appointed me as principal of Long Island City High School. I was one of six principals licensed by the Board of Examiners in a two-year testing procedure so excruciating that survivors are never the same.

Donovan, buffeted about during the strike, despised by the teachers' union and cursed by the community-control activists in Brownsville, vacillated between suspending McCoy and returning him to the district. Agreements reached between the union and Board of Education were not enforced because McCoy's promises to Donovan that teachers could return safely were broken with impunity.

I learned firsthand of Donovan's weakness in dealing with community control during the summer of '68, just before the strike. I had drafted the 21 pages of CSA demands, based on committee work in member organizations, and I was the chairman of one of the negotiating sessions in which the CSA sought an agreement with the Board of Education, represented by Donovan.

Donovan mentioned that local boards would get the right to hire and dismiss supervisors. I asked him what he meant by "dismiss." He replied, "Exactly what I said." I asked, "Do you have in mind the Ocean Hill-Brownsville 'dismiss' which meant return to the central board for reassignment?" He answered, "No, I mean fired, out, through."

I retorted that his plan was unacceptable if only because of its palpable illegality. He countered that some appeal to the central board might be arranged. It was clear in July that Donovan was determined to go along with extremists on the Board of Education, notably the Reverend Milton Galamison, a black activist who supported Rhody McCoy during the strike.

Also, during negotiations with the CSA, Donovan said that he planned to recommend a black as principal of Boys High School. (I had graduated from Boys H.S. in 1932, in the Bedford-Stuyvesant section of Brooklyn where I lived. Boys H.S. was then almost all white; by 1968 it was almost all black.) I objected strongly and said such action would destroy the merit system. Donovan might have laughed because, except for his initial teaching license, he had bypassed the merit system and sat atop the system, an ex-officio member of the Board of Examiners that he would have abolished if it were in his power.

Donovan, in response to my objection, said, "A white man wouldn't be safe at Boys High." I countered, "Then, close the school." Walter Degnan, president of CSA, and on leave as principal of DeWitt Clinton High School in the Bronx, supported me in this.

Subsequently, Donovan did appoint an unlicensed black who could not control the school and was relieved of his principalship. Boys High, a very old building, was closed and a new Boys and Girls High School was built and remains a problem school to this day.

Another reputation ruined by his handling of the Brownsville governing board's refusal to abide by agreements to accept return of dismissed teachers and to protect them when they returned was that of Mayor Lindsay. He was castigated for his weakness not only by the teachers' union—even then a weighty power in city politics—but by the business community.

A national business and financial weekly excoriated the mayor not only for the "dishonesty" of his commissioners that had become "official policy," but for his "coddling of minorities and betrayal of standards [that] have led to the crisis in the public schools." (*Barron's*, October 28, 1968). *Barron's* observed that "the experimental school districts financed by the Ford Foundation and supposedly community-controlled are dominated by black power militants and, in fact, are staging grounds for mob rule. Since then lawlessness in education has run riot . . . . the militants, with the aid of Black Panther strong-arm men, subjected the teachers to threats of bodily harm. . . . To date the Board of Education, which the Mayor has thoughtfully packed with ardent advocates of decentralization, has failed to find a way to square the circle and reopen the schools."

In the school districts the mayor was pilloried for promises unkept. He had promised to use the "full resources of the city" to bring about compliance with agreements to settle the walkout. He had promised "swift and firm" action against any who harassed or intimidated teachers. A flier, published by teachers and supervisors in District 13, Brooklyn, November 4, 1968, asserted: "These were brave words, Mayor Lindsay. It's too bad that they were also empty words, as shown by your lack of action when the chips were down."

Fallout from the strike worsened race relations, especially as it affected Jews who had been major contributors to black causes, both financially and as moral supporters of expanded civil rights for minorities. Shortly after the strike ended, I wrote to Mayor Lindsay about a newspaper article that represented the mayor to be a cause of deterioration of black-Jewish relationships.

In his reply to me on November 29, 1968, Mayor Lindsay decried the newspaper report. "I am appalled," he wrote, "by the misrepresentation of facts . . . but even more disturbed by the inflammatory reportage at a time when the entire City of New York is deeply concerned over the increasing racial and religious polarization taking place in our midst."

The mayor enclosed in his letter a release by the Anti-Defamation League of B'nai B'rith which held to be false "newspaper reports quoting Mayor Lindsay as having charged that 'New York Jews were destroying' his administration and that 'You Jews have made me use up all my Negro credit cards.' " The mayor had stated, according to the ADL, that he was "using all the influence he had in the black community and in so doing was using up his credit cards in order to bring about a peaceful solution."

Early in the strike Mayor Lindsay saw the racial implications. There could be no overlooking the fact that the Brownsville governing board was almost entirely black. McCoy was black and the 10 teachers dismissed without due process were all Jewish.

In an effort to extricate himself from direct involvement, the mayor called on State Commissioner of Education James E. Allen to intervene. Allen had said that he could not, but changed his mind when Superintendent Donovan called to say that the Board of Education (controlled by Lindsay appointees) had voted to request his intervention.

After a number of aborted plans by Allen in which the governing board was first suspended and then restored and the teachers were temporarily assigned to board headquarters, Allen came up with a plan. It had been suggested to him by Max

149

THE LAST ANGRY PRINCIPAL

Rubin, a lawyer and a past president of the Board of Education.

In the final settlement of the strike a State Supervisory Commission was empowered to close any school where teachers' rights were violated. A trusteeship was established in Brownsville and the governing board was dissolved. Four of the eight principals appointed by the governing board were ousted. (They were to be returned within a year, after the New York State Court of Appeals held that they had been legally appointed to the demonstration school district.) The trustees had the power to countermand orders from principals or McCoy. A month after the trustees took over, McCoy was dismissed for not following orders of the trustees.

As part of the settlement, instructional days lost by students were to be made up from holidays and by lengthening the school day during the remainder of the school year. This meant that teachers and supervisors would make up most of their lost pay, and there was public criticism. Teachers had given up 14 days of pay as a result of the 1967 strike and had been criticized for not offering to make up the instructional time. It was a no-win situation made more ugly by the action of some students who protested the loss of holidays and the lengthening of some school days.

Students at LIC accepted this provision of the settlement without any disturbance, but a few weeks after the return to school I heard students chanting outside our windows. I terminated a faculty meeting since it was just about over and went into the street. I found about 200 students from other schools milling about on our sidewalk and across the street. They were attempting to persuade our students who were entering the building to join them in protesting the lengthened school days throughout the system.

One girl addressed me in four-letter language. I told her that if she would just remain around for a few minutes, I would be glad to have her arrested.

About 15 minutes after the incident two squad cars arrived from the local precinct and the students were dispersed. The offending girl had disappeared.

On November 19, 1968, the first day of my return to LIC

150

after the strike, I used our public address system to speak to the students.

"Boys and Girls:

"I know you will give me your undivided attention for the next few minutes. I have spoken to you on two previous occasions this term. Each time I welcomed you back. This time, I hope, on behalf of all of us, that I am welcoming you back for good.

"We wish that we might have kept in closer touch with you during the school closing. We did send two letters to your parents and we distributed two circulars in the community. We also tried to relieve your anxiety a little bit through our interim schools. [We had set up a school in a local synagogue where some teachers conducted classes for the few students who availed themselves of the program.] But it may well be that after 36 days of strike, some of you are still confused as to the reasons for the school crisis into which you were plunged.

"Tens of millions of words have been written about the school strike; even more millions have been spoken. Your principal, and many of your teachers, devoted themselves full-time to explaining the issues to the public and to each other. We cannot at this time go into all of the reasons for the work stoppage. But I must assure you that we were concerned not only about ourselves but about you. We were convinced—and we remain convinced—that is *was* impossible and that it *will be* impossible to give you the kind of education you deserve in the atmosphere of racism and terrorism which existed in Ocean Hill-Brownsville and which had resulted in the ousting of school supervisors and teachers by vigilante action, even before the first strike on September 9.

"We now have reason to hope that we shall be able to conduct schools in an atmosphere of safety and dignity. Of course there will be incidents in various parts of the city and our newspapers will report them. But the strength the teachers and supervisors of our public school system have shown will be your assurance that in the long run your education will not be interrupted by the disgraceful behavior of a handful of people who would have destroyed public education in our city.

THE LAST ANGRY PRINCIPAL

"We, the faculty of Long Island City High School, are especially grateful to you and your parents for the patience you have shown during these awful weeks. There was not a day that we did not want to return. The fact is that we never wanted to leave for as much as a day. We had a choice. We could teach in safe schools where the rights of teachers were respected, or we could live a life of fear that would be ruinous to our self-respect and destructive of the education that we have been trained to give you.

"Our first order of business is to get down to work at LIC. We shall not try to have you do two days of work in one. We shall proceed in each class at the usual pace. When the school day is lengthened, and if days are added to the school year, we shall then seek to complete more of the regular term's work. None of you will lose your diploma, or suffer any lowering of marks because of the strike. Seniors will be given special assistance so that their opportunities for college entrance or jobs will not be hurt. You have been hurt enough.

"As principal of the school, I shall work with teachers and supervisors to make your education as meaningful as possible. I shall confer regularly with your elected school representatives on matters of broad concern, as I have in the past. We have reason to believe that your parents will participate much more actively in school affairs.

"We have gotten along well together at LIC. We shall continue to work together. I am proud to be the principal of this high school. I am proud of the faculty and I am proud of the good judgment you have exercised during 36 terrible days. It promises well for our future together."

Our future together would have been fine if only Long Island City High School could have operated in a vacuum. It is not, however, possible to insulate a school completely from the surrounding society. Seemingly, the bitter strike of '68 had been won by the union. The teachers and supervisors whose return to Brownsville was part of the settlement soon drifted off to other assignments. The system was never the same. It was to be ravaged by the Vietnam War protests, weakened by the students' rights movement and disgraced by a racial-ethnic spoils system that the strike had not averted.

Bitterness at LIC was evident in the relations between the faculty and the two teachers who had asked to enter the building. Meyers, the black, a good biology teacher and a valuable Dean of Boys, soon resigned from the system and was admitted to a medical school in Tennessee. I learned about him from another fine black teacher, Theodore Arrington, who did not seek to enter the school. Meyers, on the first day of the strike, had pointed to Arrington, seated in his car, and alleged that he, too, wanted to enter the building. I heard from Ted that Meyers had graduated from medical school. I was to learn later that Meyers died soon after starting his medical practice.

The white teacher did not resign from the system and stayed at LIC. No teacher in the school spoke to him. Only I spoke to him on professional matters for the nine years after the strike that I remained the principal. After my retirement we would meet accidentally in the neighborhood of LIC, when I was en route or returning from Manhattan television or radio appearances. (LIC was on the Queens side of the East River that separated the two boroughs.) We talked about what was happening in the schools, but I never alluded to the '68 strike that had started us on the toboggan.

Not only did teachers remember the strikebreakers, but parents in many districts were polarized by the strike. They had divided over keeping the schools closed and would not work together on school projects after the strike. Bella Abzug, a parent and political activist, had sought to keep schools open. She incurred the lasting enmity of the UFT that opposed her every move for public office.

Two decades after he had been retired from public office by popular demand, John Lindsay continued to pontificate on race relations. It was a time—1988—when Mayor Edward I. Koch was exchanging recriminations with black militants whom the mayor denounced as anti-Semites. He had been vilified unfairly as a racist, although he had appointed to high offices more blacks than any previous mayor, including Lindsay.

THE LAST ANGRY PRINCIPAL

Lindsay, in a letter to the "Living Section" of *The New York Times* (January 27, 1988), wrote in praise of a *Times* writer whom he said, "did a great service in laying on the line the depth of prejudice that has always smoldered in our society. My observation over many years," he wrote, "has been that these dark prejudices have always been there . . . and always will be. But the function of leadership is to keep those dark sides of human nature under control—'suppressed' if you will. But the climate in the United States in recent years has done just the opposite and has permitted these dangerous prejudices to come forward and even reign. It is a climate that has been set by the President [Ronald Reagan] and his many followers, and pursued by other politicians who have gained and won on it."

It is typical of Lindsay not to see the mote in his own eye. During the strike he had given way to his own prejudice in favoring the black militants in Brownsville out of his patrician sympathy for the minority. He failed to see that it is one thing to treat a minority fairly, or indeed any part of the population, and another to favor the minority in such a way as to create a reverse type of discrimination.

At the time of the strike I hoped that a union victory would prevent race from replacing merit as a major consideration in appointment of teachers and supervisors. But a radical change in the school population in the past two decades has made a minority the majority. In 1988 over 75 percent of the nearly one million children in the pubic schools of New York City are black and Puerto Rican. These same minorities are almost half of the population of the city. It should not follow that the teachers and supervisors must reflect the racial-ethnic origins of the pupils; that is, if merit is the basis on which appointments are made. Black and Puerto Rican parents should want—and do want in my opinion—good teachers for their children without regard to race or national origin. But the racist line—now the dominant one in the school system—dictates that faculty match the race and national origin of the student population.

The effort to appease black militants, as I see it, has resulted in deteriorating race relations throughout the country. No amount of special treatment can satisfy the militants because it is their business to agitate and stir racial hatred on which they thrive. Minorities who are disadvantaged should be helped without regard to race. It is the injection of race as a condition of preferment that festers under the skin and produces rashes of hatred that disfigure our society.

XI

DECENTRALIZATION: CUTTING THE BIG APPLE INTO SMALL PIECES

THE LESSON LEARNED from the strike of '68 was not lost on legislators who changed the governance of New York City public schools in 1969. Community control, as practiced by the dismantled Brownsville demonstration school district, was seen to be as revolutionary as its proponents proclaimed it to be.

Leaders of the three demonstration school districts (Brownsville, Two Bridges in lower Manhattan and Intermediate School 201 in East Harlem) declared their unalterable opposition to any decentralization plan that did not give them community control of the schools in their local districts. The three districts were abolished by the New York State legislature when its plan was signed by Governor Nelson Rockefeller.

Rhody McCoy, before he was dismissed by a state trustee, warned, "My community won't turn the schools back to the people who had them before." David Spencer, I.S. 201 Harlem agitator, declared, "Decentralization gives you nothing. You must be able to control your personnel; we are hung up on this tenure nonsense."

The community control advocates demanded freedom to handle all funds to be granted to the community by the New York City government. Unlike other school districts in the state, New York City did not (and does not now) levy a school tax. The local people, therefore, were not paying a separate tax for the support of their schools.

156

DECENTRALIZATION

In addition community control would have meant the right to hire and fire school personnel, maintain and construct buildings, purchase of supplies; in brief, control of all school operations entrusted to boards of education in school districts nationwide.

Decentralization—the division of a large school district into smaller, presumably more manageable parts—was not unknown in New York City's experience. However, the experience lay sufficiently far in the past so that it was the preserve of historians, not legislators.

From 1842 to 1897 local control of the schools was almost complete in New York City. Each of the city's wards (election districts) was treated as a separate school district with most of the power in the hands of elected trustees.

Under the ward system laymen appointed all teachers and janitors, nominated principals and vice-principals for promotion, furnished school supplies, contracted for repairs, purchased school sites and built schools. Opportunities for graft and patronage were seized upon and became entrenched in the school system.

The 19th-century decentralized system was replaced by the reformers who won out in 1898 when New York City, then just Manhattan and the Bronx, added the other boroughs and became Greater New York. Under consolidation each borough had its own Board of Education and its own Superintendent of Schools. The new city charter also established a city Board of Education, a city Superintendent of Schools and a Board of Examiners for the testing of applicants for teaching positions.

The division between a central board and borough boards did not work smoothly and complete centralization was attained with charter revision in 1901. It was this centralized system that continued in New York City until the state legislature passed the decentralization law of 1969.

The first 30 years of my experience in the New York City public schools, beginning in the late 1930's, was under the centralized system. I shall not pretend that those were good old days. Teachers in those days were products of excruciatingly difficult examinations administered by a feared Board of Examiners. Promotional examinations for positions as assistant principal, chairman of department in high schools and principal were so difficult and keenly competitive that most teachers did not attempt to move out of the classroom. Examinations and eventual appointment for the few who were successful took years.

In 1937 I passed a teacher-in-training examination in history and civics. I was first on a list of 38. Over a thousand applicants took the exam and many thousands did not attempt to take the test. I served for a year, teaching two and three classes—not a full program of five classes—and was closely supervised by the department chairman at Grover Cleveland High School in Queens.

In 1939 I passed a regular teachers' examination. It was an ordeal of written, oral, interview, teaching tests, evaluation of record, physical examination, etc. that would be unthinkable today. By the time I was appointed, six years later, I had been inducted into the armed forces and was serving with the U.S. Army Air Force at a base near Calcutta. I did not have to think twice about asking the commanding general to return me to the states for teaching duty.

The Board of Examiners, established in 1898, was retained under the new decentralization law. It has continued to license pedagogical personnel in over 200 specialties. The Examiners have been greatly weakened now that its lists are qualifying rather than competitive. Pressure to pass minorities has become so great that lists are long and exams much watered down as a consequence of court orders. The exams were seen to be discriminatory when blacks and Puerto Ricans did not pass them in proportion to their numbers in the general population. As a single example of the length of lists, when I was licensed as a high school principal in 1965 there were seven people on the list. Today, there are hundreds who have qualified as a high school principal. Teachers' lists have been described as laundry lists.

The Board of Examiners has been under constant attack and there has not been a year in the past twenty when a bill to abolish it has not been before the legislature. I have favored its retention in the hope that it will be in place should we ever get back to the time when the quality of candidates and their numbers will allow for the rigorous, objective testing that made the New York City public schools outstanding.

Teachers under the centralized system were complainers, as are most teachers everywhere under any system of school governance. The first teachers' union in New York City was formed during World War I. It was not, however, until after World War II that the union gained strength and won its first collective bargaining agreement with the Board of Education in 1962.

Complaints under the centralized system centered on low salaries, oversize classes and demands for meeting health care—the latter fringe benefit is now so firm a part of teachers' contracts nationwide that "fringe" is hardly descriptive of benefits that add substantially to teachers' salaries.

Criticism of the centralized system did not stem from teachers' dissatisfaction with their union contract—almost all teachers in the city were union members. The impetus came from reformers unhappy with the decline in performance of children in the schools and militant minorities who believed that local control of schools would ensure better learning, especially by disadvantaged children.

By the late 1960's when the decentralization movement was in full swing, the composition of the New York City public schools had changed drastically. The majority of the million children were black and Puerto Rican. Almost half of the children came from homes with family incomes below the poverty level defined by the federal government. An ever larger number came from single-parent homes and homes where the mother was working outside the home and unavailable during the school day. The system was further disrupted by court orders to move children around the schools to achieve a racial balance—not that there was agreement on the right balance. Racial balancing to achieve integration became impossible as whites fled to the suburbs. Into this steaming decentralization pot there was spilled the poison of racial hatred brewed largely by black militants who saw local control of their schools as salvation.

It became apparent in the late 1960's that some kind of decentralization had to be devised if only to bring about a cosmetic change in the school image. In the demonstration (experimental) school districts, it had been real surgery—community control—that was demanded. Community control was feared by teachers and supervisors leery of any change in governance that might make a difficult school system worse. The Board of Education had been talking about decentralization since the 1950's, but there, too, community control was rejected. The kind of decentralization that intrigued board members was the possibility of defusing mounting criticisms that were laid at the door of headquarters at 110 Livingston Street. How nice it would be if the complainants were scattered among community school districts in the five boroughs.

In a city in which the mayor is a powerful figure, lent strength by a charter that emasculates the city legislature (City Council), the mayor's position on decentralization was significant. Although any change in school governance had to be enacted by the state legislature, the mayor's influence and that of legislators coming from the city could not help but be given great weight by a legislature in which out-of-city legislators were the majority.

John V. Lindsay, mayor at the time, was gung ho for decentralization. His deference to minorities increased racial polarization of the city. In encouraging community control in the experimental school districts, he alientated the teachers and strong labor unions in the city.

So hostile did the opposition to the mayor become that "Deport Lindsay" was the legend on one of the political buttons remarked upon by *The New York Times* (July 26, 1968). I favored deportation when I wrote to Governor Rockefeller recommending Lindsay's appointment to a U.S. Senate seat that had become vacant. I saw it as a form of state aid that could not be measured in dollars and cents. Our city, I wrote, "is afflicted with a mayor whose dulcet tones range between prim inanities and invitations to violence. His most recent example of the latter is his advice to the Board of Education that if decentralization is not accomplished by September, he would not be responsible for the people's behavior."

DECENTRALIZATION

In furtherance of his advocacy of decentralization, Lindsay, a year before the strike of '68, had appointed McGeorge Bundy, president of the Ford Foundation, to head a panel on decentralization. Bundy fell short of suggesting community control, but his recommendations signaled a radical departure from anything the Board of Education had been thinking about for a decade. Bundy saw the public schools as "caught in a spiral of decline." He attributed the white flight from the public schools to loss of confidence in the schools and recommended that control of all schools be given to autonomous local districts—30 to 60 of them. In contradictory fashion, he proposed enlarged control of the schools by the mayor.

The state legislature waited until the end of the '68 strike before agreeing on a decentralization law. If politics is truly the art of compromise, the New York State legislators qualified as master artists. The bundle of compromises that emerged in 1969 made the work of the Founding Fathers look like a straight line between two points.

The state legislators took a look at Bundy, listened to the screams of community-control fanatics, and agreed that while they were likely to satisfy no one, change for the sake of change was the order of the day.

In the 1969 decentralization law, the single-district Big Apple was carved into 32 somewhat unequal pieces that quickly became more unequal. The districts range from about 15,000 to 30,000 pupils in size. A lump sum budget is granted each of the districts by the central board which retained direct control of the high schools, since high schools in the city cut across district lines. The central board also has overall policy-making power, including the right to suspend community school boards. A few times in the past two decades, local boards have been suspended and replaced by a trustee appointed by the central board and then restored to power after the violation was corrected by the community school board.

The seven-member central board (five at first) was not to be elected, since elections would run afoul of the one-man-one-vote principle handed down by the U.S. Supreme Court. Each of the five borough presidents (Brooklyn, Manhattan, Queens, Bronx and Staten Island) appoints one member and the mayor appoints two members. They have been paid since 1970, unlike any other board of education in the country, for what is supposed to be a part-time community service. At this time the pay is $160 a day and the members manage to claim $36,600 a year for 210 days (although the school year is 180 days). There are other perquisites, including chauffeur-driven cars, lush offices, highly paid administrative aides, paid expenses for junkets to educational meetings in appropriately salubrious climes depending on the month of the year, etc. The members have even voted to include themselves in a pension plan.

In contrast, the nine-member community school boards are unpaid and elected by voters in the district. Few people bother to vote in the elections, although decentralization was boosted as a means of bringing people closer to schools in their community. In 1970, 15 percent of the eligible voters went to the polls on a day other than the regular election day. The voting is by proportional representation and election results are not known for days and weeks after the polls close. Since 1970 the percentage of voters has never reached 10 percent and has sunk to as little as 6 percent.

Candidates for the community school board are virtually unknown to the voters. This has permitted the teachers' union, church groups, poverty agencies, political clubs and others with special interests to dominate the elections and control the board members. The United Federation of Teachers usually elects two-thirds or more of the 288 candidates who stand for election every three years. While observing that the union does well in the election, Albert Shanker, when he was the UFT president, saw decentralization as a costly failure resulting in 32 "minibureaucracies" as well as waste, patronage, corruption and misuse of funds.

In 1987 a Bronx grand jury investigating community school boards reported that "School board members have rewarded friends with jobs, traded jobs with each other and given supervisory jobs to individuals because they were recommended by local political club leaders . . . some supervisors got their jobs by paying bribes to local board members . . . one school board member aided his wife in obtaining a position with the Board of Education by personally exerting influence on a principal, deputy superintendent, and a member of the Central School Board."

Steven Franse, the Bronx member of the central board, was an active member of the club headed by former Bronx Borough President Stanley Simon, who resigned early in '87 so that he might give full time to defend himself against bribery charges. Efforts by Mayor Koch to get Franse to resign had nothing to do with Franse's political connections. The mayor wanted the spot on the board for a Hispanic member to satisfy the clamor of Hispanic militants for representation on the board. The mayor had to be satisfied with the resignation of his appointee, a Manhattan lawyer, so that he might appoint a Hispanic. This interjection of ethnic politics at all levels of the school system has become endemic.

Brazen intervention in appointments by community school board members has become commonplace. A Brooklyn community school board member engineered the appointment of his son, Dominic Lavelle, as principal of Junior High School 111, Brooklyn, in his district. The son was found guilty of serious misconduct and conflict of interest when he obtained $6,000 in loans, allegedly for his father's re-election, from a teacher seeking promotion. He repaid the loan when the teacher, now an assistant principal, pressed him with a lawyer's letter.

Lavelle was fined $4,500 by a central board administrative panel. The central board regarded the fine as "far from sufficient" and announced that it would appeal the decision in an effort to obtain Lavelle's dismissal. In 1988 Lavelle remains in place and his father seeks to have him appointed a deputy superintendent in the district. Chancellor Nathan Quinones, in turn, directed the removal of Lavelle's father from the school board because it has proof that the senior Lavelle does not live in the district, a requirement of the decentralization law. The Lavelles were no doubt comforted when Quinones retired on December 31, 1987.

The decentralization law changed the title of the central

board's chief executive officer from that of superintendent to chancellor. The central board selects its chancellor and local boards select their superintendents. These have proved to be short-lived with changes so rapid that one district had eight superintendents in seven years.

That racial-ethnic politics characterizes decentralization is evident at the highest levels. The community school boards choose superintendents for their $90,000-a-year posts. Increasingly, district superintendents reflect the racial-ethnic composition of the district residents. According to the Office of Community School District Affairs at the central board, 14 of the 32 community school superintendents are either black or Hispanic.

Superintendents are selected on the basis of an interview. There are paper credentials based on education courses taken. Prior experience is largely irrelevant. The matching of the applicant with the predominant minority in the community is now in almost every instance a vital factor in the selection process. In District 6, Manhattan, the person selected as superintendent was a reading teacher prior to appointment as a superintendent. She was, however, of Hispanic origin in a predominantly Hispanic district. When she was subsequently removed because the district was held to be in a shambles by then Chancellor Quinones, she was replaced by another Hispanic.

At least six community school boards are currently under investigation by the central board's Inspector General. Allegations range from misappropriation of funds to improper hiring procedures. One candidate for a superintendency told me that he was asked for $10,000 up-front as a condition of his appointment. When he refused to make the payment, the job went to someone else.

The president of the central board, Robert F. Wagner, Jr., son of a former mayor, sees in appointments to school posts "a pattern of political involvement that seems to be pervasive." Wagner, Mayor Koch and Governor Mario Cuomo are agreed on one word to describe the New York City public schools in '88. They are a "disgrace." They have not, however, given up on decentralization. One beauty of it is that it has deflected some of the criticism of the schools from the central board and the mayor to the community school boards. In a city where black militants have organized "days of outrage," tying up city services, it is no small boon to have expressions of dissatisfaction with the schools diffused rather than concentrated at central board headquarters.

Current moves in the legislature to amend the decentralization law have induced considerable nervousness in its defenders. Dennis R. Coleman, secretary of the New York City School Boards Association, denounced Wagner's proposals for change that would give more power to the mayor as "a smokescreen" designed to divert attention from the central board's own "continuous failures" and "disarray."

Philip Kaplan, president of the Community School Boards Association, snapped, "Why don't they clean out their own house first?" He charged that moves against community school boards are "political." However, Kaplan stated that the school board elections have become politically charged. "Do we have a system that elects minorities and parents and puts them on the school board?" Kaplan asked the state assembly education committee at a hearing in the late '80s. "I say no," Kaplan continued. "Instead we have unions and political clubs that spend a fortune to get parent candidates knocked off the ballot."

Sandra Feldman, now president of the United Federation of Teachers, who was active as a full-time union worker in Brownsville before and during the strike of '68, does "think it is a good time to take a good hard look at decentralization," but "we must be careful not to throw the baby out with the bathwater."

The UFT is opposed to the central board's proposal to remove its employees from membership on the 32 community school boards in the city. Under the existing decentralization law, teachers and other school employees may stand for election to school boards in districts other than the one in which they are employed. Of the 288 people on the boards, 45 are currently employed by the central board as teachers and administrators, and 28 work in the elementary, intermediate and junior high schools run by the local school boards. These members were all supported by the UFT, along with others who received UFT assistance and are beholden to the union.

THE LAST ANGRY PRINCIPAL

Into the maelstrom of decentralization, mired in an ethnic-racial spoils system, there looms an éminence grise, Anthony Alvarado. His rise, fall and phoenix-like rise again dramatize the depth to which the New York City public schools have sunk.

Alvarado was the center of a scandal that forced him in 1984 to resign as schools' chancellor after a year on the job. If anyone had predicted at that time the return of Alvarado to the schools, the response would have made the bitter "Cry of the Children" sound like a madrigal. Yet, three years later, on July 1, 1987, Alvarado was installed as the community superintendent of District 2, Manhattan, encompassing Greenwich Village.

Alvarado was born June 10, 1942 in the Bronx. He is the only son of Victoria Alvarado, who moved to New York from Puerto Rico, and Juan Alvarado, a native of Cuba. He attended parochial schools in the Bronx and was graduated from Fordham University in 1964. His first school job was obtained in 1966 as a junior high school English teacher. By 1973 he was the community school superintendent of East Harlem's District 4 (Spanish Harlem).

Alvarado acquired a reputation as an innovative educator. Among the innovations that he claimed when being considered for the chancellorship was his establishment of alternative schools in District 4. Alternative schools—set up for children with special problems or accomplishments—were nothing new, but Alvarado's approach to setting them up was distinctly novel. The approach was resented by superintendents in neighboring districts. They charged that Alvarado was attracting children—in fact, the best students—to District 4 alternative schools in violation of a Board of Education rule that children were required to attend school in the community in which they resided.

Alvarado set up 24 alternative schools in his district. Most of them occupied a floor or more in the 13 school buildings in the district. The schools were intended to attract above-average children whose parents were dissatisfied with the programs being offered in their own districts. In a central board report, it was estimated that over 1,000 children were improperly enrolled in District 4 schools.

As a byproduct of the foregoing innovation, Alvarado's district had 12 more principals than it had schools. *The New York Times*, on June 27, 1977, reported: "An examination of payroll records, which turned up this unusual hiring practice, showed that seven of the 32 principals are not even working in schools as principals normally do, one to a school, but are instead sitting at administrative desks in district headquarters." Irving Anker, chancellor at the time, said he was "concerned" about the situation but doubted that he had "the authority to change it."

Alvarado defended his hiring practices by saying that the principal-administrators in the district office were necessary to carry on the small-school philosophy of the district. He held that he was not spending any more money than other districts. Later, he confessed that he had overspent each year. In the year before he was elevated to the chancellorship, for example, he had overspent $1.6 million.

In setting up his alternative schools, Alvarado admitted that he showed parents from outside his district how they could get around the rule. He advised them to yank their kids out of the home school without explanation. The students were then registered in District 4 as first-time entrants into the system, creating new sets of records and identification numbers for the children.

In response to criticisms of his actions, Alvarado stated, "Education is not just following the rules."

The effect of enrollment in District 4 of above-average pupils was to raise reading scores in the district. Since so much stress is placed on improved reading scores, then and now, as an indicator of school effectiveness, the boost in reading scores was claimed as a credit by Alvarado.

In interviews for the chancellorship Alvarado made no mention of the means whereby he recruited above-average children for his alternative schools. And his overspending did not weigh with a Board of Education that was weighing his Hispanic origins as a major qualification for the post.

Racial-ethnic considerations became a top priority in politicking for the chancellor's post by a fluke. In 1983 the Board of Education had selected Bob Wagner, who incidentally is white.

THE LAST ANGRY PRINCIPAL

He could not wait to turn the education system around and began visiting schools before being installed as chancellor. Suddenly, he was toppled from the heights by a bolt from State Commissioner of Education Gordon Ambach who found that Wagner lacked the education courses required for the job.

Wagner, who had not served for a day as a teacher or supervisor in any school, was humbled. Mayor Koch, who had backed him for the job and held the controlling votes in the Board of Education, was outraged. Both Koch and Wagner were experienced politicians and they saw at once that the chancellor's position had to be filled by a black or Hispanic. The cry of the minorities, muted by the City Hall nominee, could no longer be restrained.

Thomas Minter, a black, the Deputy Superintendent, was next in line. He was backed by black militants who called stridently for a minority chancellor. The board, under pressure to appoint a black, saw that a retreat from Minter might not be conceived of as a rout if it held to the black demand for a *minority* member to be chancellor.

The spotlight was focused on Alvarado, who in contrast to Minter was fiery. He outlined plans for the public schools that glowed for board members. Alvarado got the job and moved his act as the "great innovator" from East Harlem to downtown Brooklyn, headquarters of the massive bureaucracy astride the schools.

Among his first initiatives was a proposal to establish a theme high school. The theme was to be writing and he planned to use as home for the theme the abandoned High School of Performing Arts in the New York theatre district. At the time, I wrote of the proposal, "Theme high schools, especially one for writing, are not so much innovative as foolish when you consider that most high school students cannot complete a paragraph without egregious errors." The writing-theme high school never got off the drawing board.

Five days after he became chancellor, Alvarado proposed changing the city's half-day kindergartens into all-day sessions. He did so in the fall of '83. The citywide program is still flawed by overcrowding, supply shortages and cost overruns. From the first, opinions differed as to whether all-day kindergartens were needed for the education of children or as a stopgap to meet the needs of working mothers. One Brooklyn elementary school principal told me that in his school, "The tots were so tired at the end of the day that most of them were asleep on the floor."

Also, early in his one-year chancellorship, Alvarado, without high school experience, launched PREP—Program to Raise Educational Performance. It was designed to allow ninth-graders, who had already been held over for a year or two, to enter high school and take courses for credit, along with special remedial classes in reading and math.

A school watchdog group, the Educational Priorities Panel, was to say of PREP in its 48-page report that the $5.6 million program was marked by confusion among high school principals about eligibility requirements and about the focus of the program. It held the ninth-grade remedial program was underfunded and poorly planned. Alvarado and his top aides conceded that he was impatient with planning and that his staff was disorganized.

Alvarado's downfall might never have come about, so enamored was the media with this "innovator," had it not been for the gunshots fired into a Westside apartment by John Chin, a Board of Education employee.

Police obtained a search warrant for the purpose of finding the gun that Chin had used to fire into a neighbor's apartment. The police also found checks made out to Chin and signed by Alvarado.

Chin had been an assistant to a deputy superintendent. After Alvarado became chancellor on April 28, 1983, Chin was given a job with the central board at Livingston Street.

The Board of Education investigation that got under way following the Chin shooting revealed that Alvarado had borrowed heavily from Chin, who held the title to Alvarado's automobile. The 1980 Toyota took center stage when it came out that Alvarado and his wife, a teacher in District 4, owed $2,100 in parking tickets. Among the 15 charges leveled against Alvarado by the Board of Education was one alleging that he had failed to report to the board the rumor that Chin was involved in drug sales and carried a gun.

Chin, it developed, was not the only subordinate from whom Alvarado had borrowed. Alvarado, under questioning, admitted that he had borrowed almost $100,000 from a dozen board employees when he was the district superintendent and during his one-year tenure as chancellor.

The money, it appeared, had been used in part for real estate operations in which Alvarado was engaged. In this connection the district attorneys of Brooklyn and Manhattan involved in the investigations determined that Alvarado had falsified mortgage applications at Citibank, a bank fraud charge that carried with it a two-year prison term and a $5,000 fine.

In the charges against Alvarado, assembled by the city chief administrative law judge, Richard C. Failla, employed by the Board of Education to hear the case against Alvarado, the link between his borrowing from school employees and the extra-pay jobs they were given was listed. Alvarado did not appear to face board charges, because he resigned a few days before the hearings were to begin.

In some cases the amount of extra pay equaled or exceeded the loans. In yet another case, it was charged that Alvarado authorized payment to a board employee for the school work her husband had done. In this category of charges, it was held that he had improperly used "per session funds"—money used to pay board employees for work performed outside their regular duties. He used Board of Education employees to paint his Brooklyn home and babysit for his family during the summer of '83. The charge read: Alvarado "certified for the purpose of payment by the Board of Education that the employee had worked full time serving the Board of Education during that two-week vacation period."

In the months following the Chin gunblasts that ignited the wide-ranging investigations of Alvarado, the chancellor sought to explain his actions. Speaking to students and faculty at the City College campus in Harlem, he said, everyone "has things you would rather not have to reveal." He compared the methods by which he was being judged to the communist witch-hunting of the McCarthy era. "We went through the 50's when a lot of people, particularly in institutions of higher learning, were not heard." Alvarado added, "The result of that: numerous lives, numerous talents were thrown aside. I think that kind of experience should not allow itself to be repeated. I think the process of due course (sic) will show a fallible human being but not a venal one."

Later, as it seemed certain that his promise not to resign could not be kept, Alvarado became more open in admitting the charges against him and offered explanations for his dishonesty. He conceded that his values were different from the values by which he was being judged. "If you're being judged by those values, of course, you come out wanting."

Finally, in his letter of resignation, May 11, 1984, he was especially perceptive. His remarks have a special meaning in a city enveloped in so many scandals that some political scientists have concluded that the corruption in the Koch administration has been systemic throughout the years in New York City government operations.

Alvarado wrote that the mounting charges against him had caused him to "reject the easy and superficial explanation; it has meant laying aside the psychological cover of interpreting one's actions in the best possible light. . . . I have previously taken full responsibility for the poor judgment of borrowing from friends and colleagues. The judgment was not merely 'poor,' it was horrendous, and the lenders were not only my 'friends and colleagues' but my subordinates."

Alvarado's rise to the top of the system had been meteroric. After a mere seven years as a junior high school teacher, he became a superintendent. There is no accounting for this rise other than ethnic politics.

When Alvarado wrested the chancellorship from Minter, blacks figured that it was their turn next. Immediately following the board's vote for Alvarado in the Hall of the Board of Education at 110 Livingston Street, on April 29, 1983, a black spokesman, Hazel Dukes, president of the New York State Conference of the National Association for the Advancement of Colored People Branches, told the board: "Do not think that by naming Mr. Alvarado as the next chancellor you have succeeded in di-

THE LAST ANGRY PRINCIPAL

viding and conquering the black and Hispanic communities. Without the black community vision and protest, Mr. Alvarado would not have been selected by you in any rounds of your closed-door politics. Therefore, he serves at our pleasure—not yours."

The expectations of the black community were evident when a mere year after his accession, Alvarado was besmirched and gone. Minter had resigned as deputy chancellor and was consoled by a City College professorship, but there was no shortage of blacks for the job.

To the consternation of blacks, however, a complication arose. Alvarado was perceived to have disgraced the Hispanic community. His second in command was Nathan Quinones, a Hispanic, who was Deputy Chancellor. How would it look if a qualified Hispanic were bypassed for a black? Might it not seem that Mayor Koch and the Board of Education had soured on Hispanics; that they could not be trusted? While it was true that Hispanics were a smaller percentage of the total city population than blacks—together they comprised about 50 percent—there was political danger in a repudiation of a potentially powerful segment of the voting population. Quinones got the job. He was to last three years before retiring.

During the three years that Quinones disported himself on the Livingston Street throne, Alvarado scrounged around for jobs. For a short time he was enveloped by shadows cast by investigations into his wrongdoing by U.S. Attorneys in Brooklyn and Manhattan and District Attorneys in both boroughs. The New York City Department of Investigation Commissioner had completed his report accusing Alvarado of a variety of improper, unethical and illegal acts, including fraud, forgery and tax evasion. Impending indictments fell between the cracks as rival attorneys jostled for the privilege of prosecuting Alvarado.

It was the Teamsters' Union, appropriately enough, that offered a hand to the fallen Alvarado and gave him the job of combating illiteracy among their members. Another job he held for a brief time was as a consultant for a private research group where he worked on a paper about community colleges.

The first outcry against any return to the schools by Alvarado, through whatever door, followed his employment in 1985 by Albert Shanker, president of the American Federation of Teachers. Alvarado was to represent the 600,000-member union in areas of educational reform and public policy. Shanker, conscious of the need for cultivating the growing minorities, may have thought that resuscitating Alvarado would be remembered by a grateful Hispanic community.

Shanker was compelled to withdraw the appointment when local union leaders told him that Alvarado "was a negative role model" and "would tarnish the image of teachers and the union." Susan Glass, a spokesman for the United Federation of Teachers, said that she had received "several thousand" letters, petitions and phone calls, protesting the Alvarado appointment by Shanker.

It was four years after his widely publicized skullduggery that Alvarado blitzed community school boards with resumés seeking interviews for the position of superintendent. He counted on the public's short-lived memory and could not have been more right.

As a guest on a radio talk show, I reviewed Alvarado's record and expressed abhorrence with the prospect of his return to the schools in any capacity. When the show was over, the host asked me who Alvarado was. This was astounding because the host has a fabulous memory in foreign and domestic fields.

The memory of Myrna Albert, a District 3 school board member, however, was keen. When Alvarado was turned down for the position, she stated: "We would prefer someone who didn't have the high visibility and notoriety of Mr. Alvarado. We are a changing district, on the way up in every respect. We don't need all the hoopla he would bring."

The re-entry of Alvarado to the schools was eased by David Dinkins, a black, who is president of the Borough of Manhattan. Dinkins may have calculated that a friendly pat on the back for a prominent, albeit disgraced Hispanic, might make for a closer coalition with the Hispanic community. Hispanics, in my opinion, would just as soon have forgotten about Alvarado. It is unjust to hold an ethnic group responsible for the depredations of one of its members. Dinkins selected Alvarado to lead a panel charged with reviewing school decentralization. In one of my columns, I remarked that Dinkins had "placed the fox in the chicken coop."

Alvarado was also embraced by central board president Wagner and Mayor Koch. They remembered him as a great innovator. Neither man was remotely qualified to judge innovations and both must have been politically motivated to encourage his adoption by any school board.

The New York Times rationalized its forgetfulness when it learned of Alvarado's quest for a superintendency. It held in an editorial that his past difficulties should not "bar him from consideration. . . . Society can be stern without being vindictive. . . ." Three years earlier, *The Times* had pleaded: "Is there no decency, vision or just plain common sense left in Anthony Alvarado. . . . ? Why, even now, have the Board and Mayor not yet thundered? And why does Mr. Alvarado insist on leaving himself to twist slowly in the wind?"

Alvarado no longer twists in the wind. Since July 1, 1987, he has been the community school superintendent in District 2, Manhattan. I have devoted some pages to his infamous career because it illustrates the immorality of New York City school authorities in setting before schoolchildren the example of an Anthony Alvarado.

Just at the time that Alvarado was returning to the schools, Chancellor Nathan Quinones announced his impending retirement. There may have been a buzzing in Alvarado's ears, but they were deafened by the instantaneous shout of black militants that they would not again be denied the top prize in what has become the biggest patronage pool in the city.

The Board of Education under President Wagner announced that it would select a search committee for a new chancellor. Quinones was scheduled for departure on December 31, 1987 and months went by as the board bungled in its quest for a committee containing a proper balance of blacks, Hispanics, whites, males and females.

The search committee recommended three candidates—a black man, a black woman and a white man. Each of the three held a superintendency in a school system. Any thought that the white school superintendent would get the job bordered on the ludicrous. The candidate may have seen the humor of it and withdrew saying that he could not leave unfinished business in Pittsburgh. The black woman superintendent in Philadelphia was vetoed by the teachers' union. "Too rigid"—meaning anti-union—said Sandra Feldman, president of the UFT, speaking through the union's boy on the board, Jim Regan. Regan, a former Staten Island teacher and political hack, has been on the board for almost two decades.

The board had agreed to select only from among the applicants recommended by the search committee. But one black, Bernard Gifford, who had been deputy chancellor at the age of 29 in the 1970's, had not been recommended by the search committee.

Gifford, after resigning from his New York City school post, eventually landed at the University of California, Berkeley, where he is dean of the school of education. He had campaigned for the job of chancellor for six months and had been honored at a reception in which Sandy Feldman played a key role. Gifford was the union's choice.

I had confronted Gifford in 1975 at a meeting of the Council of Supervisors and Administrators when I was vice-president. He had addressed us, calling for more black supervisors. I responded with a defense of the merit system and told him blacks would be welcome to join us when they passed the objective tests of the Board of Examiners, as we had.

The union clamored for Gifford's addition to the trio and the board yielded, granting Gifford an interview. Board members may have been soured by Bernie's ego when he had earlier demanded resignations of all top level personnel as a condition of his acceptance. Furthermore, there was the pledge to the search committee.

The board in a close vote, later made unanimous at a public meeting, selected Richard Green, the Minneapolis superintendent of schools, a black, as the new chancellor who took office March 1, 1988.

The jockeying for positions at the top of the New York City public school system infects it at all levels. The merit system that had characterized teaching and supervisory appointments for decades began to disintegrate with the advent of decentralization in 1970. Instant dismay was voiced by opponents of decentralization, joined by some reformers who had mistakenly believed that local participation in running the schools would assure better governance. Decentralization defenders, determined to protect their turf, dug in to protect their interests.

XII

RACIAL-ETHNIC SPOILS SYSTEM SPOILS SCHOOLS

"MARSHAL. ARREST DR. HURWITZ!"

I heard these words from U.S. District Court Judge Jack B. Weinstein, in Brooklyn, New York, on June 23, 1976.

My legs felt a little weak as I walked with the marshall to the courthouse door. Before we could reach it, Judge Weinstein called to the marshal to return me to the table (not raised bench) at which he was conducting the trial.

I had been on trial before Judge Weinstein (no jury) because of my refusal to submit to the Office for Civil Rights, then part of the Department of Health, Education and Welfare (HEW), an ethnic survey.

All schools in the United States were required then and now to complete a questionnaire identifying teachers, supervisors and students by race and national origin.

I, along with 135 New York City elementary, junior high and senior high school principals, had refused to submit the survey results. At Long Island City I had refused to allow the survey to be conducted and no report was available.

All of us were ordered by Judge Weinstein to appear before him. Fifty of us appeared in court, a day before my trial. The others promised to comply with the court order to supply the data.

The judge made it clear in his opening statement to us that failure to comply with his order would mean trial and imprisonment until the data was submitted to him.

Why was I prepared to go to prison rather than comply with the judge's order? The submission of racial-ethnic data was intended to achieve the affirmative action set forth in executive orders of Presidents Kennedy and Johnson. It was evident that their implementation had produced reverse discrimination. Blacks and Hispanics were the new favored minorities. Other minorities who had made it into the mainstream the hard way were to remain silent while they were edged out of jobs or denied promotions so that past discrimination against the now favored minorities might be corrected. I saw that the new discrimination would not correct past discrimination but would, on the contrary, poison race relations. Race and national origin were to be substituted for merit as a requirement for teachers and supervisors.

My sense of outrage peaked as I sat with my fellow principals, assembled in the courtroom of Judge Weinstein. We had met the day before at the Council of Supervisors and Administrators (CSA) and had pledged not to submit the data. Almost all of us were Jews, and we required no review of history to remind us of the direction in which we were heading. The non-Jews in the courtroom, including Peter O'Brien, CSA president, who sat across the aisle from me, had studied the same history.

Judge Weinstein asked each principal in turn, by name, "Will you or will you not comply?"

Each of the principals replied, "I will comply." Some explained that it was against their consciences to comply. They said that they foresaw in the ethnic surveys the kind of experience that their relatives had undergone in Nazi Germany. They were frank in stating that they were yielding the ethnic data only because they did not want to go to jail.

Since the majority of teachers and supervisors in the New York City public schools were Jewish, they feared that a quota system would surely follow the submission of racial-ethnic data. Whites, Jews included, would be discriminated against. All they wanted was that merit, not race or national origin, should be the determinant for school jobs.

When the judge reached me, he asked:

"Howard Hurwitz, will you or will you not comply?"

I alone among all of the principals replied, "Your honor, I shall not comply." I said nothing else.

The judge said, "I shall hold you for trial."

I listened to the capitulations of my fellow principals all morning and then went up to Judge Weinstein to ask him for permission to return to my school because of decisions I had to make on graduation of students. A few students awaited my decision as to whether they would or would not be granted diplomas. Occasionally, when one failing mark stood between a student and a diploma, that teacher would have a change of mind. I did not coerce a teacher into changing a mark, but it was my practice to talk with a teacher under the circumstances.

Judge Weinstein permitted me to return to school after I assured him that I would remain in school until 6 p.m. and would be at home at 7 p.m. to receive his phone call fixing the time of my trial. It was to be 1 p.m. on June 23, 1976.

My notes of June 22 read: "As of this moment, Nettie who has shingles, has been shielded from all this. I hate to do it, but I shall go to jail if necessary. I shall never complete the survey, or at least not until it reaches the U.S. Supreme Court and I'll decide then."

At the trial I was defended by a CSA attorney. Also in court at my side was Paul Windels, Jr., the attorney for Senator James L. Buckley whom I had kept informed on my stand against ethnic surveys. Mr. Windels suggested that there be a factual inquiry into the survey before final action was taken, and that "the court grant individuals who felt as a matter of conscience that they could not comply without exhausting all remedies, that they be allowed to do so."

Clearly, Judge Weinstein did not want to send me to prison. "You will hold the key to the jail in your hands," he told me before he called upon the marshall. "You can open the door at any time." He said that if I would agree to cooperate in completing the survey, I could give him the results and he would "keep them 'under seal' until all legal challenges were exhausted."

I thanked the judge for his offer, but said, "I just can't do this. I want to stand for something in my own mind."

Judge Weinstein then said, "Under the circumstances, you leave me no alternative. Call the marshal."

As I was being marched off, Mr. Windels, according to *The*

THE LAST ANGRY PRINCIPAL

New York Times (June 24, 1976), asked if the court could extend itself and defer placing the principal in custody pending appeal.

Judge Weinstein agreed. As I stood before him, he said, "I have no desire to punish such a distinguished and valuable member of the community. In conducting an educational war, we can't afford to lose our generals."

Later, as I left the court, *The Times* reported me as saying, "I am deeply grateful to Judge Weinstein for his compassion. He had his duty to do and I had mine."

Judge Weinstein was not only compassionate but a man of common sense. My trial was being covered by every newspaper, radio and TV station in New York. It would have made little sense to send me to jail at a time when muggers, pimps, drug dealers, rapists, vandals, burglars, white collar and blue collar crooks of all kinds were free in the streets of the world's greatest city.

The judge had paroled me pending my appeal to the Second Circuit Court of Appeals. During the summer a U.S. Attorney made several unsuccessful efforts to persuade Judge Weinstein to put me in jail, no doubt to discourage other principals in the city, state and nation who might be emboldened by my continued non-compliance with a court order to supply the federal survey data. My wife, meantime, received phone calls from the U.S. Attorney's office in which an assistant attorney said, "I want to help your husband." When she replied that I had not changed my mind, he asked, "What day in the week would it be convenient for your husband to report for confinement?" Judge Weinstein had designated the Community Treatment Center in Manhattan as the place for my jailing as long as I refused to complete the questionnaires. I was not at home when the attorney called because I was busy with my attorney preparing our brief in defense of my refusal to complete the survey.

Early in the fall term, the jail sentence hanging over me was lifted. The government's attorney let Judge Weinstein know that the regional office of HEW had received forms from Long Island City High School. "Although certain information not preserved in the school's records was not provided," the letter said, "these instruments are considered by the OCR to have been satisfactorily completed to the extent now feasible and practical.

"Accordingly, the United States of America requests that the order requiring temporary confinement of Howard L. Hurwitz to compel the completion of these instruments be dissolved."

Judge Weinstein's clerk called immediately upon receipt of the letter to tell me that I was no longer in contempt of court.

What had happened was that in late June, when there were no classes, a federal marshal came to demand that I hand over to him the survey results. I noted the gun that was visible on his person. I had not lost my sense of humor and asked, "Are you going to shoot me if I refuse?"

The marshal left my office and along with several other agents walked through the building. They emerged with what they considered an accurate estimate of the racial-ethnic composition of teachers and supervisors. At no time had either I or any of my subordinates sought to complete the survey.

In his column, "Only Human," in the New York *Daily News* (July 8, 1976), Sidney Fields reported: "Dr. Howard L. Hurwitz is undoubtedly the only principal in the U.S. who finished the school year under suspension and contempt of court. He wears both like badges of honor." (Fields was mistaken about the suspension. It had been lifted when I emerged from behind the barricades in late March.)

"The 2,500 people present at graduation in Long Island City High School . . . gave him a five minute standing ovation." Fields quoted my reaction to the HEW survey: "It's not a survey, it's an inquisition. . . . It's 38 pages with about 100 questions. Principals are asked to list under the ethnic origins of their pupils the number graduated, suspended, referred to mental health services, to drug/alcohol abuse programs, the number not promoted.

"It's weighted to show that minority students are not given more opportunities. . . . Teachers and administrators here and all over America have made great strides, at great cost and pain, in helping disadvantaged children regardless of ethnic origin.

But this is the most willful type of reverse discrimination."

Fields had interviewed me and his long column reviewed my past clashes with the chancellor and aspects of my personal life. He concluded with a quote from me: "Without my wife, Nettie, I don't think I could take this. She's sick over it. . . . But she's never asked me to quit. I won't."

My stand on the HEW survey had, in fact, emboldened other principals to join me. This time it was a state ethnic survey I refused to complete and two elementary school principals were subjected to the same charges leveled against me by Chancellor Anker. We were charged with "conduct unbecoming a teacher" and "neglect of duty" for failing to supply the survey data.

It must have been clear to Anker that I had refused to comply with a federal court order, and the likelihood of my knuckling under to the state was remote. He decided to follow the same tactic as the feds and alleged that he had somehow been able to acquire the data without my assistance. Accordingly, the Board of Education dropped the charges that had been leveled against the three of us.

There followed a reprimand from Chancellor Anker in which he set forth his position on my refusal to supply the ethnic data and his stand on ethnic surveys.

On April 12, 1977, I wrote to Anker:

"I am responding to your letter of reprimand, dated March 22, 1977.

"I take pride in my continued refusal to submit ethnic data to you or to anyone else. In this instance, I refused to submit ethnic and racial data that you sought on behalf of the State Education Department. Last May, I refused to submit comparable data that you sought on behalf of the federal government. In the latter case, I was sentenced to jail by a federal district court judge. I was ready to stay in jail indefinitely, and I so told the judge. I was relieved of the contempt charge when the U.S. Attorney alleged to the judge that he had somehow obtained all the data that was feasible at the time without my help.

"I am at least consistent in maintaining a moral stand based on conscience and the questionable constitutionality of your order. How moral are you? You have the effrontery to inform the

State Commissioner of Education that you have collected the ethnic and racial data in my school and many others. The fact is that on March 11, you sent in seven underlings who roamed the halls of my school for one-half hour, peeking into classrooms. Their report included the number of students with Spanish surnames. Even you must concede the impossibility of determining a student's last name visually.

"According to the Council of Supervisors and Administrators, 250 principals reported to their union that they gave you no ethnic or racial data. Yet, you allege that the New York State Department of Education now knows the precise breakdown of 1.1 million children who are 'Black not of Hispanic Origin,' 'American Indian or Alaskan Native,' 'Asian or Pacific Islander,' 'Puerto Rican,' 'Other Spanish Surnamed American,' and 'White not of Hispanic Origin.'

"You gathered these statistics in 30 minutes in my school of 3,000. It would have taken me several hundred hours of teacher time to gather the information. Your assertion that you have collected the required ethnic and racial data should undermine your credibility with the state.

"In your letter, you concede: 'It is possible that such data might be misused. Collectively we must guard against such a possibility, and I would be in the forefront of any battle to protect the integrity of the data and the manner in which they are used.'

"I would no more put you in the forefront of that battle than I would employ a fox to guard a chicken coop. You are bent upon appeasing the Office for Civil Rights which has charged you with discrimination against black and Puerto Rican children and failing to hire the proper quota of black and Puerto Rican teachers and supervisors. You are furthering an ethnic spoils system by offering a fresh statistical base for reverse discrimination.

"You charge that I have 'damaged the New York City public schools and the children whom they serve . . . because Commissioner Nyquist, acting under the law . . . would direct his staff to stop flow of funds to any community school district which had not complied' with his directive. . . . I say you are first in line for 30 pieces of silver.

THE LAST ANGRY PRINCIPAL

"You write to me about 'professionalism' and your resistance to 'anarchic behavior that jeopardizes education in this city. . . .' You state that 'Since all of the required data have been collected, there is no further point to be gained by continuing charges against you. I am recommending, therefore, that the charges be rescinded. Your actions are a matter of record, and this letter will serve to document them. . . .'

"Instead of bringing charges against me and my fellow principals, dropping the charges when their number and trial costs give you pause, and then sending by messenger self-righteous reprimands, you should be grateful that hundreds of principals have a sense of history.

"Soon, teachers will show the same courage as principals who have defied you. Will you then compose thousands of letters of reprimand, or will you look into that mirror on the wall and perceive that the teachers and principals who confront you are no different from the courageous blacks whose acts of continued disobedience we both applauded when they refused to go to the back of the bus.

"I charge you with taking and carrying out orders that are destroying race relations in this city and nation; that can only make innocent white people suffer for acts of discrimination they have never committed; that can only demean black people who are making it the hard way (as you and I and other minorities have made it in this nation of immigrants).

"You warn me that you are placing a letter of reprimand in my official file. I am entitled, under Board of Education policy, to have my response attached to yours in the same file. I shall inspect my file to be sure that the requirement is met.

"Some day the file may by pored over by historians of a dying school system of which you are the caretaker and order-taker. Let the people judge: Which of us is the Judas?"

I sent copies of my letter to the state commissioner, the CSA and a half-dozen school officials in top posts at the Board of Education. It was the topic of my regular weekly column in the *Ridgewood Times* (April 14, 1977) headed, "Which One of Us Is The Judas?" As a frequent speaker in the metropolitan area, I had occasion to assess the impact of ethnic surveys on the public schools. Media coverage of my stand was considerable. I predicted, correctly as it turned out, that the merit system would be scuttled and that race and national origin would become prime determinants in appointments to school positions.

Compliance with the federal and state demands for ethnic surveys was continued by Anker's successor. In 1979, Chancellor Frank Macchiarola threatened to suspend Community School Board 29 in southwestern Queens when it refused to provide the data. The board then voted to supply the data that included a racial listing of students who had been suspended as a disciplinary measure.

The single negative vote against compliance was cast by a black school board member who insisted that the data "would provide no useful purpose." Other members of the board felt that withholding the data "wasn't worth the risk" of their being suspended.

Then entering the picture was the Office for Civil Rights, continued when the "E" (Education) in HEW was removed in 1979 and established as the Department of Education. The Secretary of Education became the thirteenth member of the President's cabinet.

OCR sent Chancellor Macchiarola an analysis of student suspensions, derived from survey reports submitted by principals and forwarded by the chancellor, that showed minority students were being suspended out of proportion to their numbers in the individual school population. OCR ruled that if non-white students are suspended at a rate greater than 1.25 times the rate for white students, the school must respond to "apparent disparity." This interpretation of suspension statistics further befouled discipline in the schools.

Macchiarola was quick to take action at the direction of OCR. He notified principals of the suspension stand taken by OCR and the effect was further erosion of the disciplinary power of principals in a ravaged school system.

Yielding to threats is standard in the school hierarchy. Macchiarola, as did chancellors before him and after him, crumbled when the OCR threatened withdrawal of all federal funds from the schools if compliance did not follow its notification of alleged discrimination. Principals yield no matter how wrong the directive. It is better to surrender than to take a principled stand and fight back.

Influencing and supporting the invidious federal influence on the schools are the worst elements in the school world—militant blacks and Hispanics, poverty groups, the American Civil Liberties Union—who have undermined schools for two decades. There is little resistance to their destruction of school discipline and their stirring of racial issues where none exist.

Invariably, blacks will be discipline cases out of proportion to their numbers in the general school population. It is a fact of school life, as it is a fact in our prisons where blacks who comprise 12 percent of the general population in the United States are over 50 percent of the prison population. Understandably, black people who are law-abiding are hurt by these statistics. Sadly, race has become an omnipresent factor in reporting a wide range of conditions in our society.

In my experience in the schools, blacks were not only *not* discriminated against by principals, but my colleagues let it be known that they bent over backwards to overlook offenses by black students that would have incurred suspensions for white students. This was not my approach. I did not patronize black students who were sent to me when deans could no longer handle them. I treated such students as I would any other student. Students knew that they would be treated firmly but fairly. Black parents were unanimous in backing me in all of my principled confrontations with chancellors and boards whose policies have deeply damaged a once great school system.

Chancellor Macchiarola's order to principals that they "monitor ethnic data in student suspensions" was hammered at by Ted Elsberg, president of the Council of Supervisors and Administrators. In a letter to *The New York Times* (March 16, 1981), Elsberg noted that "several high school principals were cited by their superintendent for allegedly excessive suspensions of an ethnic group, suspensions that were out of proportion to the number of such pupils in the schools. The stupidity and the harm of this policy have now come full circle.

"Essentially," Elsberg continued, "what does monitoring

186

of suspension by ethnicity mean? It means that the offenses—be they mugging of students, beating of teachers and supervisors, drug pushing or whatever—are deemed less important than the ethnic label of the offenders.

"Maintenance of discipline in the schools for the sake of pupils of all origins becomes irrelevant. . . .

"For too many years the leadership of the school system bent to every social pull and pressure until standards of decent behavior were surrendered in a 'do your own thing' anarchy. We were forced to tolerate excesses in language, in manners, in dress, in behavior, until we were afloat in a sea of permissiveness. Authority was first challenged, then increasingly eroded.

"Let us not label as discrimination the firm and fair exercise of authority and discipline. The criterion for suspension should be seriousness of the offense committed by the pupil, and not his ethnic background. We cannot and must not accept disruptive or violent behavior, no matter what its label or origin."

At the time Elsberg wrote, and Macchiarola was contributing to the destruction of school discipline, I had been retired for four years. I was writing my columns (two-a-week, as I am doing up to this moment), lecturing nationally, appearing on radio and TV, visiting schools, keeping up my contacts with school teachers and supervisors and carrying on a full program of professional activity. I was sure of one thing—Macchiarola and his successors would not have received from me any ethnic breakdowns of suspensions or ethnic data of any kind.

It is because too many principals are unprincipled that they obey orders no matter how subversive of discipline they may be. It was the failure of principals to unite and refuse such orders by the chancellor that has fused the depth charge which exploded the schools.

Schools have been weakened by the racial manipulations of the federal government that seeks to achieve greater employment of blacks through intimidating charges of discrimination derived from statistical analysis.

I was very conscious of the racial pressure to employ blacks, but had no thought of employing anyone whom I did not think deserved consideration on the basis of merit.

THE LAST ANGRY PRINCIPAL

Two of the blacks to whom I gave substitute jobs at LIC, one in physical education and the other in mathematics, turned out to be disasters. I had the department chairmen work with them in an effort to improve their teaching and looked in on them myself. They were not only poor teachers but irresponsible. One of them was reading a newspaper in class when he was supposed to be teaching from bell to bell. Another failed repeatedly to meet her class on time or handle the most routine relationships with either students or colleagues. I dismissed both of them at the end of the term. No black organization contacted me about the terminations and none of the other black teachers in the school suggested that I had been unfair. Any school is strengthened by the dismissal of incompetents regardless of color.

In contrast with the experience of the two black substitute teachers, I had other blacks on the faculty who were diamonds that helped me cut through many a problem. One was a guidance counselor, who had been a biology teacher in the school. He had a quiet manner and was highly professional. I melted him down a little over the years to the point where he told me about his children and the difficulty one of them was having at an out-of-town college.

Another black was the chairman of the Girls' Health Education Department. She was a tall, athletic, no-nonsense type whom I gave the position after interviewing her and checking with her principal as to her performance on the job as a teacher. She had passed the chairman's examination—no small accomplishment during the early 1970's when exams were still exams, especially for supervisory positions.

This black woman had ambitions to rise in the system and I helped her. She asked me to correct her English. I did so as tactfully as possible and certainly not in front of anyone else. She was to become a high school principal and remained one for a few years. The pressure in the early 1980's became too much for her, although she had been assigned to a Brooklyn high school that was almost 100 percent black. It does not follow that a black principal assigned to a predominantly black school has any easier time of it than a white principal in such a school.

RACIAL-ETHNIC SPOILS SYSTEM SPOILS SCHOOLS

My relations with black teachers were more extensive than the foregoing recollections. In general, my experience with them was positive, and I held them to the same high standards as other teachers. I believe that they appreciated my treating them no differently than I did white and Asian teachers whom I supervised.

There were also teachers' aides (styled paraprofessionals), almost all of whom were black, with whom I worked. I was especially pleased with the work of two of the black aides who lived in the neighborhood and had children in LIC. Both assisted in the guidance office.

One of the black women had a son who was an outstanding basketball player at the school and a fine young man. He was disappointed some years later when he was dropped quickly from a professional basketball team, but went on to coach basketball at an upstate college.

The other black woman had an excellent relationship with the teachers and students. Except for her lack of college credentials, she would have made a fine teacher. Some aides have completed college and have joined the system as teachers.

Strangely, these two women clashed and I was "Mr. In-between." The woman with the basketball-playing son was offered a higher-paying job at a distant all-black high school and I reluctantly let her go. A year later she returned and asked for her job back. In the interim, she had been replaced by the other black woman. When I explained that it would not be possible for me to make the change, she was resentful. Some years later I met her while she was escorting a class of youngsters through a Long Island historical site and we chatted cordially. She was a fine woman who raised a good family.

Although I have spoken favorably of my experiences with teachers' aides and have not recounted my experiences with those whom I dismissed after a few days or weeks, I believe that the employment of teachers' aides is excessive. Over 20,000 of them are employed in New York City public schools.

Teachers, of course, are becoming increasingly accustomed to aides who assist in putting on the coats of kindergartners, taking children to the toilet, patrolling the cafeteria, taking door assignments at entrances and elsewhere, assisting in reading lessons, etc. Generations of teachers have undertaken these assignments and I do not see that teachers' aides have moderated teachers' complaints about working conditions. The smaller class size now prevailing makes the assistance of aides less necessary, apart from the expenditure that would be better devoted to the employment of additional teachers.

Another classification of school aide is the security guard. These are the "police" of the school. They have been employed in ever larger numbers to improve school security. Some of them are bigger problems than the students they are supposed to assist in controlling. Some have been dismissed over the years for trafficking in drugs and otherwise interfering with the operations of the school.

I was prevailed upon by the superintendent in the early 70's to take my first security guard. He explained that if I refused to do so, it would reflect on other principals who were taking them, as many as four to a high school. I countered that the day I required a security guard to help me keep order in the school would be the day I retired. I took the guard. And I was to take others over the years.

I talked with them—both men and women—when they first arrived, as I would to a teacher. I explained what I expected of them and encouraged them to ask questions and to come to me if they had any problem. I emphasized that they were not employed to counsel or fraternize with students or with each other. (I had two at a time when other schools had eight and roving squads of 15 during emergencies.) Some worked out well in the specific assignments I gave them, usually at doors where outsiders might seek to enter. I did not want guards wandering about the school, because they become responsible for nothing and get lost in the building.

I found that the better security guards did not last long on the job. They found better jobs. One of them apologized profusely for taking a job as a bus driver, which paid twice as much as he was earning as a security guard. I wished him well.

I continue to feel that security guards—and they are now in

almost every elementary and high school in the city—reflect the failure of discipline in the schools. It is a sad commentary on schools that employ them because teachers and the principal cannot handle disruptive students or outsiders. I prefer that schools have closer ties with the police precinct.

Valiant efforts are being made to train security guards so that they can be of assistance in those schools that simply must have them. Inner-city schools, particularly, are menaced by drug-pushers and addicts. Security guards may help to fend them off, absent adequate police cooperation with the school. However, those schools that are not subject to intrusion by outsiders should be free to decline assignment of security guards.

I am not persuaded that because security guards and teachers' aides are very largely black and Hispanic that reduction in their numbers would add to minority employment problems. Consideration of race and national origin as a factor in school employment has distorted the main mission of schools.

The emphasis on race in the assignment of children has created havoc in schools. No good purpose has been served by forced busing under court order intended to achieve integration. Learning has suffered and race relations have been poisoned. Almost all forced busing has been of blacks to predominantly white schools. This in itself is discriminatory and has been so identified by blacks. Where whites have been bused to black schools, the resistance has been almost total. Whites have either fled the public schools or sought white schools in the suburbs.

To the integration vocabulary of the past three decades— segregation, desegregation, forced busing—there has been added resegregation, for that is clearly the case in some 300 metropolitan areas of the country. Where once blacks were the minority in the public schools, they are now the majority. There are simply too few whites to allow for forced integration. The few court orders that have sought to integrate city and suburban school districts, as in Wilmington, Delaware, have speeded white flight from the public schools.

Blacks and Hispanics have been linked in recent studies of resegregated public schools. There is the University of Chicago study, "School Segregation in the 1980's," that found the level of segregation to be virtually unchanged in the past two decades. Nearly two-thirds of blacks attend predominantly minority schools. Hispanic children are increasingly attending segregated schools and New York is the most segregated state of all for students.

In the few schools where it is alleged that integration is working, it has not led to social integration. Children, especially in the secondary schools, tend to divide along racial lines in lunchrooms. At the close of the school day, buses hurry children to their home neighborhoods. Bus schedules curb whatever integration might be encouraged in after-school hours.

Forcibly integrated schools have not contributed to better race relations. They have added to other stresses in society so that the races in some respects are further apart despite expanded entrance of blacks to job markets, especially government service. Politically, too, blacks have made substantial advances. Thousands of blacks hold public office, including constituencies where blacks are in the minority.

It is in the schools that affirmative action and its corollary forced integration have failed most conspicuously. Where schools have not been impacted by court-ordered racial balancing, chances for survival improved. LIC is one such school. It is a neighborhood high school. Blacks and Hispanics in the school were there because they lived in the neighborhood housing projects. This factor helps to explain why there was not a single racial brawl in the school, apart from school discipline that made a fight of any kind rare.

There was an element of luck in our record of racial peace at LIC, but it was also owing to feelers—students, parents, police community workers—in the surrounding community and the widespread knowledge that fights inside or outside the school would bring about sure disciplinary action.

When my deans told me that something racial was brewing, I called in black and white students, individually, never as a group or even two at a time. I would talk to the student and tell him what I had heard. I asked the student to tell me what he knew so that together we might head off any confrontation that would hurt all of us. Students understood that if I learned of their involvement in any racial fighting, suspension and transfer out of our school would almost certainly follow.

If you are thinking that what a kid does outside of school is none of the principal's business, you share in the conventional wisdom. I never felt that way. Schools train the young for citizenship. If a youth misbehaves outside of school, he reflects on the school's training. I was concerned with the behavior of kids in school and in the neighborhood. It paid off. It is not the easy route to travel, but nothing worth accomplishing in the increasingly tough school world is easy to come by.

The great growth of minorities in the public schools has complicated and made more difficult the teaching of children. There is a range of ability among minorities as there is among whites, but the home and street factors weigh more heavily against blacks and Hispanics than they do in handicapping whites. This condition, however, does not justify lower aspirations for minorities, a charge so often made by militants. It is incumbent upon the schools to strive strenuously to raise the level of learning among minority schoolchildren. Apart from the fact that we shall be increasingly reliant upon minorities in our labor and professional forces, teaching them effectively is the decent thing to do.

XIII

BILINGUAL EDUCATION: POLITICAL RIP-OFF

RACIAL-ETHNIC POLITICS plaguing schools has been exacerbated by the unprecedented offensive of a minority to impose its language—Spanish—as the language to be used in the schools by Hispanic children who must learn English. Never before has a minority in our nation of minorities organized so extensively and effectively to establish a foreign language as co-equal to English.

The bilingual-bicultural program espoused by Hispanic militants has gained more than a foothold—it is a stranglehold—in schools where there are a substantial number of Puerto Rican and Mexican-American children.

So intrusive is Spanish in schools and some cities that it has given rise to two national organizations—US English and English First—that seek a constitutional amendment to make English the official language of the United States. Thirteen states have enacted legislation making English the official language in the state. Such a law was passed in California in 1987 by a landslide vote, but bilingual education has been unaffected. The law was a simple statement with no qualifications or explanations, just as is the proposed amendment to the U.S. Constitution. Although there is no law mandating bilingual education in California, a factor that favors its continuance is that opponents are called racists. This is not the case, for opponents of bilingual education seek only to speed the acquisition of English by Hispanic and other limited English proficient (LEP) children.

It is the Congress that unwittingly advanced the cause of Hispanic militants. When Congress passed the Bilingual Education Act of 1968, it did not intend that foreign-born children be educated in their native language. The act was seized upon by Mexican-American and Puerto Rican militants as a means of ensuring the permanence of the Spanish language and culture for their constituents.

Although Hispanic-American politicians now in office never spent a day in a bilingual education classroom, they are almost to a man in the bilingual education camp. I made this point when I debated Congressman Robert Garcia (New York) on WABC-TV in the mid-80's.

The 1968 act has been amended three times, most recently in 1984, and each time reliance on the child's native language as a transition to English is strengthened. In the Bilingual Education Act of 1984 it is provided that 96 percent of federal funds for teaching English to LEP students be granted to bilingual education to the exclusion of any other method.

In some school districts children have been retained in the bilingual program for years after they have acquired sufficient English from the streets, radio, television and contacts with American children in and out of school. Even worse, children are forced into the program on the basis of their Spanish surnames, although they speak an idiomatic English. In my personal visits to schools where there are bilingual programs, I have talked with children who emerge from classrooms where the instruction has been in Spanish and they talk to me in idiomatic English. I asked one child in a Bronx junior high school, "Why are you studying science in Spanish?" She replied, "I do what they tell me to do."

This state of bilingual education is no secret to congressmen, but they have done nothing to change the law. Representative James Scheuer (New York) said on the floor of the House in 1984, ". . . its original purposes were perverted and politicized. I was an original sponsor of the Bilingual Education Act . . . and I remember very well that it was clearly intended . . . to be a pressure cooker exposure for the kids [from foreign language homes] to learn English."

Another false base for militant claims to a bilingual education program is that it was mandated by the U.S. Supreme Court in *Lau v. Nichols* (1974). Nothing could be further from the truth. The case arose when parents of non-English speaking Chinese children in San Francisco brought a class action suit against the school district alleging that the schools had failed to teach the children English. The court, in finding for the Chinese students, grounded its decision on violations of the Civil Rights Act of 1964.

The Court did not rule on the appropriateness of any particular language program since it was not presented with that issue. Justice William Douglas, writing for the court, held, "No specific remedy is urged upon us. Teaching English to the students of Chinese ancestry who do not speak the language is one choice. Giving instructions to this group in Chinese is another. There may be others. Petitioner asks only that the Board of Education be directed to apply its expertise directed to the problem and rectify the situation."

The real reasons for the fervor with which Hispanic militants impose bilingual education on the schools were set forth in the "Aspira National Think Tank Report: Bilingual Education" (1973) a year before *Lau*. (Aspira is a Puerto Rican advocacy group.) The exclusive use of English in U.S. schools was assailed as an "unthinking, immoral, attempt to forcibly assimilate, linguistically, the Spanish-speaking population of the United States. . . ."

The "Think Tank" was fueled by Hispanic militants who inveighed against "racist North American society" that tells children "that to be Hispanic is bad, that one has to be American because that is the best thing one can be. . . . In order to fight American racism," it was "necessary to draw a line and state 'not an inch further,' or links to native culture gradually dissolve."

It was candidly stated by "Think Tank" contributors that teaching Puerto Rican children in Spanish would ease their return to the island since they would not fall behind in subjects being taught. In this connection it should be noted that in the high schools to this day bilingual education requires that science, mathematics and social studies be taught in the native language.

Bilingual education was seen as requiring the employment

of Spanish-speaking teachers who might not otherwise obtain school employment. "Native speakers preferably from the same community as the students are the best qualified to teach in Spanish," it was added.

Another dividend that flowed from the continued use of Spanish in U.S. classrooms was the assurance that Hispanic-American candidates for public office would be reelected in barrios where Spanish remained the language of the community. "The existence of such a community," it was observed, "will undoubtedly meet with opposition in a society geared to impose conformity on all its members."

I oppose bilingual education, but not because I desire conformity. The United States is not a melting pot. People do adhere to their own cultures, and the country is enriched by this diversity. English, however, is the common language of the nation and it is a unifying force. Hispanic militants, more so than any immigrant group in our history, are campaigning for Spanish as a language equal to English. They have been successful in influencing the government to finance the teaching of Spanish in U.S. schools. While bilingual education advocates seek to justify use of the native language as a transition to English, the excessive time that children are kept in the program and the wide use of Spanish in the schools and community make evident their intent to diminish English as the official language of the country.

No reasonable person would deny the desirability of fluency in more than one language. It is, however, one thing to learn a foreign language in school and another to learn English through the native tongue. Our schools have done a poor job in teaching any foreign language. Few students emerge from our foreign language courses capable of ordering a meal in a language they have studied for years. We are largely reliant for second-language fluency (bilingualism) on foreign-born Americans and those who have retained fluency in the foreign language spoken by parents and grandparents.

At LIC I encouraged Spanish-speaking youngsters to enroll in our "Spanish for Natives" course. I learned from the teacher that many of the Spanish-speaking students spoke Spanish badly, wrote it ungrammatically and read below grade. In this they were not alone, for many American-born students have comparable failings in *our* native language.

In my experience non-English speaking children who enter our schools learn English through English. This eliminates the requirement for native speakers, always in short supply, especially for Asian languages. Orientals have been brought into the program by Hispanics who seek to deflect criticism that they alone benefit from the perquisites of bilingual ed—employment of teachers, supervisors, state and federal department personnel, etc.

The method of teaching English-as-a-Second Language (ESL) has been used effectively for a half-century and bilingual education teachers are supposed to use it as a component in their heavy concentration on the native language. I gained first-hand experience with ESL in the early 1950's, at Seward Park High School in lower Manhattan, a few blocks from Chinatown. We had large numbers of Chinese teenagers, and I programmed them for ESL. We had classes in basic, intermediate and advanced English. I set them up in parallel classes to ease movement of students from one level to another without waiting until the end of the term.

The Chinese children spent three non-consecutive periods a day in ESL and were mingled with American kids in physical education, music, art, typewriting, mathematics, lunch and some other subjects. They learned to speak English and entered regular classes in a maximum of a year and a half. No doubt, radio, TV and the streets helped them to learn English quickly.

At LIC we had children from Asian countries, Latin America and Europe—especially Greeks and Italians. In all, some 40 countries sent us children whom we were determined to make unhyphenated Americans as quickly as possible. We followed the same ESL program that had worked at Seward Park and many other schools.

I never met a foreign-born child who could not speak English in a year and a half or less. I remember well the Korean boy and girl with whom I had occasion to talk because they had helped to produce our most recent school publication, a Korean magazine written in English.

Both youngsters spoke an idiomatic English, almost entirely free of an accent.

"How many years of English did you study in Korea?" I asked.

"None, Dr. Hurwitz."

"But, surely, you spoke a little English when you came to the United States."

"I didn't know the word for 'please,' Dr. Hurwitz," the boy told me.

The girl echoed similar experience.

The Korean youths had been in our ESL classes for only a year. They had been in the same room with boys and girls from Vietnam, China, India, Greece, Italy, Israel, Colombia, Haiti and other countries. They had not been permitted to sit alongside of each other or other Koreans in the class. In this way reliance on their native tongues was reduced. Their immersion in English was facilitated by attendance in regular classes, as at Seward, where the need for English was not so demanding. They heard English in the cafeteria, the street, on radio and television. Above all, they had a strong desire to learn English so that they might swim in mainstream America.

I was determined to keep bilingual education, which I saw as a political ploy, out of LIC. It would likely impose upon us teachers who spoke English imperfectly and who were less than competent to teach the solid subjects—science, mathematics and social studies—to which they were assigned. I knew this from my observation of them in other schools and from the information given me by frustrated colleagues.

The pressure from Hispanic agitators to accept bilingual education was relentless, and the chancellor and Board of Education bowed to their tactics. LIC was just about the only high school in the city with a substantial number of Hispanic students that held out.

I have remarked before that it was necessary to retain a little humor in order to remain alive in the New York City public schools in the 1970's. I got a laugh from my colleague, David Gordon, president of the High School Principals Association, who sent us a letter on the "consent decree" that Aspira had gained from a federal judge and that was interpreted as mandating bilingual education.

Dave, in a two-page, single-spaced polemic on shocking-pink paper, made my day on February 11, 1976, when he wrote: "Humans get conditioned through their experiences. One day, when I opened the mail, I felt that something was missing and was uneasy—until I realized I hadn't received a request for a report from the city Office of Bilingual Education. It's hard to tell whether the repetition and continuing clerical confusion is planned or merely 'fray as you go.' Such undeviating consistency could hardly be created by sheer chance.

"The testing [level of English proficiency] has been a continuing daymare, reinforced by threats of confinement for contempt. Jail may yet prove preferable. . . ."

At LIC we tested the kids and sent in the reports with the regularity of flak in an air attack. I was not, however, planning to succumb to the bilingual offensive. I decided to enlist Hispanic parents in our battle to preserve ESL. Although 15 percent of our students were of Hispanic origin, they came from South and Central America, not Puerto Rico or Mexico. I reached a selected number with a letter translated into Spanish by our Chairman of the Foreign Language Department. There followed on a Saturday morning in the spring of '75, a meeting in my office of 11 parents. They required no persuasion that learning English through English was the way they wanted their children taught. We decided to enter court to establish what I knew to be the case from my reading of *Lau*, that bilingual education was *not* mandated.

I worked with an attorney on the preparation of a deposition presented to the U.S. District Court, Southern District of New York, sworn to by Rodrigo Cepeda, an LIC parent, "together with 10 other parents" named in the deposition. Mr. Cepeda denied that Aspira "represented the interests of all 'Hispanic' children and their parents; and that all such children and parents had common interests which made it appropriate to classify this action [mandating bilingual education] as a class action. . . ." He denied that *Lau v. Nichols* directed that bilingual instruction "shall be given to Hispanic children who cannot speak, read, write, or understand the English language. In practice," he continued, "such bilingual instruction is being given entirely in the Spanish language by teachers who were appointed as bilingual teachers without the education experience qualifications required of other teachers. . . . As a result, the Hispanic children who are now being given such bilingual instruction are now learning even less of the English language than before such bilingual instruction was given. . . . Moreover, most of the recently appointed bilingual teachers are of Puerto Rican origin, and they speak a Spanish dialect which is different from the Spanish language dialects spoken in South American countries, including Colombia, where I was born."

The LIC parents were under no obligation to prove in their deposition that ESL was a superior method to bilingual education; they simply resented the compulsion to have their children taught in Spanish rather than English and a dialect of Spanish that they did not speak.

U.S. District Judge Marvin E. Frankel listened to our arguments and on July 11, 1975 handed down a memorandum that affirmed our stand that bilingual education had not been mandated either by the U.S. Supreme Court or the Federal District Court, despite the claims of Aspira adhered to by a compliant chancellor and Board of Education.

Of Aspira's argument that bilingual education was the only permissible method of teaching foreign-language children, Judge Frankel stated it "is overborne because, in addition to misconceiving the court's powers and purposes in this case, they have allowed their zeal for bilingual education to sweep them momentarily past deeper concerns for freedom. . . . We would go outside the bounds of law and good sense if we held rigidly to the court's decree as the only permitted regimen for repairing English-language deficiencies."

Judge Frankel cited other cases that permitted "opting out" by parents who did not want their children to learn English through bilingual education. The "details of content, style, and method," the judge said, "remain broadly within the free judgment of parents and those they enlist to assist them as a matter of free choice.

THE LAST ANGRY PRINCIPAL

"Nothing in this court's decree could or did invade such liberties. It would be presumptuous indeed for a judge in this City—where the history of education in English and other things, has been so varied and the roads to effective citizenship so diverse—to command enrollment in a court-ordered program of bilingual instruction as the only permissible course open to Spanish-speaking children and their concerned parents. No such command was ever sought or given."

An article, "Bilingual Education Curbed Sharply by Federal Court Judge," in the *CSA Newsletter* (August 28,1975) was challenged by Chancellor Anker. He alleged in a letter to CSA President Peter O'Brien that he had "consistently maintained" that bilingual education was "optional."

O'Brien responded: ". . it was not *you* but the Long Island City parents who went into court and achieved this clear statement that the consent decree does *not* mandate bilingual education. . . . Up to this very moment, including your most recent Special Circular . . . , you are forcing bilingual education upon schools. . . .

"We wonder whether there is any responsible educator in New York who views your pronouncements as offering bilingual education as an 'option.' In fact, you specifically deny principals the right to criticize the program you have forced upon the schools. . . .

"We call upon you to reaffirm the right of educators to criticize the bilingual education program and to make clear that it is, in fact, optional."

In my columns, I have frequently exposed bilingual education as "political rip-off." The column appears occasionally in *Human Events*, a national conservative weekly that is read by President Reagan. He was to recommend me for appointment to the Department of Education's National Advisory Council on Bilingual Education. I served for two years (1984–1986) and prepared the council's Ninth and Tenth Annual Reports which were sent to the President, heads of Senate and House and the Secretary of Education.

In the reports we remarked on the one-sidedness of the Bilingual Education Act. Secretary of Education William J. Bennett was moved to follow "New Directions in Late '80s," the title I gave the Ninth Annual Report. In an address to the Association For A Better New York, on September 26, 1985, he said: "Educational research does not lend itself to hard conclusions as to whether one method of teaching children English is better than another. Nevertheless, there is a growing body of opinion that counsels expansion of barely used alternatives to bilingual education. One such approach is English-as-a-Second Language. . . .

"Congress . . . prescribed education in the student's native language as the sole method local school districts seeking funds could use. Why this change? Not because research had established the superiority of this method. . . .

"This, then, is where we stand: After 17 years of federal involvement, and $1.7 billion of federal funding, we have no evidence that the children whom we sought to help . . . have benefited. . . .

"What then are we to do? . . . . Continue down the same failed path on which we have been traveling? . . . ."

The answer would seem to be yes. Legislation intended to amend the Bilingual Education Act has been lost on Capitol Hill. The small but influential Congressional Hispanic Caucus is protective of the bilingual-bicultural program that ensures their continuance in office.

Tentacles of the federal octopus have ensnared local schools not only in its grasp of native languages but in racial skewing of schools, making it appear that normal operations in assignment of teachers and disciplining of students are discriminatory.

Although the federal contribution to the costs of school operation have not yet reached 10 percent of the total costs, the federal tail has come near to exhausting the school dog. Schools have been dogged by racial-ethnic strains that have made them prey to divisive forces.

XIV

A PROFESSION AT RISK

SINCE THERE IS no more important ingredient in the school mix than the teacher, I have kept a first-hand acquaintance with the caliber of new entrants to the profession.

Recently, as an assistant to the Board of Examiners, I interviewed an applicant for a teaching license in the New York City public schools. He was a man in his late twenties who sought a license as a teacher of common branches (grades 1-6). He told me that he was a graduate of a university in Texas where he had majored in consumer science and merchandising.

"What degree did you get?" I asked.

"A B.S."

"Did you take any physics?"

"No."

"Did you take any chemistry?"

"No."

"Did you take any biology?"

"No."

He was telling me what passes for a Bachelor of Science degree today. It is both watered down in most of the country's 3,300 colleges and emptied of meaningful content. The limitations of the B.S. degree are true also of the B.A. (Bachelor of Arts), a catchall for the liberal arts—English, history, foreign languages, philosophy.

I tried to pin the young man down on what he had actually studied at the Texas college. It seems that in consumer science, he learned about the laws that protected consumers from fraud.

In merchandising, he learned how to make window displays attractive.

The Houston youth reflected the kind of preparation for teaching that many new entrants in the school system have been receiving from colleges that offer a multiplicity of education courses. These courses are largely without substance and deprive both the undergraduate and graduate student of the grounding in solid subjects—science, mathematics, history—so essential in teacher preparation. The lack of a diet of solid subjects is especially harmful to elementary school teachers, many of whom are at a loss in teaching science and arithmetic because they have been deprived of contact with content. Teacher applicants who have been immersed in ed courses often lack a cultural background.

Others who are now seeking teaching jobs seem to have attended trade schools rather than traditional colleges. In the latter, both science and liberal arts students were expected to study and survive cultural subjects. Science students had to suffer through English composition, literature, history, foreign languages, etc. Liberal arts students studied a laboratory science—biology, physics, chemistry, geology—and some higher mathematics.

Today, most colleges are offering courses that lead to jobs—or so they allege. They are in competition for the declining pool of high school graduates and do everything but guarantee a job to the graduate. As a consequence, English is widely known as "communications arts." Students learn about TV, radio and newspapers. Business subjects have proliferated. The B.B.A. (Bachelor of Business Administration) is being sought by students with the avidity that knights once sought the Holy Grail. Accounting is a must and calculus a no-no. The study of history is almost dead, although dismay with the ignorance of today's high school and college graduates has caused some rumbling. Might not one reasonably expect a college graduate to complete a sentence about the Renaissance, or place the Civil War in the right half of the 19th century?

Employers among Fortune's 500 and lesser-endowed businessmen are distraught by the deficiencies of today's high school and college graduates. Whereas a high school diploma or a college degree once carried with it the guarantee of adequate preparation for learning on the job, such confidence has evaporated. It is for that reason that corporations now must take the time to impart in employees basic skills that they were supposed to have acquired in schools and colleges prior to entering the job world.

My major interest is in the quality of teacher applicants. All of them are required to be college graduates and in some states a year of graduate work is required before the teacher can be granted full certification by the state department of education. Despite the formal preparation, many are poorly prepared for the classroom because of the impoverished standards to which they have been held. Fortunately, there are a few who rise above the poor preparation and will not be discouraged from obtaining a teaching position. These young people who are our future hope are being reinforced by well-educated women in their fifties whose children are now adults. They attended college at a time when the American mind had not yet closed, as attested to by Allan Bloom in *The Closing of the American Mind* (1987), a devastating critique of what passes for a college education today.

The recent college graduates can scarcely complete a grammatical sentence. Their speech is studded with "ya know," "I mean," "all right" and "O.K." Some "ax" a question but do not "ask" it. In content areas their gaps in knowledge make the Great Divide look like a hole in your backyard. Their writing is scarred by errors.

I have heard the anguished cries of my colleagues in colleges nationwide, for I was president of the University Professors for Academic Order (UPAO), 1985–88. Only a week before writing this, I received a letter from an English professor at a university in the Far West. It was on UPAO business, but he remarked that he would get to the project, on which I had asked him to work "as soon as I get an English grammar test out of the way—yuz got dat? . . . . So back to grammar . . . . It's depressing to be teaching in college what I learned in the sixth grade!"

And it is depressing to contemplate what is ahead for American education if we must depend on teachers who are badly prepared for the arduous job of teaching our young. The demand for teachers is accelerating as evidenced by mounting enrollments of children in the primary grades and an increase in early retirement of teachers.

There are some fundamental problems connected with staffing our schools. There is the matter of women's rejection of teaching as a fitting career. The distaff side has been the main source of teachers, especially in the first eight grades, for more than a century. But women today have less exhausting opportunities beckoning.

In my lecture trips around the nation, I am interviewed by media reporters. Women interviewers invariably tell me that they were once teachers, but quit after a few years. No, it was not the pay. It was the lack of respect, ranging from the teacher spat upon by a third-grader to those who buckled under the daily strain and hostility of kids, parents and community.

If teaching is once again to become an attractive profession, its image will have to be changed drastically. I do not believe that the low salaries of the past will be the prime consideration in the future in deterring young people from entering the profession. In New York City the salary range under the most recent contract between the United Federation of Teachers and the Board of Education is $25,000 to $50,000 for a 180-day school year. In the nation the average teacher salary is now about $27,000. These salaries are likely to go up substantially as teachers' unions benefit from the law of supply and demand.

A major deterrent to recruitment and retention of teachers is the breakdown of discipline in the school, a subject on which I have already remarked upon (Chapter IX).

There are other elements as well tarnishing the teachers' image that are given insufficient weight. Take, for example, so simple a matter as teacher dress. A principal in Paterson, New Jersey, told a teacher that it was improper to wear sandals in school. The teacher filed a grievance against the principal for interfering with his right to dress as he pleased. The teachers' union defended the teacher's right to wear sandals. An arbitrator overruled the principal.

There was a time when male teachers wore a jacket and tie

and women wore dresses or skirts and blouses. Their mere appearance instilled respect in children and served as an example to children. Styles have changed, to be sure, but these elementary requirements of dress, widely prevalent in the business community today, have broken down in the schools. It should not be necessary for teacher dress to be specified in a code. Teachers should adhere to reasonable dress in class in their own self-interest.

In visiting schools countrywide during the past decade, I have been disheartened by the appearance of many teachers. I would not have them in any school I headed—and I did not when I was a high school principal in the 60's and 70's. An occasional teacher would tell me that his colleagues in other schools wore sneakers, jeans and sports shirts. I told him that teachers in other schools had to teach behind locked doors to prevent intrusion by outsiders; that teachers at LIC were neither threatened nor assaulted; that there is a connection between teacher dress and student behavior. A tie, I said, was a small price to pay for the privilege of teaching in a safe school.

Almost without exception, teachers at LIC dressed appropriately as befitted professionals. I rarely had to speak to a teacher about his appearance. There was no dress code and a code would be demeaning to the profession. The New York State Commissioner of Education had declared that he would not enforce a dress code for teachers or students, but he was protecting the kind of attire that contributed to the low esteem in which teachers are held.

Teachers' unions have done much to improve teachers' salaries and working conditions. But, in defending slovenly teachers, they do the profession a disservice. Today, in many schools, teachers cannot be distinguished from students, clad in the jeans, sneakers and tee-shirt that are supposed to signify non-conformity. Together, they lower school tone and pollute the climate for learning.

Boards of education that take a stand on teacher dress should be supported by state commissioners of education. The courts would do well to leave matters of dress to the school board. There is no constitutional right to look like a slob and teach at the same time.

The teachers' image is also impaired in the public mind by the strike ritual at the beginning of the school year—and often in mid-year. There were no teacher strikes in the United States until the early 1960's. These strikes are comparatively few and may affect a mere million of the 45 million children attending school, but they do teachers harm. A strike in the smallest school district is reported in the national press and, of course, is front-page news in the community newspaper. Apart from the fact that all of these strikes are illegal—contrary to state laws that prohibit strikes by public employees—teachers on picket lines seem incongruous. No matter how justified the strike action in the minds of participating teachers and the union, the bottom line in the public mind is that teachers rank the children below their self-interest. The argument that a contented teacher will do a better job in the classroom may satisfy some teachers, but parents with kids out of school, at times for weeks during the school year, are not impressed.

Teachers are also faulted for failing to teach values. I am no great believer in teaching morality *per se* in the public schools. I think that morality is best taught at home and inculcated by example. Teachers can set a good example for children. Students can learn to be punctual, honest, respectful of the rights of others, responsible for assignments, cooperative, etc. These attributes contribute to a moral code which the school can help the child to develop.

It is also possible to pose moral problems, appropriate to an age level, for discussion purposes. The danger here is that the teacher may allow for differences of opinion that may push morality out the window.

More serious than the charge that teachers are failing to teach moral values is the charge that they are teaching immorality. The charge is shocking, but not so bizarre as to be excluded from consideration by federal courts. Schools have been charged with teaching secular humanism. There is controversy as to whether secular humanism *is* a religion, but for those who contend that it *is*, there is agreement that it is a religion that places emphasis on the human being, who can make moral decision without reference to creeds.

Secular humanism may have a strange sound, but it is a bell-ringer in Alabama and other Southern states. In one case in the mid-80's, Alabama parents cited passages from textbooks that state "moral values are made by men" and that school textbooks ignore religion. The court ruled that the plaintiffs were not denied their First Amendment right to free exercise of religion.

To the extent that history textbooks give scant space to religious freedom as a motive for settlement of the colonies, there is reason to complain. Exception may also be made to omission of the history of religion as a continual force in shaping the American family and institutions. It is, however, one thing to teach about religion and another to inculcate religious values.

Religious values are tied to morality and parents are nearly unanimous in wanting schools to teach morality. Although few would contend that Bible-reading and non-denominational prayer in public schools assured that morality was being taught, their prohibition by the U.S. Supreme Court in the early 1960's weighed heavily on public perception of the schools. The high court after 150 years discovered that both practices were violations of the establishment clause in the First Amendment. A breach in the wall separating church and state was discerned by the justices. The court crackdown elicited the cry of "Godlessness" and added to distrust of our public schools.

There is the widespread feeling among people who hold to traditional Judeo-Christian values that morality is not being taught in the public schools. In support of this charge, curricula are cited—especially sex education guides—in which decision-making is taught as a responsibility of the child. It is the child who must determine for himself what is right or wrong.

There are situations in which a child must be told what is right or wrong. It would be rare for me to substitute a child's judgment for my own. I do not believe this firmness destroys a child's capacity for exercising his own judgment.

It is in the area of sex education that morality is being

shoved out the school window. The frenzy over expansion of sex education has been induced by the million teenage pregnancies each year that are part of the sexual revolution in which children and adults have become co-equal hedonists.

So all-inclusive is teaching about sex that the New York City curriculum guide, *Family Living Including Sex Education*, offers lessons from pre-kindergarten through the 12th year. The syllabus has been drawn upon liberally by school systems outside of New York. Short on family living and long on sex, it contains information on the use of nine contraceptive techniques with addresses and phone numbers of abortion clinics. The guide is stacked with role-playing suggestions in which boy and girl in class play roles in which the boy is the seducer. The class, coeducational as required by the federal government, is invited to evaluate the players. (Federal regulations for more than a decade require that boys and girls take physical and health education together, just as classes are open to both sexes in shop subjects, homemaking and other traditional one-sex classes. Failure to conform to the coed requirement can result in loss of federal aid as punishment for violation of the civil rights law prohibiting sex discrimination.)

Although the requirement that boys and girls be in the same health education class already existed, I chose to ignore it. Parents of LIC students would not have taken kindly to coed classes in sensitive areas. The superintendent of Queens high schools either overlooked my determination that classes were to be separated by sex or decided that the battle would not be worth fighting on moral grounds.

Most teachers would like nothing better than to be excused from teaching about sex, but there are those who pitch in with every intention of imposing their own values. I shall not forget the young physical education teacher at LIC who implemented the syllabus that had the precise title of the current syllabus although its emphases were vastly different. The old syllabus had stressed chastity and was devoid of any references to contraception or abortion.

I dropped in on the teacher who was in the middle of a lesson and he must have been too slow to shift gears. He was telling the boys how they might satisfy girls in foreplay. I sent word to the teacher to see me before he left school for the day. Any probability that he would ever again teach health education along the lines I heard was banished.

I see kids today as being titillated, not educated in sex courses. These are now being expanded to include teaching about AIDS (acquired immune deficiency syndrome). The United States Department of Health and Human Services has descended on schools with an avalanche of booklets and guides intended to prevent the spread of AIDS. Although abstinence is recommended, the use of condoms as a preventive is suggested. In some schools where there are health clinics, condoms are given free to students who say they are active sexually. So contrary to a moral code is the counsel of condom use for schoolchildren that three conservatives resigned from the Reagan administration's Panel on Teen Pregnancy Prevention, charging that it is doing more to promote teenage sex than prevent it. One of the three panel members who resigned, said of the panel, "They have substituted their own ideology and course of action; that is, the wholesale distribution of condoms to teenagers supported by so-called value-free advice about sexuality" (*The New York Times*, March 5, 1988).

In furtherance of the belief that AIDS be combated through the schools, the New York City Board of Education commissioned a film, "Sex, Drugs and AIDS." The dialogue between the actress who plays the role of the teacher and teenagers allows for exchanges on the differences between homosexual and heterosexual sex. Use of condoms as protection is urged upon the youths.

The film became the basis for a book with the same title, published by Bantam Books. Bantam's marketing director for school and college books stated, "It is being sold to schools and we are getting good solid orders and re-orders from our school jobbers" (*The New York Times*, March 19, 1988). Bantam's boost for the book was in response to the New York City Board of Education's refusal to approve purchase of the book for school use—not because of its explicitness, but because the book was based on the first edition of the film and not the one in use in the

New York City schools. The board had insisted that the film be changed to show more boys rather than girls, almost exclusively. The film-makers had made the change in the film, but the change had not been picked up in the book.

The film is currently available for use in the city's 116 high schools and 178 junior high schools, but the book is not yet on the approved list. The producer of the film, a former reading teacher, found it ironic that the board would reject a book that was specifically written for teenagers who read below grade. "They're always talking about how kids cannot read," she said, "This is written for fourth-grade level reading."

So aggressive have gays become in forcing schools to accept their aberrant sexual behavior that many of them are now teachers in communities where they are protected against alleged discrimination on grounds of "sexual orientation." By including homosexuals among the protected minorities, legislators have been protecting civil wrongs, not civil rights.

Sex education courses in the schools have provided homosexuals (including lesbians) with a springboard for introducing their way of life as an alternative to homosexuality. The National Gay Task Force (gays are activist homosexuals) demands that homosexuality be presented as an alternative lifestyle and this view has been adopted in many sex education guides. In the New York City sex syllabus, for example, students are encouraged to discuss "a wide range of preferences" in "sexual expression," including "homosexual preference," "gay," "lesbian," and "bi-sexual." In defense of homosexuals, the syllabus states, "Most child molesters are heterosexual males and not homosexuals." This is true if only because heterosexuals greatly outnumber homosexuals in the population.

Gays' boldness is boundless. They have invited teachers to join gay teachers' organizations through advertising in such publications as the *New York Teachers Bulletin* of the teachers' union. They are emboldened to flaunt their perversity by the New York City Board of Education and other boards that have stated homosexuality is no bar to a teaching license.

In the mid-80's the New York City Board of Education established the Harvey Milk School in Greenwich Village, named after a murdered San Francisco city official. The school's small enrollment is limited to homosexual and lesbian teenagers who have had difficulty in their home schools and request admission. The teachers are professed homosexuals.

A school for homosexuals is a concession to gross immorality, apart from acknowledgment that regular schools do not prevent harassment of students. And I believe further that persons who engage in homosexual practices should be barred from teaching.

I have encountered a few homosexual and lesbian teachers, but in only one case was I forced to take action. The young man was a good teacher whose ability to repair office machinery caused me to call on him frequently. He showed me pictures of his girl friend and said that he expected to marry soon. There was no reason to suspect Lem. As is the case with many homosexuals, there was nothing in his manner to suggest any abnormality.

I learned from Lem's department chairman about complaints from boys that they had been molested by him. Before I could be satisfied that there was substance to the complaints, I was visited by one 15-year-old boy's parents and male relatives who insisted on meeting the teacher. I persuaded them that I would take care of the matter and that the boy need have no fears.

Lem must have learned of the Friday afternoon visit, for on Saturday night, when my wife and I were out for the evening, he came to my home and pleaded for admission. My son had been instructed to answer the bell for no one. When we came home after midnight, my son told us what had happened and I knew that it was a frightened Lem who had come to seek my help.

I talked with Lem and we agreed that his transfer from LIC could not be avoided. I decided not to prefer charges against him, and the superintendent was easily persuaded to arrange his assignment to 110 Livingston Street, board headquarters. Lem was to remain at the board doing clerical work for five years. A few months after my retirement, he was assigned to an all boys' high school in the city.

I have said that Lem was a good teacher. He, of course,

was a homosexual who engaged overtly in sexual practice in the school. There are other homosexuals who are not overt but whose homosexuality is known to the students. These, too, may be good teachers. The overriding consideration, however, is that students who know their teacher is a homosexual conclude that there is nothing wrong with homosexuality, for their teacher is one. This is another type of cancer that our sick schools cannot abide.

Encouragement of homosexuality—certainly forbearance—is a small but significant failing of current sex syllabi. Their overriding fault is in introducing sexual activity to children long before they are ready for it. It is morally wrong for teachers to offer options in sexuality to teenagers and to encourage them to make the choice. Decision-making by children is the essence of sex syllabi. This approach has reinforced approbation of sexual activity outside of marriage that is the hourly fare on TV, a staple in movies and a preoccupation of the print media.

Schools should not be vehicles for moving children into sexual activity. Traditional separate sex hygiene courses and coed biology classes, supplemented by family living units that stress responsibility, were adequate to sustain the generative powers of millions never exposed to sex education current style. The new sex syllabi have not stemmed the growth of pregnancies and attendant trauma, but rather inflamed the sexual revolution.

Teenagers whose curiosity about sex is not satisfied by the kind of sex education that abjures techniques, contraception and abortion will have no difficulty in finding supplementary reading in the storehouse of books, pamphlets, magazine articles, etc., devoted to human sexuality. The only requirement for savoring this cornucopia of sexual knowledge is the ability to read. It is in the development of this basic skill that schools are failing. It is mastery of reading for comprehension that can unlock career doors for youth, expand cultural interests and, perhaps, curb recreational sex that is wrecking their lives and contributing to the decay of morality in our society.

Decision-making by children in moral matters is one peril; decision-making by teachers in all school matters is another. The hottest item in proposed reform of the schools is decision-making by teachers. The Carnegie Task Force on Teaching as a Profession in its report, "A Nation Prepared: Teachers for the 21st Century" (1986), recommended: "Giving teachers a greater voice in the decisions that affect the school will make teaching more attractive to good teachers who are already in our schools as well as people considering teaching as a career. . . . If the schools are to compete successfully with medicine, architecture and accounting for staff, then teachers will have to have comparable authority in making key decisions about the services they render." The task force conceded that goals for students should be "set by state and local policymakers"; but, it cautioned, "teachers . . . must be free to exercise their professional judgment as to the best way to achieve these goals."

The 14-member Carnegie Task Force did not include a single school administrator. It did, however, include Albert Shanker, president of the American Federation of Teachers (AFL-CIO). A belief that is fundamental with Shanker is that supervisors (used interchangeably with administrators) get in the way of teachers. He sees them as unimaginative bureaucrats who hold teachers to daily lesson plans and otherwise restrict their creativity.

Following the task force recommendation on decision-making power for teachers, the AFT met in Chicago, and Shanker let the delegates know that the time has come for teachers to take over. He sketched the outline for their future in the experience of ALCOA (Aluminum Company of America) workers in Arkansas that "ended 45 years of adversarial labor-management relations by establishing autonomous work crews which almost entirely eliminated the need for plant supervision. The workers made their own decisions about how their jobs could best be done."

Carried away by his vision of teachers emulating ALCOA workers, Shanker predicted, "A generation from now may well look back and see that the Task Force's proposals were our teachers' way of 'buying into' our schools and marked the beginning of the revitalization of American public education."

What Shanker never developed in his few years as a junior high school teacher in New York City public schools was a feel for the classroom and an understanding of the role that supervisors have played and must continue to play if the schools are not to be rudderless ships.

As a teacher and principal with 40 years of experience, I know a good teacher when I observe one. Many a good teacher has elected to stay in the classroom where he is in charge, rather than undertake the arduous upward climb and added responsibilities that go with the rank of supervisor. Other good teachers— and some not so good—have advanced in the profession.

Any good supervisor will tell you that he works *with* teachers and must rely on their strength. It is one policy, however, to consult teachers regularly and another to share decision-making.

The Carnegie Task Force inveighs against "school systems based on bureaucratic authority." Once having established to its satisfaction that it is dealing with hated "bureaucracy," the task force sees that bureaucrats "must be replaced by schools in which authority is grounded in the professional competence of the teacher."

The Carnegie Task Force saw the principal—"the single model for leadership found in most schools"—as "better suited to business or government than to the function of education." In support of this incredible judgment, the task force would have "schools headed by the lead teachers acting as a committee, one of whom acts like a managing partner in a professional partnership. In such schools the teachers might hire the administrators, rather than the other way around."

The Carnegie people did not leave any loose ends around. The task force proposal that there be a new National Board for Professional Teaching Standards is now the fact. It is composed of educators, executives, political leaders and others who are charged with creating the first national system for certifying teachers' varying levels of competence.

The board is a private one, not a creation of the federal government, and it will be up to state and local governments to decide whether to license teachers certified by the National Board. There will be an Advanced Teachers Certificate for lead or master teachers who will be paid top dollar. A cut below will be certified teachers—the majority of the teaching force.

THE LAST ANGRY PRINCIPAL

The taking of the Carnegie test will be voluntary. The private national board will be bucking up against some 44 states that now rely on the National Teachers' Examination, prepared by the Educational Testing Service (Princeton, New Jersey). The new board may be seen as an outsider undercutting their authority.

Supervisors, too, are unhappy about the prospect of being overshadowed by teachers certified as "distinguished." Salaries projected for such lead teachers are in excess of those paid to supervisors. This is consistent with the Carnegie prescription that teaching becomes a profession only when teachers make the determination as to who will or will not enter the classroom.

The projected high-power testing is scheduled to begin operation at the very time that half of the 2.2 million teaching staff will have to be replaced owing largely to retirements and resignations by the mid-90's. If the tests hold to a high standard, who will be around to pass them? Not the present caliber of candidate drawn from the bottom of the college barrel. About six percent of current undergraduates have expressed an interest in teaching as a career and these score lowest in such standardized measurements as the Scholastic Aptitude Tests. At that, there are far too few undergraduates who plan teaching careers to satisfy the burgeoning need.

I doubt whether intensive testing, desirable though it is, will make it easier to staff schools with good teachers. If the new system of Carnegie testing should work—and certified teachers turn out to be a big cut above the current crop—we shall have witnessed a miracle.

Reform proposals are not coming from the teaching staff. State legislatures that provide most of the money for funding schools have become increasingly concerned with what goes on in the classroom. They are led by governors who are loud in their concern about the on-going educational crisis. They are embarked on a plan for minimum competency testing of already licensed and on-the-job teachers.

Texas, Arkansas and Georgia have already imposed such testing of employed teachers. Yelps coming from Lone Star State teachers, who had their feet put to the test fires, are scaring teachers nationwide. While the tests reflect public dissatisfaction with teacher performance, teachers see it as an undeserved public whipping. Some three percent of the teachers have failed the tests and these are permitted to retake the tests after enrolling in university courses of a remedial nature.

Is it possible for a teacher who has been performing satisfactorily in the classroom for decades to fail a paper and pencil test? Might an automotive shop teacher who entered the school shop after years in a garage forget commas in sequence? As anyone who has ever taken a test knows, there is a degree of nervousness; also, skills grow rusty and there is a rate of forgetting. Test-taking is a skill in itself. It requires polishing. Teachers are accustomed to giving tests, not taking them. At that, nearly one hundred percent of the teachers required to take the tests have passed them. I can understand that they find the tests insulting. It does not follow that kids will learn better if their teachers are required to pass tests in the basic skills they are supposed to be transmitting to their children.

There is little argument against requiring would-be teachers to take tests *before* they can be licensed to teach. All states but two (Alaska and Iowa) now require such testing. Requiring teachers to take tests *after* they are licensed and on the job is locking the barn door after the horse is stolen; or, worse yet, shooting ol' Dobbin.

What would be more to the point is far stiffer tests for those who would enter the classroom. They should then be closely supervised and rated before they are granted tenure. There are too many teachers, especially those licensed within the past two decades, who should not be in the classroom. They were not good from the first day, but protections afforded unsatisfactory teachers make Miranda rights for criminals look like candy bars.

State legislators would do better to rework the laws that keep unsatisfactory teachers in the schools. They are entitled to due process—fundamental fairness—but not the inordinate grievance procedures encased in collective bargaining contracts that ensure long careers for poor teachers. Such procedures do a disservice to children and to colleagues who suffer from a lowered image of the profession.

THE LAST ANGRY PRINCIPAL

In addition to granting decision-making powers to teachers, reformers would distinguish among teachers by rewarding the better ones with higher pay. Under existing union contracts that cover almost all teachers, they are placed on salary steps and receive increases automatically until the final step is reached. Teachers thus proceed from minimum to maximum salaries over a 15-year period, or whatever span is provided for in the agreement between the teachers' union and the board of education.

Merit pay would splinter the steps crafted in collective bargaining agreements. But merit pay is seen as simple justice by reformers, especially businessmen despondent over the products emerging from the schools.

Teachers' unions—the American Federation of Teachers and National Education Association (NEA)—who speak for almost all teachers, are opposed to merit pay. No union would want to get involved in distinguishing among its members as to who should get merit pay. For their part, few teachers are so broadminded as to concede that the teacher in the next room, who may have fewer years of service, is so superior as to deserve more pay. Merit pay is seen by most teachers and their unions as a morale breaker. They reject the dictum of the Carnegie Task Force—joined by a gaggle of other task forces—that "the system's rewards do not go to those who produce the most achievement for the students and the greatest efficiency for the taxpayer."

Merit pay in one form or another is being tried in at least 30 states. It takes shape in extra pay for longer contracts (*e.g.*, 12 months instead of 10 months), salaries tied to student achievement, extra assignments for some teachers, etc.

One state that attracted considerable interest when in 1984 it introduced merit pay in the form of career ladders is Tennessee. There are three rungs and 6,000 of the 49,000–plus teachers in the state are assigned to the higher two rungs. Currently, teachers on the second level can extend their work years by one month, and teachers on the third level can extend their work years by two months, with the state paying the additional salary of $2,000 per month. The ladder was defended by one principal who said that it permitted him to make extended use of his best teachers and that they did not have to seek part-time jobs to make ends meet.

The Tennessee Education Association (the teachers' union) argues that the money financing the career ladder should be used to raise the minimum salary. Teachers turned down on the climb up the ladder object to their evaluation by outside teachers employed by the state department of education.

I like the link between higher pay and increased responsibility, such as the summer assignment of one teacher to helping six youngsters who failed 7th-grade math. I would not dismantle the ladders until teachers have had more experience climbing them.

I would eliminate any rung constructed of education courses as a requirement for advancement, or extra pay conditioned upon enrollment in an education course. These courses are thin and painful to any student or teacher with an ounce of intellectuality. Schools of education over the years have gained a hammerlock on certification requirements at the state level.

In place of education courses, prospective teachers and those seeking advanced degrees should concentrate on solid subjects. This should hold true for elementary school teachers, who might then be better grounded in science and math, as well as high school teachers, who must have solid backgrounds in the subject they are expected to teach.

Those states, notably New Jersey, that have eliminated education courses as a requirement for certification are that much ahead in recruiting liberal arts graduates who would attempt a teaching career if it did not require that they be bored in soporific education courses.

The big mistake made by school systems is in throwing new teachers directly into the classroom, often in the most difficult schools, whatever their course preparation might be. This can deter even retired army officers, among other second-career people, who are being recruited along with neophytes from Squeedunk College.

No new teachers should be entrusted with a class at any level. The new teacher should be assigned to an experienced teacher, a mentor, who will permit the beginner to take over a class from time to time. The mentor should not himself be relieved of teaching classes, since this weakens the instructional program and requires employment of substitute teachers to take the place of the mentor. The practice teaching should be observed by the mentor who seeks to strengthen it.

When the new teacher is entrusted with a full program, he should be observed frequently by an assistant principal or principal. This is the major function of the school supervisor, who is so often bogged down in paper work that he has little time for his highest priority.

There is some evidence that teacher mentors are being called upon again to ease the transition from college, or other employment, to the classroom. This can be called reform, if pleasure can be derived from renaming an old practice.

The most effective program for inducting new teachers was the teacher-in-training, as it was called in New York City in the 1930's. It was comparatively inexpensive in those days to employ a teacher and not give him a full program for a year. (As a teacher-in-training in 1938, I was paid $4.50 a day with no pay for holidays, illness, or other benefits.) Although it is expensive to undertake a teacher-mentor plan, it is more expensive to bring in the new teacher only to have him depart after burdening the children and supervisory personnel.

If teachers are to be developed on the job—the only real place where they can grow—it is imperative that strong principals be found, encouraged and retained. Strong principals have invariably been master teachers. They have progressed up the ladder through the assistant principalship to the premier position in the school. Teachers can respect a principal who has come up through the ranks and whose awareness of the classroom teachers' problems is evident. A principal, no matter how strong, as I have remarked, is dependent on a corps of good teachers. And teachers who are without the leadership of a strong principal will find their effectiveness greatly diminished. It is with this relationship of teacher and principal in mind that I reject as another manifestation of reformers' zeal the recruitment of New Jersey principals from among successful business managers who have had no school experience.

A PROFESSION AT RISK

When reformers are through ranting, teachers will still be in the front lines. They will be at risk until they are strengthened by a fresh corps of well-trained troops led by principals who have earned their stripes in the field.

XV

CAN WE SAVE OUR SINKING SCHOOLS?

A CASCADE OF national, state and foundation reports inundated schools in the 1980's. If there is a single report that is remembered, if only for its title, it is *A Nation At Risk: The Imperative For Educational Reform* by the National Commission on Excellence in Education. The very idea of this nation being at risk because its schools are so bad caught hold.

The commission was aghast at school performance and was so dismayed as to state: "If an unfriendly power had attempted to impose on America the mediocre educational performance that exists today, we might well have viewed it as an act of war. . . ."

Indicators of the risk included poor performance of students on tests. The commission found that "on 19 academic tests, American students were never first or second and, in comparison with other industrialized nations, were last seven times. . . . About 13 percent of all 17-year-olds in the United States can be considered functionally illiterate. Functional illiteracy among minority youth may run as high as 40 percent."

Three years after the nation was shocked by the commission blast, the Carnegie Task Force on Teaching as a Profession (1986) called for "highly qualified" teachers to save the nation. School districts were urged to offer higher "pay, autonomy and career opportunities. In return, teachers would agree to higher standards . . . and real accountability for student performance."

What better way could there be for holding teachers *accountable* (big word in school world) than to judge them by students' test scores? Tests are tangible, it is reasoned. Results can be compared. Have students' scores improved from year to year? How do students in one school compare with students in another school? In another state?

With states pouring money into the schools in the 1980's, as never before in our history, test results (a measure of teacher performance) held special fascination for governors and legislators who voted the appropriation bills. Reformers, too, could measure the effect of new programs by the way students tested.

Understandably, teachers do not want to be judged by test results. There are just too many factors that affect scores. A teacher of slow students, not necessarily minorities, may be doing a far better job with the kids than the teacher of bright or average students. It is not likely that the test results will favor teachers of the slow.

Test results can be affected by many factors, apart from the fact that they are imperfect measuring instruments. There are teachers who teach for the test. They go over past tests repeatedly in an effort to raise scores if only by making students familiar with the test. Others judged by the test results include the principal, superintendent and board of education.

There are schools in which students sure to lower the average test scores are somehow not tested. These may include the foreign-born who have difficulty with English, slow students, truants and trouble-makers.

The scoring of tests may not always be done with accuracy. Commercially prepared tests are usually sent outside the school for scoring, but statewide tests and local tests that are marked in school oftimes lend themselves to manipulation.

Although testing is deadly serious now that accountability is in the air, one wisecracking teacher was heard to remark, "I can imagine the governors of Texas and Oklahoma comparing notes about whose kids do best academically rather than how their football teams do."

The likelihood of more testing assuaging the governors' concern about ever-increasing school expenditures—the largest item in state budgets—is about as likely as kindergartners designing a rocket to the moon. We already have in our schools the most over-tested kids in the world. Standardized tests of every conceivable skill, aptitude, achievement, etc., are listed with reviews by educators that can fill a Manhattan-sized telephone directory. They are marketed nationwide.

For good reason reading skill remains a continuing public concern. Yet, in one study of the most recent test results available, 90 percent of school districts and 70 percent of students tested performed above average on nationally normed tests. This defies the law of averages and common sense.

Reformers are fervent in their faith in testing and want more of it. Although testing is confined largely to the states, the U.S. Senate is currently considering expansion of national testing. It is not enough that the federal government has been testing for the past 20 years a "scientific sampling" of 120,000 children every two years in the National Assessment of Educational Progress. The existing national test battery is aimed at reading and math with occasional sampling in science and history. The results reveal what we already know. Most kids couldn't tell you whether $7/8$ is greater than $3/4$ if their allowances depended on it. They not only cannot put the Civil War in the right half of the 19th century, they don't know who fought in it. A devastating documentation of the schools' failure to inculcate literacy from the earliest grades was made in 1987 by E.D. Hirsch in his *Cultural Literacy: What Every American Needs to Know*.

There was a time in the dim dead days almost beyond recall when testing consisted largely of teacher-prepared tests. Classroom tests were seen as a vital part of the instructional program. I took them as a student and gave them as a teacher. Even when objective-type, short-answer tests became fashionable—easier to mark and less subjective in grading—teachers did not use multiple-choice questions to the exclusion of essays.

There was the realization that marking a box with a pencil merely allowed for recognizing the answer. It did not allow for development of a sustained, coherent response to a broad, thought-provoking question. Mere recognition of a correct answer and a generous allowance for guessing the correct one has not advanced learning. The multiple-choice madness combined with teaching for the test has contributed, if anything, to semi-literacy.

As noted, there are factors other than the teachers' effectiveness that enter into test results—not the least of which is the influence of the home.

A fundamental flaw in any program for strengthening schools is our greatly weakened family structure. Half of all mothers with children under three and 60 percent of mothers with children between the ages of three and five are in the work force. It is clear that we need arrangements for child care and these now range from the makeshift to government provision for day-care centers. At the simplest but not necessarily the most satisfying level, children are farmed out to neighbors for a fee or harbored with the few grandmas who are not doing their own thing. Some children are placed in child-care centers (a booming business) that does not begin to supply the need for places. The centers are licensed in some cities, but inspection is weak and many small day-care facilities are improvised and unlicensed.

Some children are left alone, especially when the custodial arrangement collapses for the day or more extended periods. Children are even being left in libraries for long hours so that local ordinances are now being enacted to punish parents who seek to make babysitters of librarians.

Into the breach reformers would move an already faltering teacher corps to engage four-year-olds. If I thought that putting four-year-olds, and even smaller tots, in a school setting would ease them through the years leading to high school graduation, I would join the womb-to-classroom camp. But I believe that children suffer from too early exposure to a classroom setting; that even precocious children strain themselves in an effort to satisfy their parents' expectations; that children who are not exposed to early education catch up quickly with those who seem to have benefited from pre-kindergarten schooling.

The underlying reason for the rush to push four-year-olds into the school world is mother's rush into the world of work. There are parents, too, who believe that if their children are not started on the school road early, they will be at a competitive disadvantage with those whose parents have succumbed to the pre-kindergarten schooling that is becoming institutionalized.

Poor mothers find the cost of child care in the guise of either baby-sitting or schooling prohibitive and middle-class mothers are drained by the costs. Both see the public schools as substitute mothers for "free."

I recognize the seriousness, indeed the irrefutable argument, that many mothers go to work because they must have the income. This is especially true of single parents—half of all children will live in single-parent homes by the time they are 18. The schools, however, should not undertake to care for children who might not otherwise be provided for.

Since women are working outside of the home, it follows that they are needed by the employer. Some employers, including the government, are already making provision for the care of children below school age. I expect a great increase in the number of employers who must adapt to the needs of women who will not otherwise be available to them in the work force. Until this gap is filled, working mothers should make private provision for the care of their children. To the extent that inability to make such provision will keep some of them at home, I see an advantage to society. I do not favor government intervention, except where it is acting as an employer, to relieve parents of their primary responsibility—care of their children.

There is, to be sure, little likelihood of any substantial withdrawal of mothers of young children from the work force. We may expect, therefore, to continue paying the price imposed on society. Although the social sciences do not allow for proof positive, I do not doubt that the weakening of home influences has contributed to drug abuse by youth, unwanted pregnancies, abortions, suicides, crime and the general decline in morality that is corrupting America.

Lowering the age for school entry has appeal for the parents of toddlers. Lengthening the school day and year has appeal not only for the parents of older children but for reformers who believe that more is better.

In *A Nation At Risk*, the commission noted: "In England and other industrialized countries, it is not unusual for academic high school students to spend 8 hours a day at school, 220 days per year. In the United States, by contrast, the typical school day lasts 6 hours and the school year is 180 days."

CAN WE SAVE OUR SINKING SCHOOLS?

There has been some expansion of the school year since the 1983 blast, but the days have been added to the teachers' year, not the children's. These are charitably described as planning days. Too frequently, they are goof-off days in which teachers are supposed to be conferring with each other and administrators. Gone are the days when teachers and committees of supervisors planned curricula after school hours. Now, most planning is done on school time when students are not around. I see a school without kids as a house not a home.

Although the short school year in the United States harks back to days when we were a largely agricultural country and kids were needed for work on the farm, there is no huge outcry by kids, parents and teachers for extending day or year.

Where teaching is poor added days and hours will only intensify bad results. Where teaching is good extensive add-ons are not the answer. Good students and good teachers do not fritter away the free time that is available when school is not in session. Some of their finest hours are spent away from school—reading, developing interests, travel, recreation.

While the school year is short, the schools are often open in the evening and during the long summer for activities that include summer school. In a few school districts, building use is maximized by the year-round school. Since the children are staggered in starting the school year, it befalls some of them to attend in the summer months.

The impetus for year-round schools stems largely from the overcrowding in some school districts. Very few of the districts have used the year-round school as a means of lengthening the school year in the direction that prevails in Japan and most of Europe.

It is hard to break with tradition and a lifestyle that has been built around summer closing of schools, but some parents have adjusted to the change. The president of the school board in Los Angeles said recently, "I expect that within maybe seven years . . . almost every school in the district will be year-round." A parent chimed in, "Now I don't have to listen to my eight-year-old saying for three months that he's bored."

THE LAST ANGRY PRINCIPAL

The children are the most adaptable of all. One child spoke for many when she said, "I don't forget things over the summer anymore." Some young beavers enroll for an additional session and reduce the number of years required for graduation.

What is now being realized by those districts that have the year-round school under way is that costs are considerably in excess of the regular school year. There are not only the maintenance costs but the added pay for teachers is substantial.

Almost no commentary on the year-round school mentions the principal. He will not be around for a month, although teachers and pupils will be in full swing. Where the principal is not worth a damn, there is no loss. Where the principal is strong, the cat's-away-mice-will-play syndrome can be a big minus for year-round schools.

It is possible, especially in large school districts, that there may be in the same district both year-round schools and those with the traditional year. This evokes interest by educational choice advocates who believe that parents are too narrowly restricted in their choice of schools. The length of the school year is comparatively minor, but major is the parents' perception that some schools offer better programs than others or programs that are more in keeping with the parents' view of what should be taught in schools and how it should be taught.

Educational choice was trumpeted by the National Governors' Association in its 1986 report, *Time for Results*. The governors stated: "If we first implement choice, true choice among public schools, we unlock the values of competition in the educational marketplace. Schools that compete for students, teachers and dollars will, by virtue of the environment, make those changes that allow them to succeed. . . . Choice in the public schools is the deregulatory move needed to make schools more responsive."

Although the governors are thinking of educational choice among public schools, other proponents of choice would include private schools. Religious schools are largely out of the choice picture. Private schools have reservations about getting into the choice act, especially where vouchers are proposed as means whereby parents will make their choice of school.

The voucher issued by state or federal government would be for an amount equivalent to the cost of educating a single child in a school district. The voucher idea is not new because it has been used in Vermont since 1894.

It is Vermont that is Exhibit 1 when advocates of a voucher system to achieve educational choice are challenged. Currently, some 33 Vermont towns have no public elementary school and 95 of Vermont's 246 towns have no high school. For students in these towns, payments are made to any approved elementary or high school in or out of the state equal to the average per pupil cost of education. If the tuition of the chosen school exceeds that amount, the parents make up the difference.

The Vermont teachers' union, an affiliate of the National Education Association, is opposed to the "tuitioning out" or voucher system in Vermont. It fears that towns are being encouraged to close their public schools and go the cheaper route of paying tuition to public or private schools.

Vermont is hardly typical of most states and can scarcely be a guide in city school districts. Parents in school districts where there is one school would have no choice and where there are a few schools, they would be severely limited as to choice. They might descend en masse on the school they perceive to be most desirable. Second choice might be no choice at all.

Private schools have already let it be known that they are wary of any voucher system. They know from the experience of public schools and colleges (both public and private) that when a federal dollar is accepted either directly or from students, there follows federal control. Private schools are content to enjoy the comparative freedom to hire and fire teachers, dictate their own curricula and otherwise be free of most state-imposed constraints.

Akin to educational choice, but apart from any voucher system, is the magnet school. These have been established in some fairly large school districts, primarily to achieve integration. The magnet is supposed to attract whites to predominantly black schools, or get whites to come back to a school system from which they have fled. The school district establishes a magnet school with alleged special programs, usually in science and mathematics, or catering to special interests—art, medicine, oceanography, etc.—not available in the neighborhood school. An effect of magnet schools is to denude neighborhood schools of some of their better students, for only the parents of such children are moved to seek programs that purport to be beyond the standard school offerings.

Apart from the inability of magnet schools to achieve social integration, it is misleading to suggest that elementary school-children (most magnets are at this level) require special programs. The development of basic skills and building thereon should be the hallmark of every school. Where children are above average in ability, provision is often made for them in neighborhood schools where they are divided (tracked) according to ability. Bright students (grouped in honors classes or euphemistically designated as IGC—intellectually gifted children) are thus not slowed by average or below-average children.

Tracking is abused in some schools where honors classes are set up for the sake of having them. In schools with small enrollments it is often not possible to skim off the few children who read and do arithmetic two years or more above grade level. Tracking does remove from regular classes the few students who might spark them and stimulate teachers. The advantage, when there is real justification for the honors class, outweighs this deprivation. I reject the criticism of tracking that it is elitist. There is nothing undemocratic about making provision for children who are considerably above average or markedly below average in ability to learn.

A very limited choice of high schools is offered to students in cities where there are specialized schools (not to be confused with magnet schools). In New York City, for example, there are the Bronx High School of Science and Stuyvesant High School, open to students who score high on entrance tests. Both schools offer not only the standard curriculum for college-bound students but more advanced courses, especially in science and mathematics.

Standards in both Bronx High School of Science and Stuyvesant have been lowered in recent years to allow for the admission of more blacks and Hispanics in furtherance of the school system's integration policy. Asians attend both schools in numbers far out of proportion to their presence in the general population.

Integration in New York City high schools has also been sought by allowing blacks to choose high schools out of their zones. Instead of attending zoned high schools with boundaries drawn to achieve an even distribution of students, black students have been offered—and many have accepted—the opportunity to attend schools out of their neighborhood.

Alternative high schools offer yet another choice, but these are vastly different from the regular and specialized high schools. They have been set up in New York City—some 15 of them in a city with 116 high schools—for those students unable to adjust to the regular schools. Their maladjustment means simply that they have been failing subjects, or are absent without excuse frequently, or disrupting classes, or behaving in such a way as to make life miserable for teachers and others who come into contact with them.

In the alternative high schools in New York City, enrollment is low, perhaps 200 to 500, in contrast to regular high schools enrolling from 2,000 to 4,000 students. Efforts are made to adapt the curriculum to the abilities of these troubled youths. Invariably, attendance is poor. Teachers are often addressed by their first names, boys wear hats, smoking is ignored, etc. There is little learning and the benefits, if any, accrue to the regular schools that are relieved of a burden.

I can see alternative schools for youths under 16 because the regular schools simply cannot handle them. I am opposed to the expenditure of school funds and teacher time for those over 16. Other institutions must deal with youths over 16 who are interfering with the educational process. Schools, I deeply believe, cannot solve all of the problems of society and they are being prevented from achieving their mission by retention of youths who for whatever reason cannot or will not take advantage of the great resources offered them.

Since state law often requires compulsory education for children above the age of 16 (in New York it is up to age 21), it may be necessary for legislators to see the light and amend the compulsory education law. While they are at it, they may wish to expand state and local youth service programs. The three-year-old New Jersey Youth Corps has placed high school dropouts in programs where they have rehabilitated urban housing, served the victims of Alzheimer's disease, worked in day-care centers and helped restore Waterloo Village, an 18th-century canal town. There is the opportunity also for youth corp members to earn their high school diplomas and obtain productive jobs. Such programs permit society to say that it is not just abandoning reluctant learners to the streets.

There is, too, the possibility that some 16-year-olds, denied the holding operation of alternative schools, will seek re-entry to regular schools. There are already sufficient modifications of curricula to allow for their retention, if only they will show some respect for the rights of others.

The real choice of schools is implicit in our dual school system. Private schools, including parochial schools, now educate about 12 percent of the total number of schoolage children. Independent schools (private but nonsectarian) account for about 20 percent of non-public schools students. They are prohibitively expensive except for families with high incomes and the few who are granted scholarships, most often with the well-intentioned purpose of bringing about representation of minorities in the student body.

Although many creeds have established parochial schools, two-thirds are Roman Catholic in denomination. Tuition costs of parochial schools have risen sharply in the past decade but they continue to offer refuge from the public schools when sought by parents. Many Catholic schools enroll non-Catholic children while giving preference to children of the Catholic faith. In addition to offering an unabashedly religious education, parochial schools are less troubled by discipline problems that burden public schools. They are free to discharge (expel) students who misbehave whereas public schools are obligated to accept such problem students.

When I was principal of Long Island City High School, I had an excellent relationship with the parochial schools in the neighborhood. The few students they expelled were retained until the end of the school term so that we did not have to accept them until new classes were formed in September and February of the school year.

Many studies that compare parochial and public schools show higher test scores for parochial (and private) school students, a higher percentage going on to college and being retained in college. The alleged superiority of parochial schools is hailed along with their much lower costs of operation.

Public schools with all their problems need not slink in the shadow of parochial or private school achievements. In national contests, such as the Westinghouse Science Talent Awards, public school students both in number and in proportion outshine non-public school students. And public schools take on problems that other schools need not abide.

Above all, private and parochial schools are selective. The parents who foot the bills give a high priority to the education of their children and want their religious values to be reinforced. They tend to check more closely on their children's schoolwork. These are the factors that account for private-parochial school alleged superiority.

The lower cost of private-parochial school operation is owing in large part to the lower pay of their teachers and supervisors. The starting salary of non-public school teachers is one-third lower than that of public school teachers and their maximum salaries are usually not half of the salaries paid to public school teachers. Increasingly, private-parochial school teachers are leaving for the better-paying public schools after they acquire a few years of teaching experience. They may miss the relative peace and satisfaction of parochial school teaching, but almost all parochial teachers are now laymen—not members of religious orders—and they are not attuned to genteel poverty.

Any flight of children from the public schools is restrained by the cost barrier. The likelihood of any substantial expansion of the private-parochial schools is remote. Parents could not begin to pay the costs of such expansion. Public schools are supported by taxpayers whether or not their children attend the schools. Private schools are supported by tuition payments and donations by well-to-do parents, alumni and others.

THE LAST ANGRY PRINCIPAL

Proposals to aid parents of non-public school children through tuition-tax credits have been turned down repeatedly by a Congress disposed to save pennies while pondering a trillion dollar-plus national debt and hundred billion dollar-plus annual deficits. The proposed credits, on the order of $500 a year, are piddling for parents looking to private schools but might move more parents toward parochial schools.

Tuition-tax credits are strongly opposed by the National Education Association (NEA) and American Federation of Teachers lobbies as a threat to the public schools. Any public school so threatened is on shaky ground to begin with. There is some merit to the argument advanced by critics of the public schools that the public school "monopoly" might be stimulated to do better if the competition of private-parochial schools were encouraged by tuition-tax credits.

There are those who escape from the public schools in vast numbers who do not trouble the private-parochial schools. These are the dropouts. The numbers game played here would be hilarious if the problem were not so disheartening. The U.S. Department of Education estimates the national average to be 25 percent. In some school systems half the students drop out before graduation from high school. In other school systems the dropouts may be as few as 5 percent. The accounting is complicated by the difficulty of following up on students who disappear. Some surely have transferred to schools in other localities or states. The great majority of dropouts, however, hate school and will have no part of it.

There are considerable costs in money and staff time in returning dropouts to the schools. They tend to be disruptive when they are forcibly returned and soon depart through the revolving school door. It is enough that the schools are there for those with the sense to take advantage of the opportunity. Dropouts are free to return with the prodding of parents or change of heart induced by unfriendly streets. The blandishment of attendance teachers (truant officers) should be directed to students whose attendance has been regular but whose sudden absence cannot be accounted for by school authorities.

CAN WE SAVE OUR SINKING SCHOOLS?

The widely publicized problems of public schools and the experience of some parents with both public and private schools have spurred thousands of parents to undertake home instruction for their children. Permission to teach children at home is usually required by the school district. In some states—Oregon for example—permission is granted for one year at a time. In other states parents are threatened with fines and imprisonment if children are kept home from school for the purpose of instruction.

There are now companies that make available teaching materials for home instruction at various grade levels. Although such materials facilitate home instruction, the job remains an arduous one and few parents can continue for many years. In Oregon, where the state is comparatively friendly to such dedicated parents, the majority of children instructed at home are kept out of school for a year and a half before they are returned to school. While children in home instruction may miss the companionship of classmates and diverse school activities, their parents tend to believe that they do not acquire the bad habits that some school environments foster.

While I do not believe that compulsory education laws should be used to intimidate parents who are capable of and willing to undertake home instruction, I do not see home instruction as a viable alternative to formal schooling beyond the early elementary school grades. Home instruction will continue to be an alternative to both public and private schools. More parents will be stimulated to undertake it if schools get worse.

If any proof is required that the public schools are offering an education, it is the performance of Asian children. Asian students win science prizes and excel in mathematics. At LIC, where Asians were about 2 percent of the school population, they held five of the six positions on the Math Team and excelled in interscholastic competition.

Asians are widely recognized as our nation's super immigrant group, contributing new generations of systems analysts, engineers and other high tech professionals.

Why are Asian children doing so well in school? There are those who suggest that Asian children are naturally smarter than

American children. I do not believe that for a moment. I do believe there are differences in the role of the family that account in large part for differences in school achievement.

Asian parents place great emphasis on the education of their children and they control their children. Unlike too many American parents, they are not easily satisfied with the school performance of their children. They have no illusions about their children doing better when they mature. They want them to achieve at a high level from the very first.

The products of Asian schools are coming to the United States. More often than not, Asian immigrants are not poor. Koreans, especially, come with cash. They are the ones with get-up-and-go, so we are not getting the bottom of the Asian barrel.

Asian-Americans are an asset at a time when Asian competition from the Far East is a risk remarked upon by the National Commission of Excellence. "The risk," the commission stated, "is not only that the Japanese make automobiles more efficiently than Americans . . . . not just that the South Koreans recently built the world's most efficient steel mill. . . . It is also that these developments signify a redistribution of trained capability throughout the globe."

A risk seen by the commission is that "Secondary school curricula have been homogenized, diluted, and diffused to the point that they no longer have a central purpose." A gaggle of commissions have clucked the same refrain. I agree.

Those reformers reconciled to the idea that it is going to be one teacher in a classroom with one group of students are properly concerned about the content of subjects to be taught. The solid subjects and the amount of time to be given them in the high schools pose no great area of disagreement. Secretary of Education William J. Bennett in 1988 proposed for his mythical "James Madison High School" four years of English; three years each for social studies, math and science; two years of a foreign language; one-half year of health; one and one-half years of physical education and one-half year of art and music history.

It happens that James Madison is not at all a mythical high school. It exists this very day in Brooklyn, New York, and probably in hundreds of other school districts in the nation. The curriculum now seen as a reform was the standard curriculum in the James Madison I knew in the 1930's. It was, in fact, a stronger curriculum in that the requirement for an academic diploma included three years of one foreign language and two years of a second foreign language. I know because I had to pass those subjects at Boys High School (Class of '32), also in Brooklyn.

We need no guidance from current reformers as to what constitutes a solid curriculum devoid of Mickey Mouse courses, or electives that permit good students to evade trigonometry and physics. Superior students at LIC who resisted guidance counselors bent on programming them for solid subjects were sent to me. Seniors, in particular, argued that they had satisfied the academic requirements for a diploma and did not want to risk lowering their averages by taking tough subjects rather than such bits of confectionery as Bachelor Pad for the male destined to be single. I explained that the colleges had made the decision to admit based on the first three years of high school marks and that strong preparation for college would serve them better than soft stuff. No student ever objected to my advising him and most of them were grateful that I showed an interest. In only rare cases was it necessary for me to bring in a parent who was easily persuaded that my judgment in matters of this kind was superior to that of the child.

The danger today is that we shall ascribe the names of solid subjects to course offerings, but the contents will be weak distillations of real content. There is the further concern that today's crop of teachers are so poorly grounded in solid subjects that they simply cannot teach them as they were once taught.

There is also a lack of realism in proposing, as do reformers, that *all* students be subjected to solid subjects. Perhaps half the students in our high schools today would find solid subjects indigestible. We now are reconciled to a system of mass education in which all students are permitted to remain in high school and millions have been graduated as functional illiterates. They can read a little but have trouble with a restaurant menu and require assistance in completing an application for employment.

THE LAST ANGRY PRINCIPAL

Realism suggests that we shall continue to offer 12 years of education to all. It does not follow, however, that all must be subjected to the same curriculum. The new James Madison High School had better allow for modified courses that tap gently into solid subjects and other subjects of a vocational nature; not that vocational subjects are for non-readers. The new technology requires a level of learning that goes far beyond the non-college preparatory courses of older generations.

Imbedded in the technology is the computer. At the moment there are some 1 million computers in approximately 100,000 elementary and secondary schools in the United States. It may be that every schoolchild will be equipped with a computer because the device is suited for education and is omnipresent in business and industry.

Some reformers would expand the curriculum, at least in high schools, to one-half year of computer science. This would include hands-on learning through computers as well as understanding the importance of computers in our technological society. The implications of computers for the schools loom larger than the more familiar use of television, films, video cassettes and comparatively primitive filmstrip projectors. The older technologies have been used to supplement classroom instruction although few would contend that we have made the best use of television. The latter medium has been abused rather than used, although wise selective use by teachers can reap dividends in the classroom.

Can computers be abused in the classroom? They are already being abused in schools where they have been purchased thoughtlessly by administrators fearing that they will be accused of falling behind the times. Software—programs in subjects that are part of the curriculum—are largely lacking. These deficiencies will likely be overcome. There is nevertheless the temptation to become so reliant on tapping keys for programmed information that computer "brains" will be given priority over development of human brains entrusted to teachers.

One fear of computers that is overdrawn is fear by teachers that they will be replaced by computers. Teachers can rest easier on that score although they will be expected to be as comfortable with a computer as most of them are now with a typewriter.

Teachers must be comfortable with more than computers. To the extent that they are dismayed by existing conditions in the schools and that dismay is communicated to those who might be encouraged to enter the profession, we shall continue to be at risk.

That we continue at risk was acknowledged in the 1988 report of the Carnegie Foundation for the Advancement of Teaching. In *An Imperiled Generation: Saving Urban Schools*, the Carnegie trustees conceded: "The harsh truth is that the reform movement has largely bypassed our most troubled schools." Improvements in the past five years, the trustees observed, have not touched many schools in big cities, including New York, Los Angeles, Chicago, Houston and New Orleans. Schools in these cities function as "little more than human storehouses to keep young people off the streets."

In the spirit of the dance that moves reformers, the trustees called for more "autonomy" for teachers and principals while also making them "accountable" for student performance. "Since 1983," the trustees continued, "school reform has been at the top of the national agenda." Gains resulting from stiffer graduation requirements have been limited to "schools that are already succeeding."

In these final pages I have assessed schools today as they rock on a wave of alleged reform. Some of the reforms would beach the ship of schools. Others may do little harm and arguments generated can only stimulate thinking about the schools. The horde of presidential candidates in 1988 who decried the "education crisis" were expressing public concern.

The public is rightly concerned. We have not fully recovered from the disruption of our schools and colleges by the Vietnam War protests. The students' rights movement continues to surface as young militants find issues in U.S. foreign policy in Central America and apartheid in South Africa. The watering down of courses in high schools and colleges that followed student demands for subjects relevant to their interest and needs has reduced learning. Efforts to bring back a solid curriculum are subverted by poor preparation of students in basic skills and a weakened profession ravaged by early retirements and an influx of new teachers who have themselves been badly educated.

Changes that might revive respect for schools in the 21st century will not be brought about by reforms turning topsy-turvy the relationship of teachers and supervisors. Conferring decision-making powers on teachers who have enough to do carrying out the aim of a single lesson borders on the mindless.

When all is said and done there is only one reform—and that is *not* reform but an application of common sense to right our wronged schools. We must remove from our schools those youths who interfere with the education of others. We must recruit well-prepared teachers who will then encounter less of a class struggle.

I believe our schools will continue to sink until they are buoyed by teachers who can teach in safe schools where children learn to the best of their abilities. Is this too much to expect in a great nation that has needlessly been placed at risk?

INDEX